Understanding Microsoft Loop

Transforming Team Collaboration

Charles Waghmare

apress®

Understanding Microsoft Loop: Transforming Team Collaboration

Charles Waghmare
Mumbai, Maharashtra, India

ISBN-13 (pbk): 979-8-8688-2079-3 ISBN-13 (electronic): 979-8-8688-2080-9
https://doi.org/10.1007/979-8-8688-2080-9

Copyright © 2025 by Charles Waghmare

This work is subject to copyright. All rights are reserved by the Publisher, whether the whole or part of the material is concerned, specifically the rights of translation, reprinting, reuse of illustrations, recitation, broadcasting, reproduction on microfilms or in any other physical way, and transmission or information storage and retrieval, electronic adaptation, computer software, or by similar or dissimilar methodology now known or hereafter developed.

Trademarked names, logos, and images may appear in this book. Rather than use a trademark symbol with every occurrence of a trademarked name, logo, or image we use the names, logos, and images only in an editorial fashion and to the benefit of the trademark owner, with no intention of infringement of the trademark.

The use in this publication of trade names, trademarks, service marks, and similar terms, even if they are not identified as such, is not to be taken as an expression of opinion as to whether or not they are subject to proprietary rights.

While the advice and information in this book are believed to be true and accurate at the date of publication, neither the authors nor the editors nor the publisher can accept any legal responsibility for any errors or omissions that may be made. The publisher makes no warranty, express or implied, with respect to the material contained herein.

Managing Director, Apress Media LLC: Welmoed Spahr
Acquisitions Editor: Smriti Srivastava
Editorial Project Manager: Jessica Vakili

Cover designed by eStudioCalamar

Distributed to the book trade worldwide by Springer Science+Business Media New York, 1 New York Plaza, New York, NY 10004. Phone 1-800-SPRINGER, fax (201) 348-4505, e-mail orders-ny@springer-sbm.com, or visit www.springeronline.com. Apress Media, LLC is a Delaware LLC and the sole member (owner) is Springer Science + Business Media Finance Inc (SSBM Finance Inc). SSBM Finance Inc is a **Delaware** corporation.

For information on translations, please e-mail booktranslations@springernature.com; for reprint, paperback, or audio rights, please e-mail bookpermissions@springernature.com.

Apress titles may be purchased in bulk for academic, corporate, or promotional use. eBook versions and licenses are also available for most titles. For more information, reference our Print and eBook Bulk Sales web page at http://www.apress.com/bulk-sales.

Any source code or other supplementary material referenced by the author in this book is available to readers on GitHub. For more detailed information, please visit https://www.apress.com/gp/services/source-code.

If disposing of this product, please recycle the paper

> **"Blessed are those who find wisdom, those who gain understanding." – Proverbs 3:13**

First, I would like to say thanks to the Almighty Lord Jesus Christ for offering me yet another opportunity to author this book. I completely owe everything to Him. I take this opportunity to praise and glorify Lord Christ for all the wonderful things that He has been doing in my life. God Bless.

I humbly dedicate this book to my beloved mother, Late Mrs. Kamala David Waghmare, and my father, Mr. David Genu Waghmare, in recognition of their fundamental role in shaping my life and career. I am sincerely grateful for their unwavering support and guidance.

Also, I dedicate this book to my adorable wife, Mrs. Priya Waghmare, for her support, love, encouragement, and care.

Table of Contents

About the Author xi

About the Technical Reviewer xiii

Acknowledgments xv

Chapter 1: Introduction to Microsoft Loop: Understanding the Platform 1

  Introduction 2

  Three Elements of Microsoft Loop 3

  What Can Be Done with Loop? 12

  Common Use Cases of Loop 14

  Manage Your Tasks from Loop Task Lists 14

  Use Copilot in Loop to Draft and Add Content 21

  Keyboard Shortcuts for Microsoft Loop 23

  Benefits of Microsoft Loop 26

    Real-Time Collabaoration 26

    Modular Content Structure 27

    Deep Integration with M365 27

    Productivity 28

    Project Management 28

    Collaborative Workforce 28

    Knowledge and Information Sharing 29

    Compliance 29

    Agile Workforce 29

Chapter 2: Getting Started with Microsoft Loop 31

  Introduction 31

    Creating a New Loop Workspace 32

    Creating Pages and Subpages Within a Loop Workspace 39

TABLE OF CONTENTS

    Favoriting a Workspace 46

    Adding and Removing Loop Workspace Members 48

    Renaming and Restyling a Workspace 51

    Managing Page Versions 58

    Printing and Exporting Workspace Pages 61

    Deleting Loop Workspaces 62

Chapter 3: Co-creation and Managing Loop Components 67

  Introduction 67

    Send a Loop Voting Table Component in a Teams Communication 69

    Create a Teams Meeting Agenda Loop Component 76

    Set Up a Loop Task List Component in an Outlook Message 81

    Share a Loop Component Across Microsoft 365 Apps 86

    Find Loop Components 88

    Coauthor a Loop Component 90

    Manage Access for a Loop Component 91

    What to Know About Microsoft Loop Before Getting Started 95

  Cocreation Challenges Using Microsoft Loop 96

Chapter 4: Real-Time Collaboration Using Loop 99

  Real-Time Collaboration Using Loop 100

    Rewriting Content with Copilot Assistance 104

    Instructing Copilot to Summarize a Loop Workspace Page 109

    Asking Copilot to Brainstorm an Idea in a Loop Workspace Page 115

  Create Loop Workspace Content with Copilot 118

  Understanding the Communication Process by Comparing Microsoft Loop with Microsoft Teams, Microsoft Outlook, and OneNote 120

    Microsoft Loop vs. Microsoft Teams, Microsoft Outlook, and OneNote: A Deep-Dive Comparison 120

    Core Purpose and Philosophy 120

    Collaboration Style 121

    User Interface and Experience 122

    Integration with Microsoft 365 122

TABLE OF CONTENTS

Communication Features.. 123

Content Collaboration 123

Use Cases 124

Strengths 125

Limitations 126

Security and Compliance 127

Workflow Integration 127

AI and Copilot Integration 128

Accessibility and Mobility 128

Future Outlook 129

Conclusion 129

Chapter 5: Integrating Loop with Microsoft 365 Apps 131

Introduction 131

Integration of Microsoft Loop with Microsoft 365 Apps 133

Sharing a Collaborative Table Loop Component in an Outlook Message 133

Developing a Team Retrospective Loop Component Within a OneNote Notebook Page 155

Chapter 6: Exploring Advanced Features and Customizations 169

Task List 169

Voting Table 173

Progressive Tracker 176

Kanban Board 179

Team Retrospective 182

Q&A Session 186

Calender 189

General Features to Support and Improve Content 192

    New Subpage 194

    Table 194

    Checklist 194

    Bulleted List 195

    Numbered List 195

vii

TABLE OF CONTENTS

Date 195

Callout 196

Code 196

Mermaid 196

Math Equation 197

Table of Contents 197

Divider 197

Inline Equation 198

Paragraph 198

Heading 1 198

Heading 2 199

Heading 3 199

Collapsible Heading 1 199

Collapsible Heading 2 199

Collapsible Heading 3 200

Quote 200

Inline Code 200

Communication, Media, Microsoft, and Other Apps 201

Chapter 7: Use Cases for Team Collaboration Using Loop 203

Introduction 203

Value and Impact of Collaboration 205

Core Components of Effective Collaboration 207

Challenges in Team Collaboration 208

Strategies for Successful Collaboration 210

Collaboration in the Digital Age 212

The Role of Technology in Collaboration 214

Future of Team Collaboration 216

Use Cases with Microsoft Loop 217

Value and Impact of Collaboration 217

Core Components of Effective Collaboration 219

Challenges in Team Collaboration 220

Strategies for Successful Collaboration 222
Collaboration in the Digital Age 223
The Role of Technology in Collaboration... 225
Future of Team Collaboration... 226

Index... **229**

About the Author

Charles David Waghmare is presently a DBA (Doctor of Business Administration) scholar from the prestigious SP Jain School of Global Management and has completed his MBA from the same B-School. He has over 17 years of industry experience in IT, engineering, and energy sectors.

Charles is presently working with a global energy leader since 2019 as an Information Management Consultant in the Microsoft 365 space. Before that, he worked for Capgemini for eight years in various roles, including Viva Engage Community Manager and Manager of the Drupal-Based Enterprise Knowledge Management System. He also developed a knowledge management platform for Capgemini's Digital Customer Experience (DCX) organization using SharePoint Online to manage client references and knowledge assets related to artificial intelligence and customer experience (CX). Further, he adopted Microsoft Azure Chatbots to automate communication channels with the customers.

Charles also worked for ATOS (erstwhile SIEMENS Information Systems limited) for five years. During his tenure there, he was a Community Manager of SAP-based communities, where he utilized Technoweb 2.0 – a Viva Engage-like platform – and on-premises SharePoint to manage SAP user-based communities. Charles was also global rollout manager for a structured document management system built in on-premises SharePoint.

Charles has penned several books on Microsoft 365 technologies, such as Viva Engage, SharePoint Online, and Azure Chatbots, and on ChatGPT. Further, he loves reading motivational books in his spare time, his favorites being *The Monk Who Sold His Ferrari*, *The 5 AM Club*, and *The Everyday Hero Manifesto*.

About the Technical Reviewer

Mittal Mehta is an experienced technologist who specializes in DevOps automation, configuration, and release management process for on-premises and cloud applications. He is always eager to learn new technologies related to automation application life cycle management. He worked on Microsoft technologies like C#, .Net, Azure DevOps, Powershell, etc. Mittal currently works as a Senior Manager, DevOps, for enterprise applications in Bangalore. He specializes in setting up cloud automation and Azure DevOps processes. He has been a technical reviewer for many books on Azure DevOps, Git, and release management.

Acknowledgments

Late Mr. Anil Malvankar, ex-DGM at SIEMENS, who offered me my first job at SIEMENS – I thank him for his mentoring until his last day on earth, April 2024.

Late Mr. Alwin Fernandis, my beloved friend – he is not present with me today, but his memories exist in my heart forever.

CHAPTER 1

Introduction to Microsoft Loop: Understanding the Platform

Microsoft Loop is an innovative collaboration platform developed by Microsoft within the Microsoft 365 suite, intended to enhance team productivity in today's digital-centric environment. The platform is fundamentally composed of three key elements—Loop Components, Loop Pages, and Loop Workspaces—as follows:

- Loop Components are atomic units of productivity—such as lists, tables, notes, or tasks—that can be shared and edited in real time across multiple Microsoft 365 applications like Teams, Outlook, and Word. These components are dynamic and portable, ensuring that updates made in one location are instantly reflected everywhere else they are embedded.

- Loop Pages serve as flexible canvases where users can organize their thoughts, embed components, and collaborate asynchronously or in real time.

- Loop Workspaces are shared spaces that allow teams to group related pages and components, track progress, and manage projects collaboratively.

A key attribute of Microsoft Loop is its robust integration with the Microsoft 365 suite, allowing users to transition effortlessly between applications and maintain productivity within their existing workflows. For example, task lists created within a Loop Page can be embedded directly into Teams chats and updated in real time during meetings, ensuring immediate visibility for all participants. The platform further capitalizes on the capabilities of Microsoft 365 Copilot, an AI-driven assistant designed to assist with content generation, discussion summarization, next-step recommendations, and automation of routine processes. This integration enhances overall efficiency by minimizing manual workload and facilitating informed decision-making. Microsoft Loop is well-suited to a variety of professional scenarios, including project management, brainstorming sessions, meeting documentation, and cross-departmental collaboration. Its centralized approach to communication, content development, and task monitoring makes it especially advantageous for distributed teams.

Loop has introduced features such as guest sharing, link-based access, PDF export, and enhanced commenting capabilities, making it even more versatile and user-friendly. Security and compliance are also top priorities, with Loop leveraging SharePoint and OneDrive for data storage and offering enterprise-grade controls for administrators.

Getting started with Loop is straightforward: users can log in with their Microsoft 365 credentials, create a workspace, invite collaborators, and begin organizing content using templates and intelligent suggestions. Best practices for using Loop include maintaining clear communication, updating content in real time, leveraging templates for consistency, and aligning team efforts with defined goals.

In conclusion, Microsoft Loop constitutes a noteworthy advancement in collaborative technology by providing a flexible, intelligent, and integrated platform that enables teams to enhance their productivity and creativity. With its focus on real-time collaboration, AI-powered assistance, and seamless compatibility within the Microsoft ecosystem, it is well-positioned as a foundational tool for contemporary digital workplaces. As organizations further embrace hybrid and remote work arrangements, solutions such as Microsoft Loop are expected to play an essential role in fostering efficient, cohesive, and innovative teamwork.

Introduction

Microsoft Loop Components are portable and editable content elements that remain synchronized across all locations where they are shared. These components enable collaboration within various work contexts, such as chat, email, meetings, or documents. They include formats like lists, tables, and notes, ensuring users access the most current information in supported applications, including Microsoft Teams, Outlook, and Whiteboard. Loop component is available in Teams chat, Outlook Web App, OneNote, OneDrive, SharePoint Online, Microsoft Word Online, and Whiteboard.

CHAPTER 1   INTRODUCTION TO MICROSOFT LOOP: UNDERSTANDING THE PLATFORM

In this chapter, we will cover Introduction of Microsoft Loop, Elements such as Loop components, pages, and workspaces, respectively, details about three elements of Microsoft Loop, What can be done with Loop? Common use cases of Loop, Manage your tasks from Loop Task lists, Use Copilot in Loop to draft and add content, Keyboard shortcuts for Microsoft Loop, why it is important to know keyboards shortcuts, and benefits of Microsoft Loop.

Three Elements of Microsoft Loop

Microsoft Loop is a collaborative platform designed to bring together teams, content, and tasks across various tools and devices. Loop features a flexible canvas and portable components that can move and stay synchronized across applications, allowing teams to work together on planning and creating projects. Microsoft Loop can be accessed using `https://loop.cloud.microsoft/` and shown in Figure 1-1, home page of the Loop. Home page is segregated into Workspaces, as shown in Figure 1-1, and Recent accessed components and pages, as shown in Figure 1-2.

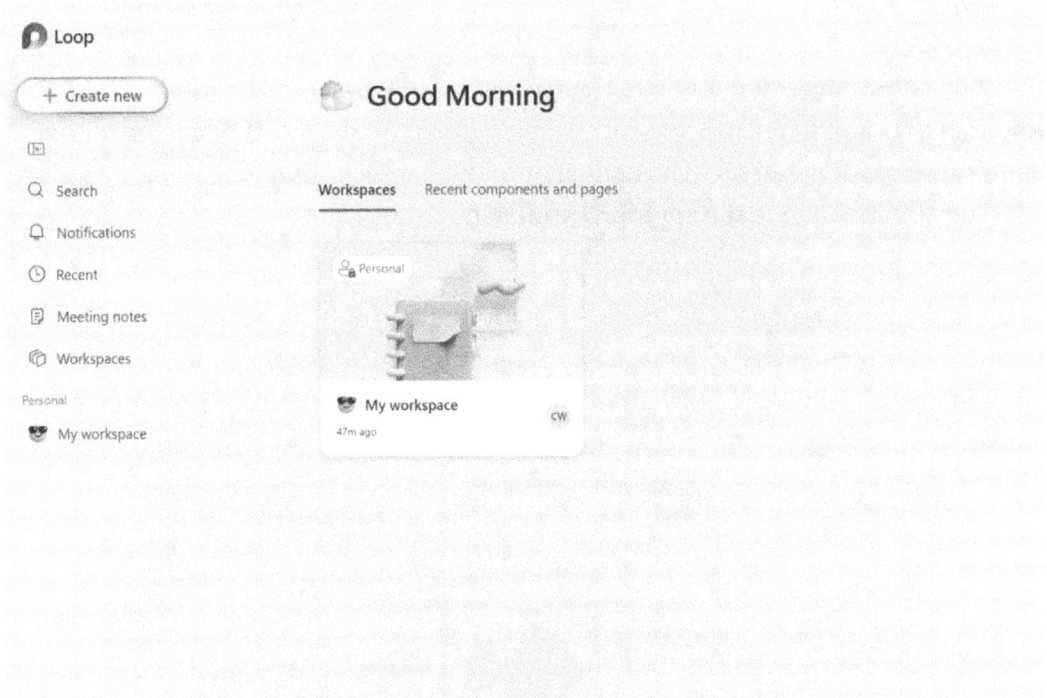

Figure 1-1. *Home page of Microsoft Loop*

CHAPTER 1 INTRODUCTION TO MICROSOFT LOOP: UNDERSTANDING THE PLATFORM

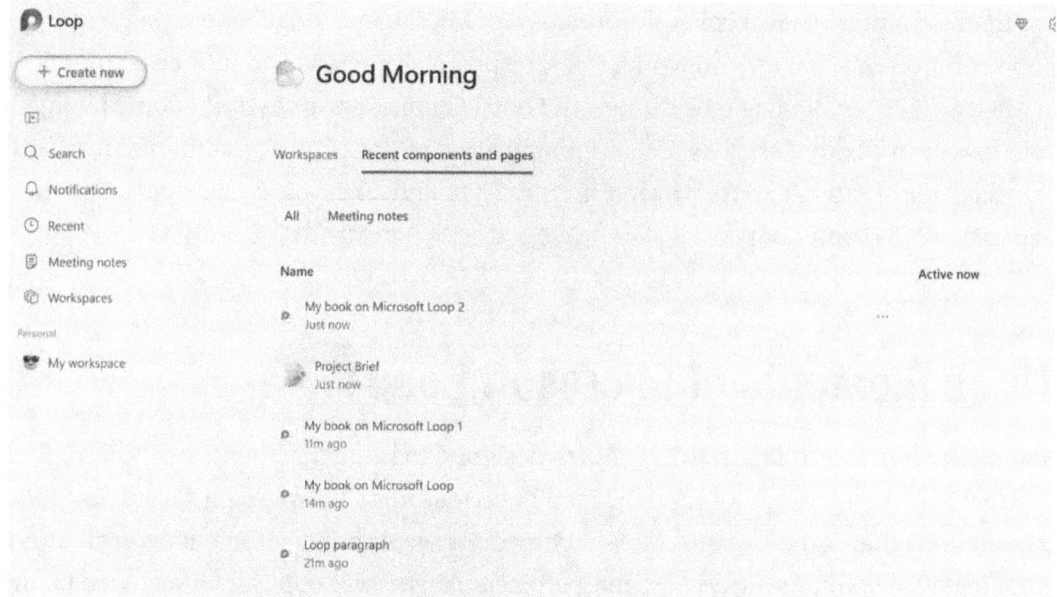

Figure 1-2. *Recently accessed components and pages in the Loop*

Let us understand Loop Components, Loop pages, and Loop pages visually since we know how Loop Homepage appears after log-in into Microsoft Loop, as shown in Figure 1-1.

Loop components are portable elements of content that remain synchronized wherever they are shared in Microsoft Teams, Outlook, OneNote, Whiteboard, or the Loop app. End users can segment content into smaller sections and distribute only the necessary information to the appropriate individuals.

To access Loop Component in Microsoft Teams:
To insert a Loop component in Teams, begin by opening either an existing chat or starting a new one. Navigate to the message input box and ensure it is empty before proceeding. Click on the Loop components icon located directly beneath the message box, as shown in Figure 1-3. Choose the desired component type, add your content, and then send your message, as shown in Figure 1-4.

CHAPTER 1 INTRODUCTION TO MICROSOFT LOOP: UNDERSTANDING THE PLATFORM

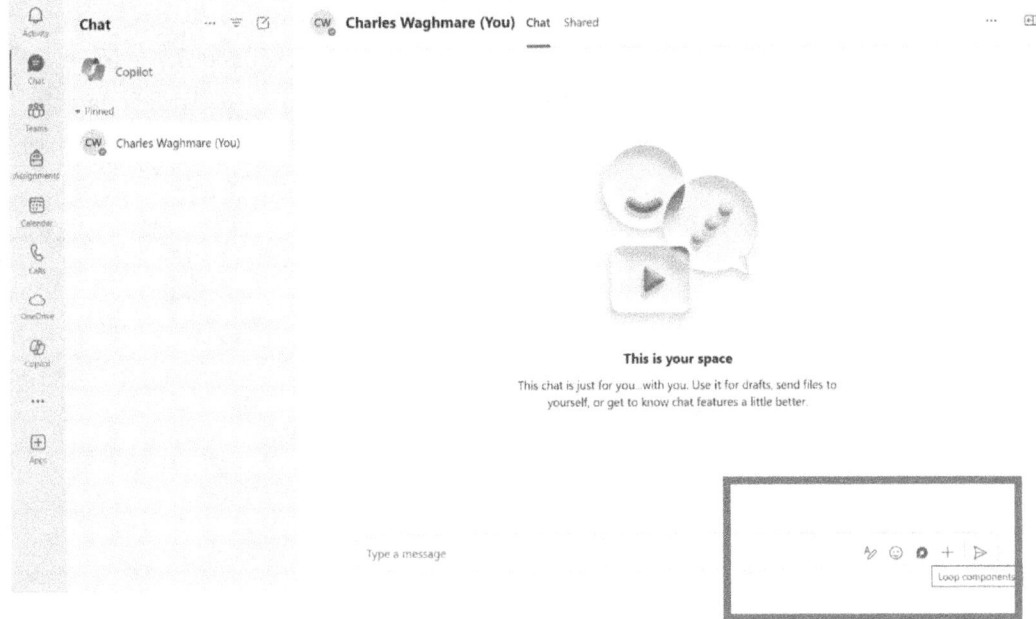

Figure 1-3. *Loop components icon*

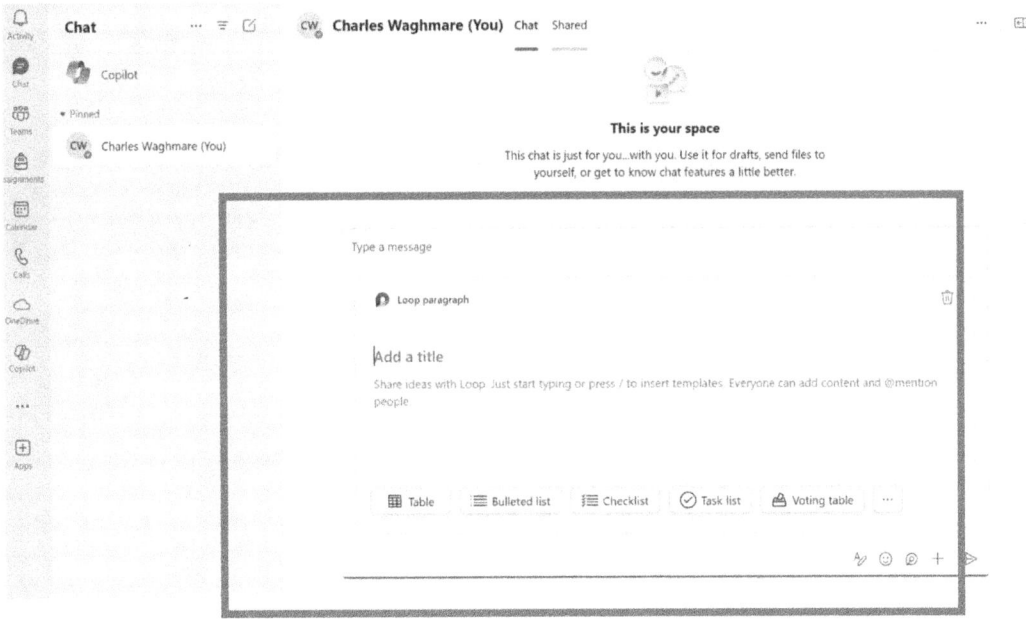

Figure 1-4. *Loop components*

CHAPTER 1   INTRODUCTION TO MICROSOFT LOOP: UNDERSTANDING THE PLATFORM

To access Loop Component in Outlook:
In Outlook, you can add a new Loop component while composing or replying to an email by selecting Insert ➤ Loop Components, as shown in Figure 1-5. Additionally, a shortcut to insert a Loop component is available as shown in Figure 1-6 in the upper grid of the message window.

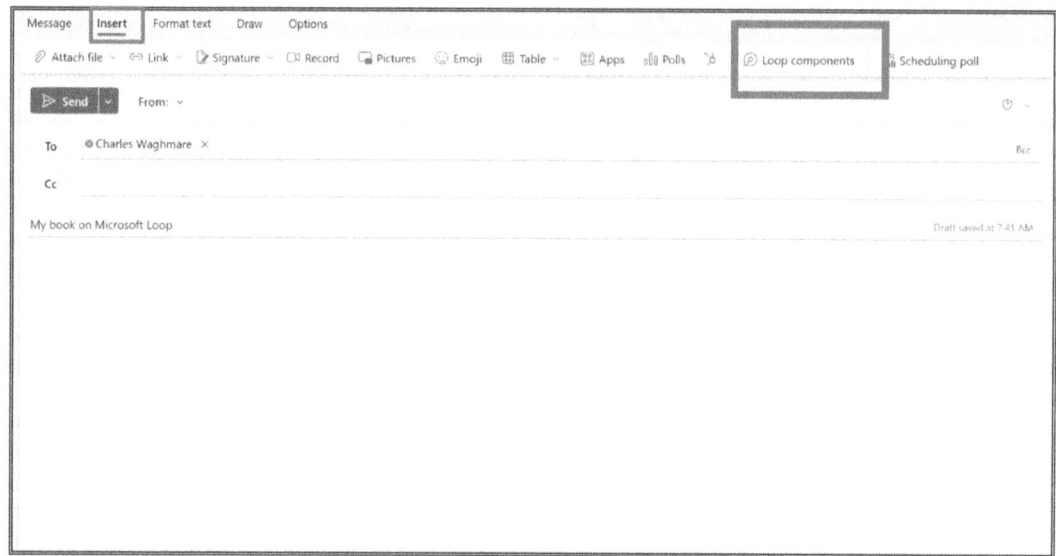

Figure 1-5. Loop components in Insert Menu

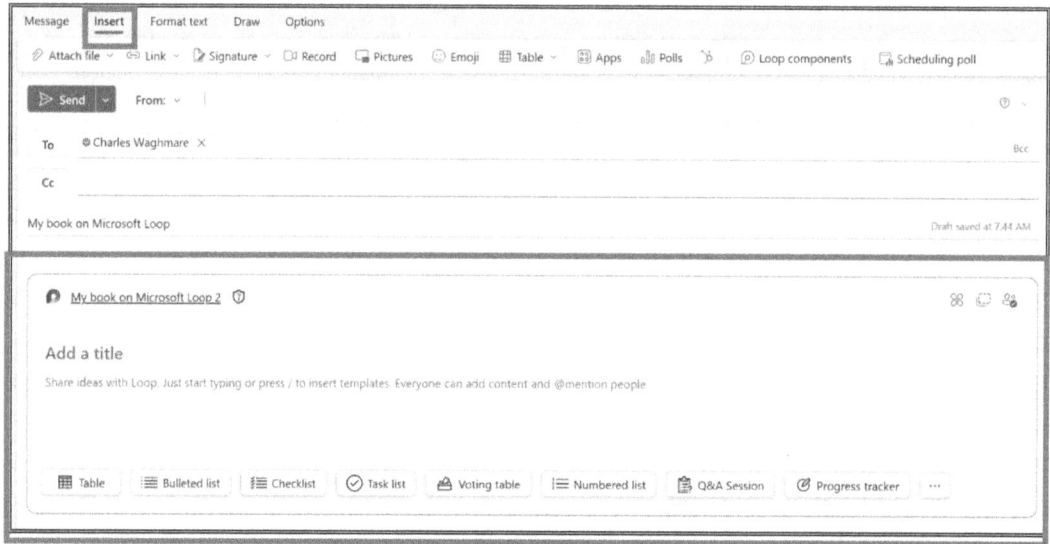

Figure 1-6. Loop components in the email

6

To access Loop Component in Whiteboard:

Existing Loop components from other M365 applications can be copied and pasted onto a whiteboard by selecting "Insert" during the paste process, as shown in Figure 1-7. At this time, it is not possible to create Loop components directly within the whiteboard application. Once you click on Look components icons, Task List, Table, Voting table, Progressive Tracker, and Checklist components are shown in Figure 1-8 and all of these components can be chosen, as shown in Figure 1-9.

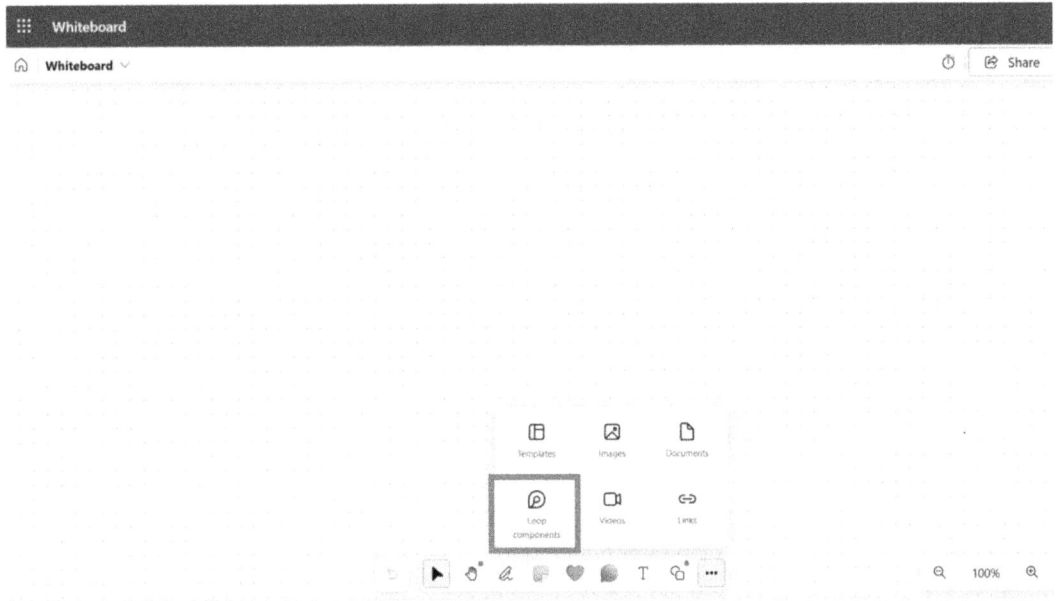

Figure 1-7. Insert Loop components in the Whiteboard

CHAPTER 1   INTRODUCTION TO MICROSOFT LOOP: UNDERSTANDING THE PLATFORM

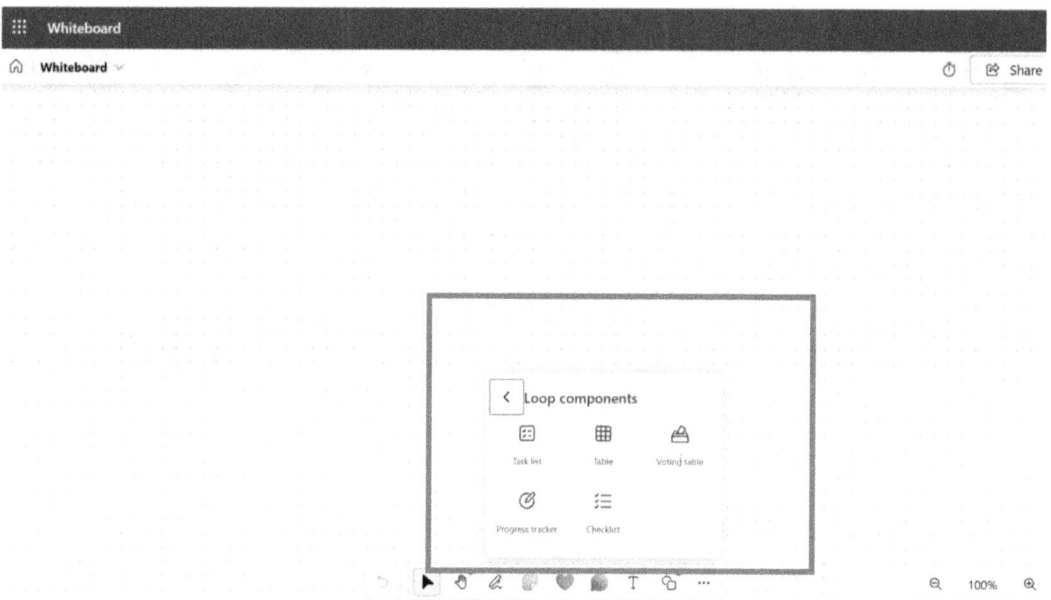

Figure 1-8. *Loop components in the Whiteboard*

Figure 1-9. *Different Loop components*

CHAPTER 1   INTRODUCTION TO MICROSOFT LOOP: UNDERSTANDING THE PLATFORM

To access Loop Component in OneNote:

Similarly, Loop component in the OneNote is available under insert Menu, as shown in Figure 1-10.

Figure 1-10. *Loop Component in OneNote*

To access Loop Component in Word:

When working in a Word document, it is possible to create a Loop component and share a link to it via Teams or email. Edits made by others will be visible immediately within the Word document. Anyone in the organization who has access to the document can edit it and view changes in real time.

To insert a Loop component, navigate to the desired location in the Word Online document. Ensure the cursor is not within a table, list, header, or footer. Select "Insert" and then choose "Loop Component" as shown in Figure 1-11. Use the drop-down menu to select the preferred type of Loop component. Enter content into the new component.

CHAPTER 1   INTRODUCTION TO MICROSOFT LOOP: UNDERSTANDING THE PLATFORM

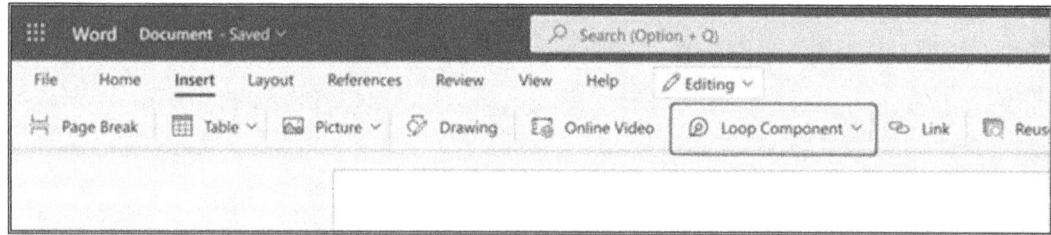

Figure 1-11. *Loop Component in Word*

Loop pages serve as versatile workspaces within the Loop app, enabling users to collaborate by integrating people, components, links, tasks, and data in a unified environment. Ensure that all necessary tools and documents for your project are systematically organized and stored together in a designated location. Pages are created under workspaces, as shown in Figure 1-12.

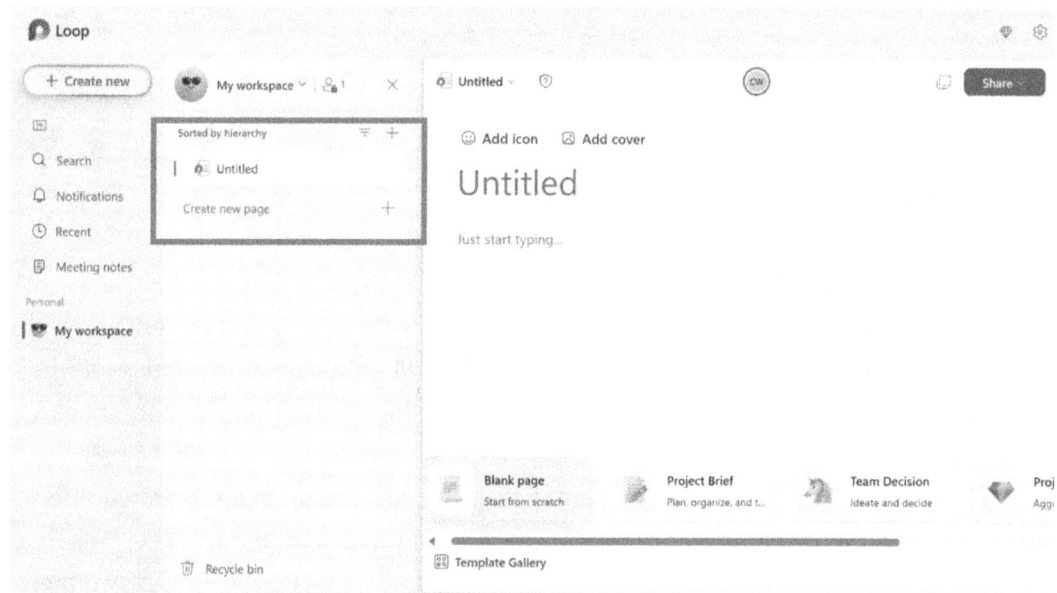

Figure 1-12. *Creation of Loop Pages*

Loop workspaces are collaborative environments designed to enable teams to view and organize all key project components efficiently. They facilitate teamwork within shared spaces, providing tools for managing tasks and projects that synchronize seamlessly across Microsoft 365 applications and services. Pages are created in Workspaces, as shown in Figure 1-13.

CHAPTER 1   INTRODUCTION TO MICROSOFT LOOP: UNDERSTANDING THE PLATFORM

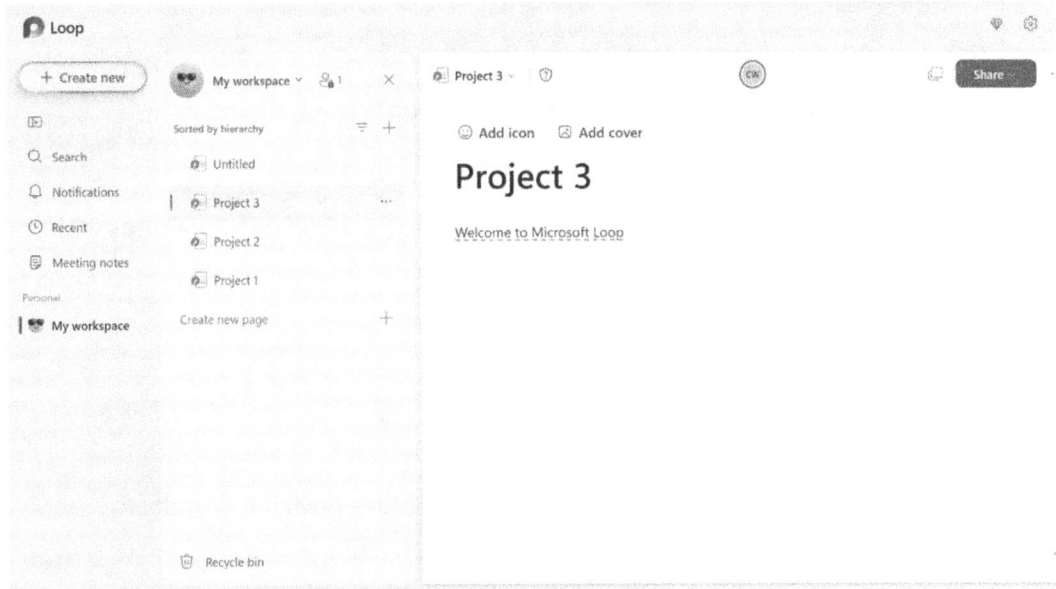

Figure 1-13. *Loop Workspaces*

Note   As we have seen, Loop components are accessible to users with permissions in Teams, Outlook, Word Online, Whiteboard, and OneNote.

The majority of features within Microsoft Loop are available to all individuals with a work or academic account (Microsoft Entra account, formerly known as Azure Active Directory account). Users who have access to the Loop app can view Loop pages and components, track recently used Loop components across other applications such as Teams and Outlook, and review Loop workspaces in which they have been included, among other functions.

To utilize the full range of features offered by the Loop app, users with work accounts (Microsoft Entra accounts) must hold one of the following Microsoft 365 subscriptions:

- Microsoft 365 Business Standard
- Microsoft 365 Business Premium
- Microsoft 365 E3
- Microsoft 365 E5
- Microsoft 365 A3

- Microsoft 365 A5
- Microsoft 365 E3, E5, A3, or A5 Extra Features (when combined with an applicable Office 365 or Microsoft 365 plan)
- Microsoft 365 Copilot

Eligibility through one of above plans provides three additional capabilities within the Loop app:

- Creating new Loop workspaces
- Adding members to Loop workspaces
- Removing members from Loop workspaces

Access to Copilot features within the Loop app requires an active Copilot for Microsoft 365 subscription.

In the section, we have seen how can we access loop, and its different elements such as Components in Microsoft Teams, Outlook, WhiteBoard, OneNote, and in Word. Later we have also, seen that Loop pages are created in the Loop Workspaces. Next, we will see what can be done with Microsoft Loop.

What Can Be Done with Loop?

There are multiple objectives which Loop can achieve to create a collaborative and work like a network environment, which includes Directing a discussion, Brainstorming, Coauthoring, data compilation, and Project management, as explained below:

Directing a discussion

A component may serve as a focused discussion area, similar to a mini breakout room, allowing participants to concentrate on a specific topic while the primary chat thread addresses broader subjects. This approach is particularly effective for facilitating alignment and finalizing decisions.

Brainstorming

Encourage colleagues to contribute their suggestions, whether you are seeking names for a new product or topics for an upcoming team meeting. Utilize a bulleted or numbered list to maintain organization and clarity.

Coauthoring

If you require assistance from your team to refine messaging, Loop components enable real-time collaboration within M365 applications. Utilize these tools to efficiently develop introductions for presentations, draft upcoming social media content, or create essential client communications.

Data Compilation

Distribute a table component with clearly defined columns and rows to your team. In each cell, specify the required data and formally @mention the individual you believe is best equipped to provide it. Additionally, a table may be utilized as an effective tool for creating a straightforward sign-up sheet.

Project Management

The task list component provides a simple method for assigning work with due dates to members of your team. Team members can be notified of their tasks through an @mention. When the assigned work is completed, everyone can mark their task as finished.

Common Use Cases of Loop

Collaborative Authoring and Task Coordination
A centralized platform designed to facilitate real-time collaboration and content creation in an organised and structured manner. This environment enables brainstorming, ideation, and efficient project task management.

Async Collaboration
Asynchronous collaboration allows individuals to contribute at times that are most convenient for them. This approach eliminates the necessity for all participants to coordinate their schedules in order to work simultaneously.

Centralize knowledge.
Look workspaces are collaborative environments that enable users to centralize and manage knowledge resources, including files, links, and data.

Email Optimization
It can be challenging to identify important messages in an overcrowded mailbox. Loop enables users to manage ad hoc tasks, ensuring that updates are reflected across all M365 applications where the component resides.

Reduction of meeting
Unproductive meetings can impede decision-making processes and reduce overall job satisfaction. Fewer meetings are required when task coordination is conducted transparently.

Manage Your Tasks from Loop Task Lists

Task lists, like other Loop components, are modular content elements that remain synchronized wherever they are shared. Microsoft Loop offers seamless integration with Planner and To Do to enhance task management for teams. Tasks generated within Loop components are automatically synchronized with Planner for efficient project oversight and with To Do for management of individual assignments. This integration facilitates real-time updates, centralized tracking, and improved collaboration across both shared workspaces and personal workflows. The methods below are currently available for creating task lists.

Add a task list in Loop app.

Loop workspaces allow users to organize project resources, including tasks. On a Loop page, typing "/" enables insertion of a task list such as Bullet and number list, as shown in Figure 1-14, and additional tasks can be added by selecting + (Add a task), as shown in Figure 1-15. Each task can be assigned to a user by mentioning or selecting their name, as shown in Figure 1-16.

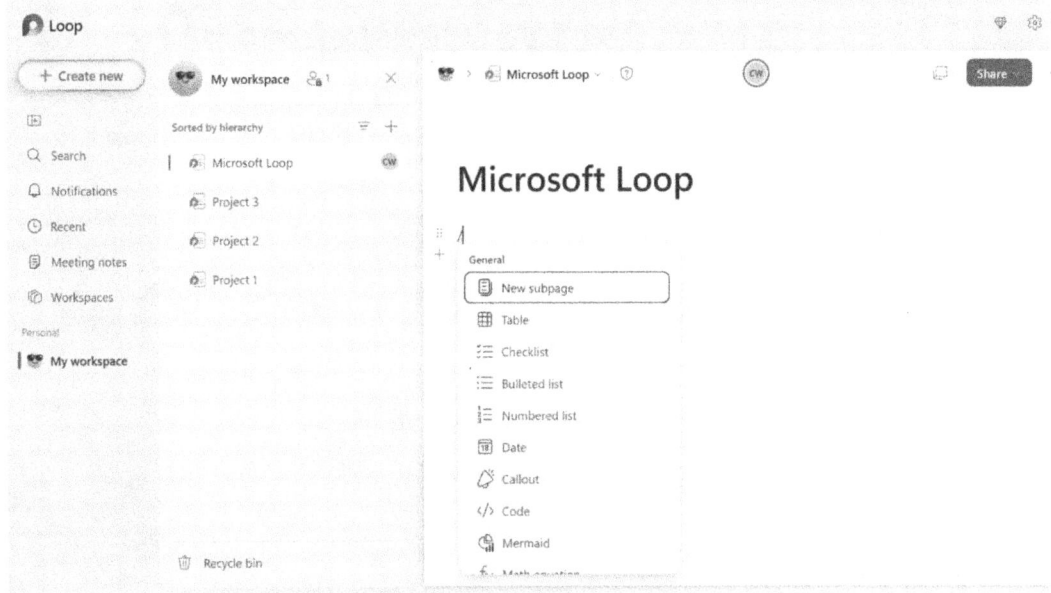

Figure 1-14. "/" enables insertion of a task

CHAPTER 1   INTRODUCTION TO MICROSOFT LOOP: UNDERSTANDING THE PLATFORM

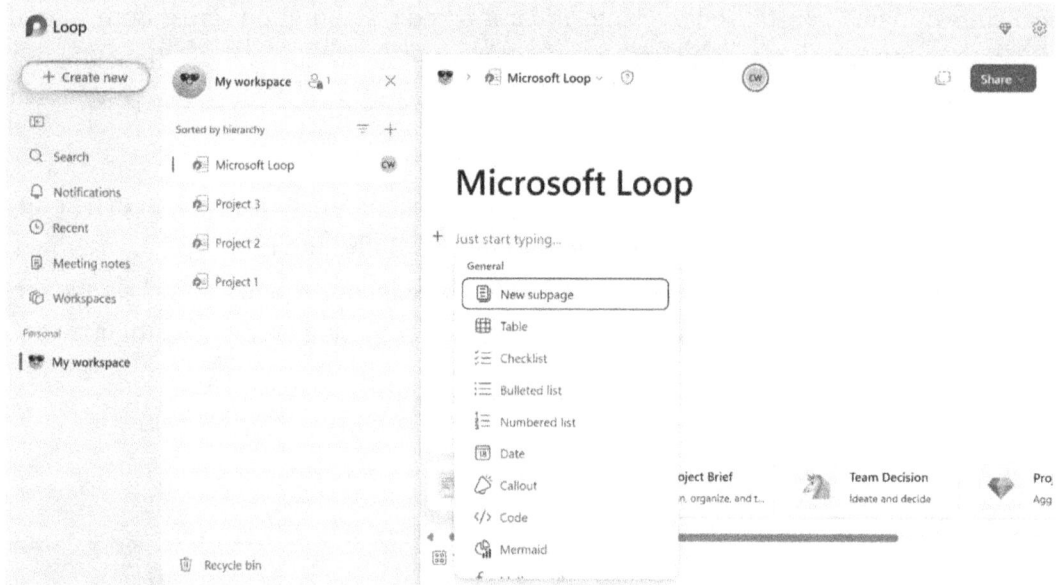

Figure 1-15. *"+" enables insertion of a task*

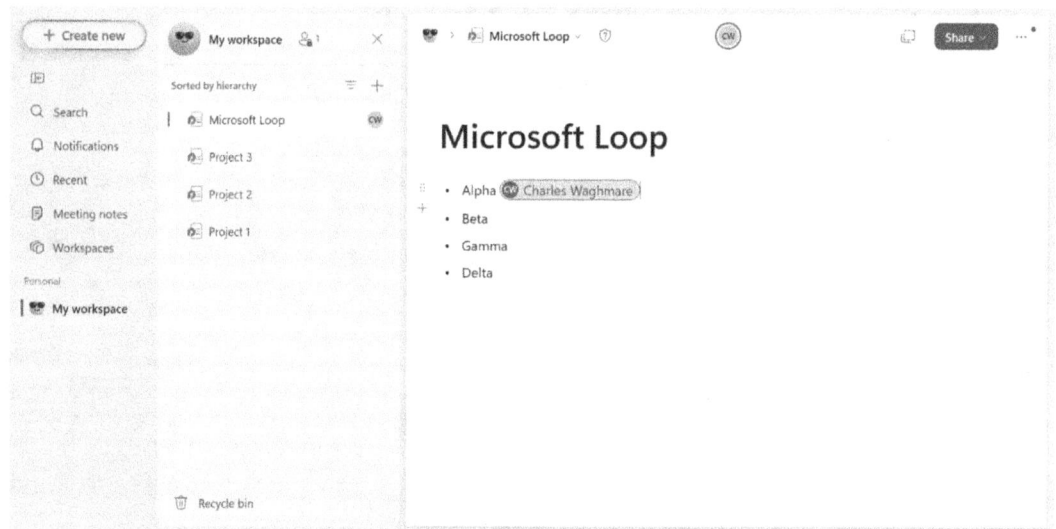

Figure 1-16. *Names assigned to Task*

16

Task lists created in Figure 1-17 can be converted into Loop components by copying, as shown in Figure 1-18, and Component URL, as shown in Figure 1-19, which can then be shared across Microsoft 365 services such as Teams chat, Outlook, and Whiteboard for the web. Updates to tasks, whether additions or completions, remain synchronized wherever the task list is shared.

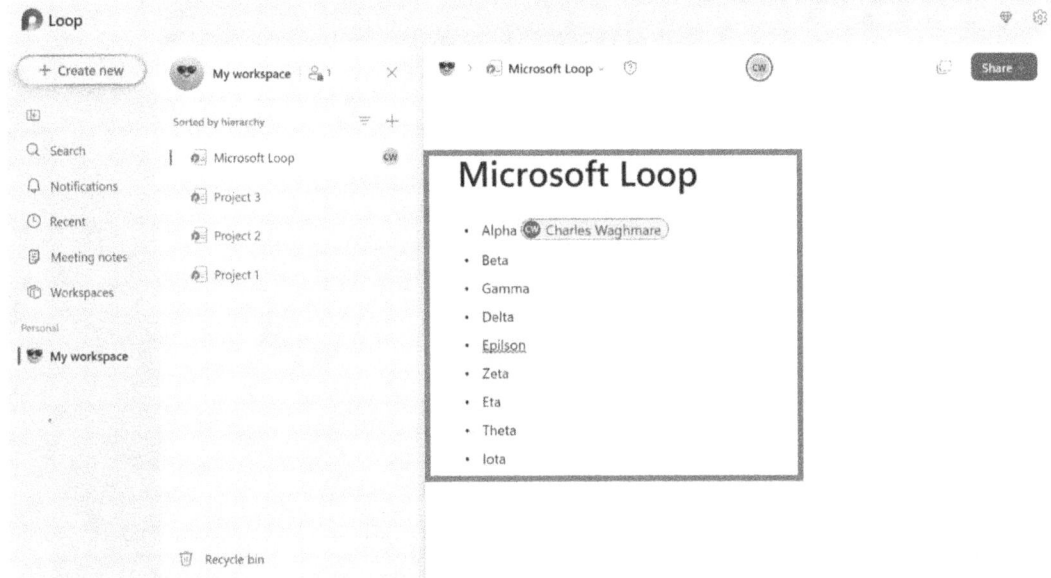

Figure 1-17. *Creation of Task list*

CHAPTER 1 INTRODUCTION TO MICROSOFT LOOP: UNDERSTANDING THE PLATFORM

Figure 1-18. Copy List as Loop Component

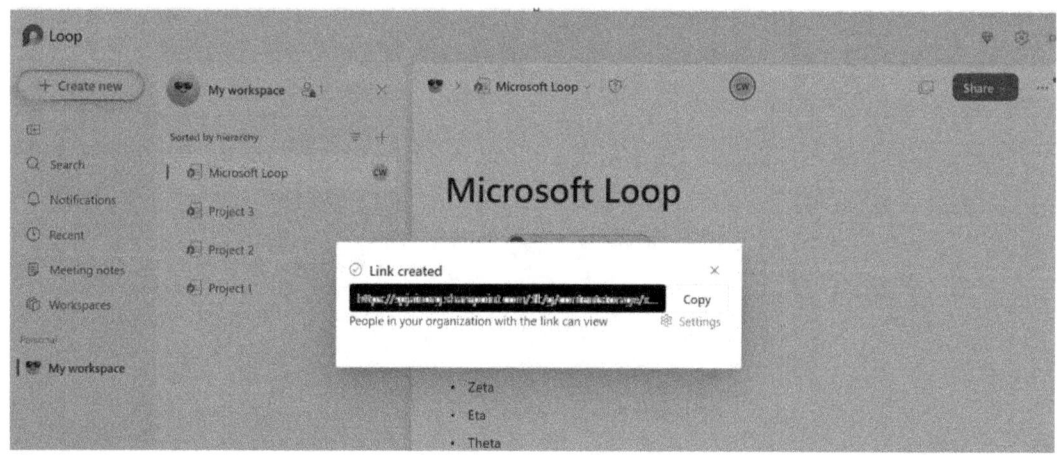

Figure 1-19. Copy URL of Loop Component

CHAPTER 1　INTRODUCTION TO MICROSOFT LOOP: UNDERSTANDING THE PLATFORM

Task list can be created in Teams by accessing Loop component, as shown in Figure 1-20, and then, copy and paste of the URL of Loop component, as shown in Figure 1-21, to display tasks.

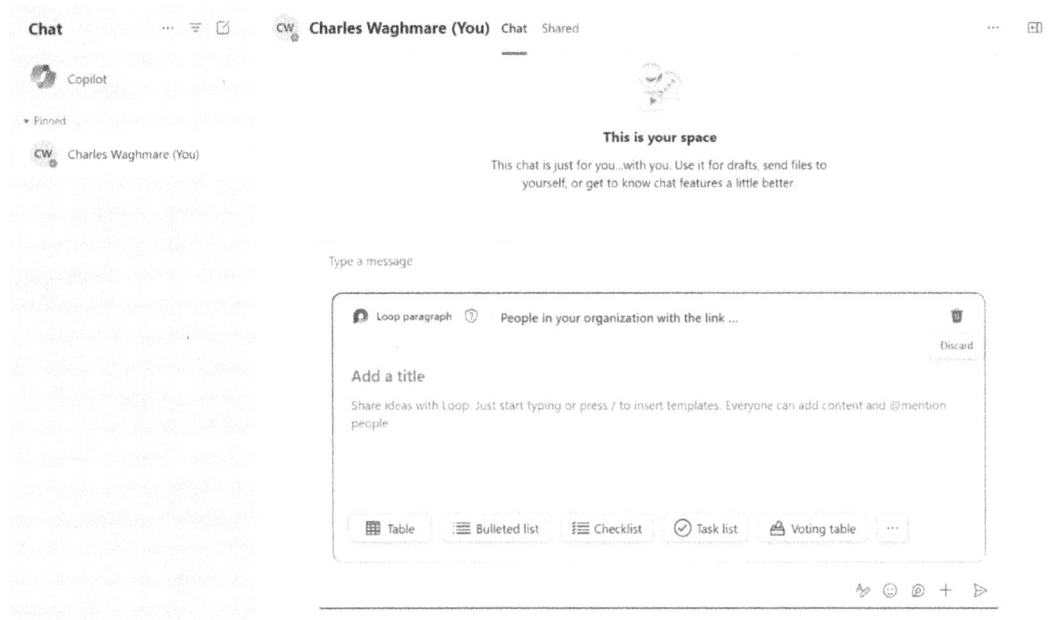

Figure 1-20. *Access Loop component in Teams Chat*

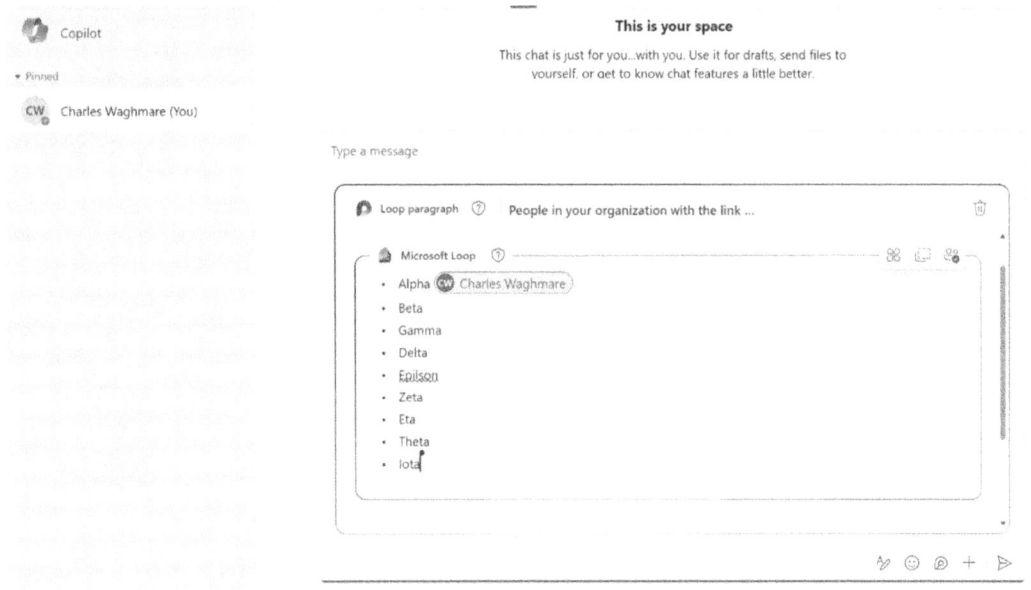

Figure 1-21. *Copy URL of Loop component to display Task list*

CHAPTER 1   INTRODUCTION TO MICROSOFT LOOP: UNDERSTANDING THE PLATFORM

Task list can be created in Outlook by accessing Loop component, as shown in Figure 1-22, and then, copy and paste of the URL of Loop component, as shown in Figure 1-23, to display tasks.

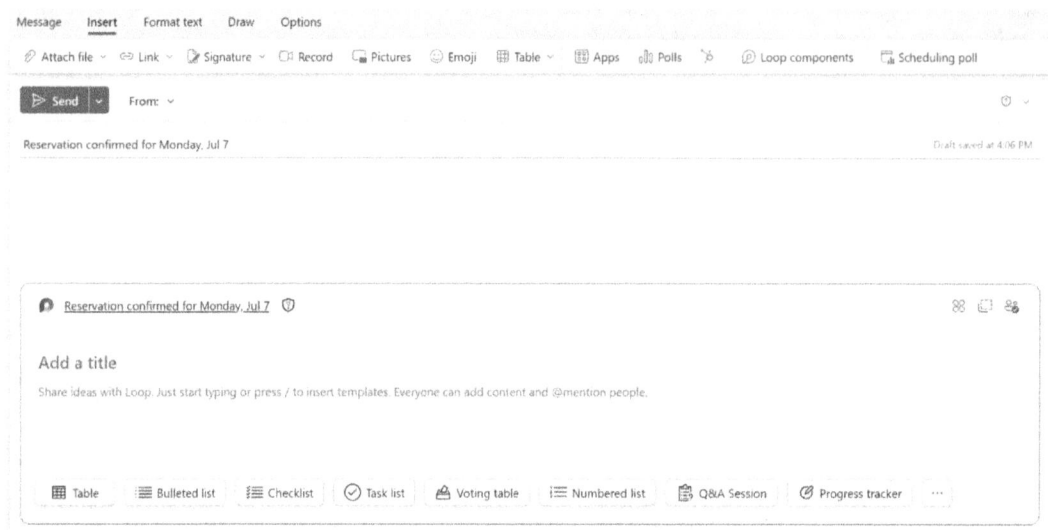

Figure 1-22. Access Loop Component in Outlook

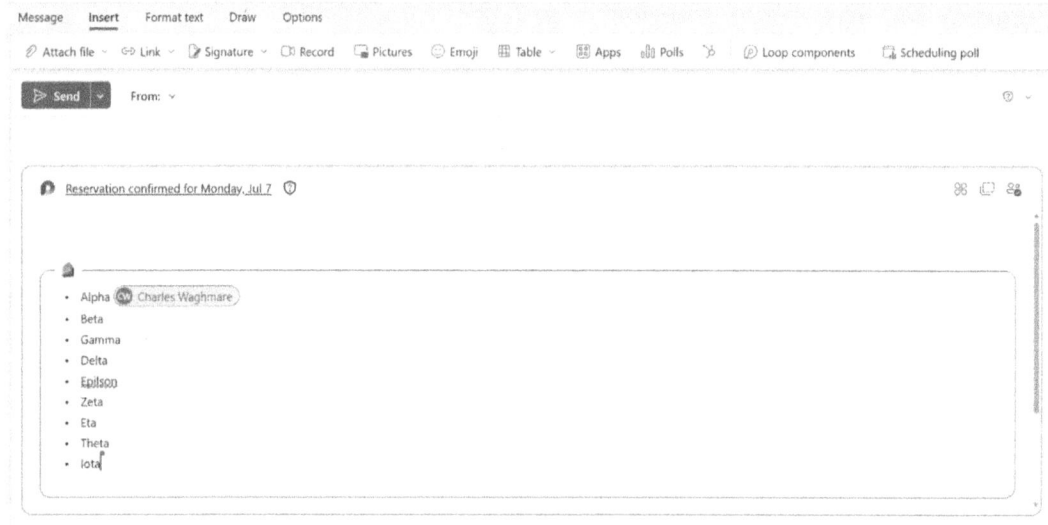

Figure 1-23. Copy URL of Loop component to display task list

Task list can be created in Whiteboard by direct copy and paste of the URL of Loop component, as shown in Figure 1-24, to display tasks.

Figure 1-24. *Copy URL of Loop component in Whiteboard to display task list*

In this section, we have seen that tasks created in Loop component can be copied into Microsoft Teams, Outlook, and Whiteboard. Tasks remain asynchronized across these M365 services and can be seamlessly updated or modified from any of the services, creating a unique seamless experience for end users.

Use Copilot in Loop to Draft and Add Content

Regardless of whether you are initiating work from a Loop component, page, or workspace, Copilot in Loop enables you to draft content, facilitate brainstorming, perform rewrites, and collaborate effectively with your team. *Copilot interprets prompts by leveraging advanced natural language processing (NLP) to analyze user language, intent, and contextual cues. It discerns key instructions and tailors its responses to suit both explicit and subtle prompts. Within Microsoft Loop, Copilot can produce a range of dynamic content to enhance collaboration and productivity, including summaries, task lists, meeting notes, project plans, brainstorming ideas, structured outlines, and more. Seamlessly integrated into Loop's adaptable workspace, Copilot facilitates real-time updates and continuous content improvement.*

CHAPTER 1   INTRODUCTION TO MICROSOFT LOOP: UNDERSTANDING THE PLATFORM

To use Copilot on a blank Loop page, follow any of these methods:

- Select + and then choose Draft page content, as shown in Figure 1-25.
- Enter / and then select Draft page content.
- Select the Copilot button at the top of your page.

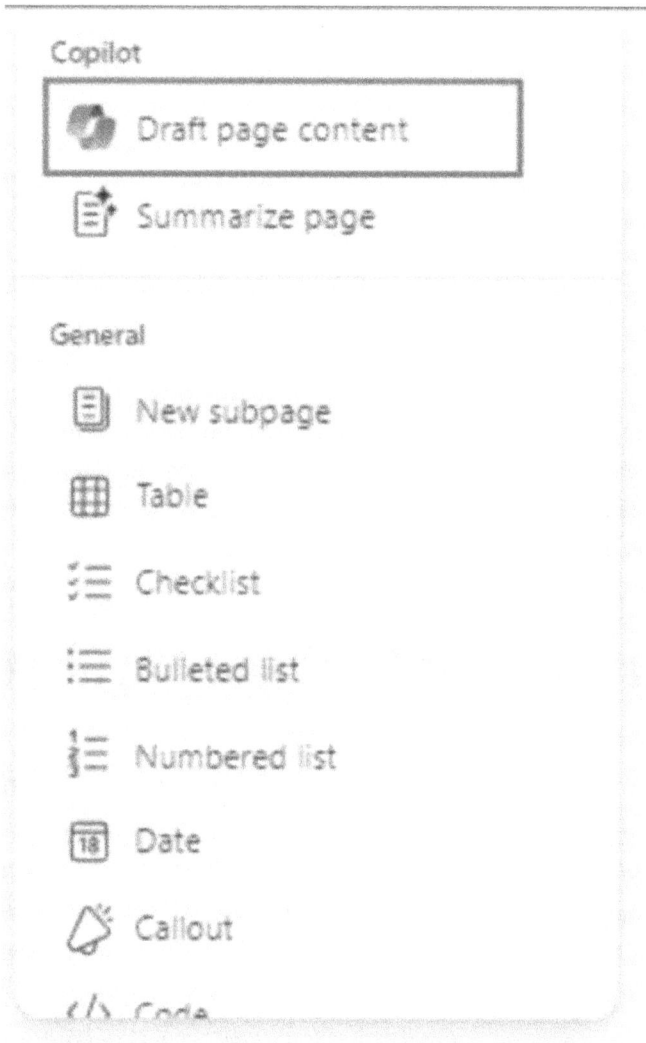

Figure 1-25. Copilot in Loop

Please enter your prompt. For instance: "draft a brochure for an underwater theme park" as shown in the Figure 1-26

Figure 1-26. *Writing a prompt in "Copilot" integrated in Loop*

Keyboard Shortcuts for Microsoft Loop

Proficiency in keyboard shortcuts is essential for enhancing efficiency, productivity, and comfort in computer usage. In an era where digital tools play a central role in professional, academic, and personal environments, the ability to navigate software swiftly and effectively constitutes a valuable skill set. Keyboard shortcuts facilitate the rapid execution of routine tasks—such as copying, pasting, saving, or switching between applications—far more efficiently than traditional mouse navigation. The cumulative effect of this increased speed can result in considerable time savings, which is particularly beneficial for individuals whose work heavily depends on computers, including writers, programmers, designers, and data analysts. By enabling users to keep their hands on the keyboard, shortcuts help maintain workflow continuity and minimize cognitive interruptions, thereby improving overall productivity and reducing mental fatigue.

Furthermore, the use of keyboard shortcuts supports ergonomic health by limiting repetitive mouse movements, aiding in the prevention of strain-related injuries such as carpal tunnel syndrome. For individuals with physical disabilities, shortcuts are critical to accessibility, allowing for more effective interaction with digital content. Mastery of keyboard shortcuts also reflects advanced digital literacy and professionalism, showcasing one's competence and adaptability in utilizing technological resources efficiently—a notable asset in any workplace. As many shortcuts are standardized across various applications and operating systems, they streamline the process of learning new software and transitioning between platforms. Additionally, in cases where mouse functionality is compromised or system responsiveness is diminished, familiarity with keyboard commands provides valuable alternatives for troubleshooting and task management.

CHAPTER 1   INTRODUCTION TO MICROSOFT LOOP: UNDERSTANDING THE PLATFORM

Standard keyboard shortcuts for navigating Microsoft LoopKeyboard shortcuts refer to individual keys or key combinations that offer an efficient alternative to tasks normally performed with a mouse. Below are several standard keyboard shortcuts for navigating Microsoft Loop. Furthermore, Microsoft Loop is compatible with Markdown syntax.

Action	Windows shortcut	Mac shortcut
Mention and alert an individual	@	@
Open Discover Menu to access components.	/	/
Access the Commanding Surface to view available formatting options.	Shift + F10	Shift + F10
Please access the six-dot menu located in the margin.	Alt + Shift + F10	Alt + Shift + F10
Insert your name as an in-line comment.	Ctrl + Alt + M	Ctrl + Alt + M
Please include an appropriate symbol or icon as needed.	Windows logo key +. (period)	^ + ⌘ + Space
Undo typing	Ctrl + Z	⌘ + Z
Redo typing	Ctrl + Y	⌘ + Y
Bold	Ctrl + B	⌘ + B
Italic	Ctrl + I	⌘ + I
Underline	Ctrl + U	⌘ + U
Strikethrough	~~ text ~~	~~ text ~~
Heading 1	Ctrl + Alt + 1or # + Spacebar	Option + ⌘ + 1 or # + Spacebar
Heading 2	Ctrl + Alt + 2or## + Spacebar	Option + ⌘ + 2 or ## + Spacebar
Heading 3	Ctrl + Alt + 3 or### + Spacebar	Option + ⌘ + 3 or### + Spacebar
Divider	--- + Spacebar	--- + Spacebar

(*continued*)

Action	Windows shortcut	Mac shortcut
Checklist commands: • Generate a checklist or a checklist item. • Mark an item as completed on a checklist. Delete a checklist item or the entire checklist.	Ctrl + 1	⌘ + 1
Create unchecked checklist	[ ] + Spacebar	[ ] + Spacebar
Create checked checklist	[x] + Spacebar	[x] + Spacebar
Create a bulleted List	Ctrl +. (period)	⌘ + . (period)
Insert hyperlink	Ctrl + K	⌘ + K
Insert inline code	`text`	`text`
Insert code block	``` + Spacebar	``` + Spacebar
Insert quote	> + Spacebar	> + Spacebar
Delete backward (word)	Ctrl + Backspace	⌘ + Delete
Delete forward (word)	Ctrl + Delete	Option + Delete
Set text alignment to LTR (left to right)	Ctrl + Shift + Alt + L	⌘ + Shift + Alt + L
Set text alignment to RTL (right to left)	Ctrl + Shift + Alt + R	⌘ + Shift + Alt + R
Increase image size	Ctrl + Shift + >	⌘ + Shift + >
Decrease image size	Ctrl + Shift + <	⌘ + Shift + <
Insert a row (only applies to table when in the last cell)	Tab	Tab
Move IP left by word	Ctrl + Left Arrow	Option + Left Arrow
Move IP right by word	Ctrl + Right Arrow	Option + Right Arrow
Move IP up by paragraph	Ctrl + Up Arrow	⌘ + Left Arrow
Move IP down by paragraph	Ctrl + Down Arrow	⌘ + Right Arrow
Move IP to beginning of line	Home	Function + Up Arrow
Move IP to end of line	End	Function + Down Arrow
Increase indent	Tab	Tab
Decrease indent	Shift + Tab	Shift + Tab

(continued)

CHAPTER 1   INTRODUCTION TO MICROSOFT LOOP: UNDERSTANDING THE PLATFORM

Action	Windows shortcut	Mac shortcut
Navigate the main regions of apps (canvas, left nav, top bar)	Ctrl + F6	⌘ + F6
Paste as plain text	Ctrl + Shift + V	⌘ + Shift + V
Paste markdown syntax and convert to rich text	Ctrl + Shift + V	⌘ + Shift + V

Keyboard shortcuts offer more than just increased efficiency; they provide a strategic approach to interacting with digital tools. By utilizing keyboard shortcuts, users can optimize their workflow, minimize physical strain, and enhance both confidence and competence in technology use. Whether optimizing academic tasks, improving workplace productivity, or seeking more ergonomic computing experience, acquiring proficiency in keyboard shortcuts constitutes a worthwhile investment with substantial benefits.

Benefits of Microsoft Loop

Microsoft Loop is an advanced collaboration platform engineered to enhance team workflows through flexible components, real-time coauthoring, and seamless integration across Microsoft 365 applications. This solution redefines productivity by prioritizing fluid and dynamic interactions around shared content, moving beyond traditional static documents. Microsoft Loop offers significant advantages, particularly in contemporary hybrid and remote work settings where adaptability, transparency, and collaboration are essential. This discussion will examine the principal benefits of Microsoft Loop, such as its real-time collaboration features, modular content architecture, integration within the Microsoft 365 suite, facilitation of increased productivity, support for project management, and contribution to a more inclusive and adaptive workplace environment.

Real-Time Collabaoration

A key advantage of Microsoft Loop is its real-time collaboration capability. Unlike traditional documents, which often require sequential editing or extensive version control, Loop enables multiple users to contribute to the same content concurrently.

As a result, updates, edits, and comments are reflected instantly, minimizing the necessity for prolonged email exchanges or meetings to coordinate changes. This immediate interaction promotes teamwork and facilitates more efficient decision-making and workflow management. Whether teams are brainstorming, drafting proposals, or overseeing projects, Loop helps ensure that all members remain aligned both operationally and strategically.

Modular Content Structure

A key benefit of Microsoft Loop lies in its modular content structure, centered around Loop components such as lists, tables, notes, and tasks. These components are not limited to a single document or application; instead, they can be embedded within Microsoft Teams, Outlook, Word, and other Microsoft 365 apps, remaining synchronized wherever they are utilized. This modular approach enables users to create content once and efficiently reuse it across various contexts, reducing inconsistencies and duplication. For example, a task list generated as a Loop component within a Teams chat can be updated via Outlook or Word, with all changes reflected universally. This flexibility supports teams in working within their preferred tools, while ensuring consistency and a sole source of truth.

Deep Integration with M365

Microsoft Loop offers comprehensive integration with Microsoft 365, thereby enhancing both its capabilities and accessibility. As a core component of the Microsoft ecosystem, Loop operates seamlessly with established applications such as Teams chat, Outlook Web App, OneNote, OneDrive, SharePoint Online, Microsoft Word Online and Whiteboard. This integration enables users to utilize Loop's collaborative functionalities while maintaining familiar workflows, which reduces the need for extensive retraining. For instance, a Loop page can be used to efficiently organize meeting notes within Teams or manage action items in Outlook. This level of interoperability reduces barriers to use and encourages broad adoption across teams and departments.

Productivity

With regard to productivity, Microsoft Loop incorporates features designed to enhance workflow efficiency and minimize cognitive burden. Its user-friendly interface and intelligent recommendations enable users to concentrate on content development rather than formatting or file organization. The collaborative canvas supports unstructured ideation and creativity, making it well-suited for brainstorming, planning documents, and innovation workshops. Furthermore, Loop facilitates project management through its capabilities to monitor changes, assign tasks, and establish deadlines within various components. This structured approach is especially beneficial for managing complex projects that require coordination among multiple stakeholders and deliverables.

Project Management

Project management is another domain where Microsoft Loop demonstrates significant utility. Thanks to its adaptable framework and real-time synchronization, Loop can function effectively as a streamlined project management solution tailored to diverse team requirements. Users have the capability to develop project pages that integrate timelines, task lists, status updates, and embedded documents within a unified workspace. These collaborative pages facilitate shared editing, offering transparent insight into project progress and delineating responsibilities. In contrast to conventional project management platforms, Loop accommodates dynamic growth and change, rendering it well-suited for both structured and agile approaches. Teams may begin with a basic checklist and incrementally expand it into a comprehensive project dashboard as their initiative advances.

Collaborative Workforce

In addition to its functional benefits, Microsoft Loop fosters an inclusive and adaptable workplace environment. Its collaborative framework supports active participation from all team members, irrespective of their location or role within the organization. By facilitating asynchronous collaboration and reducing organizational silos, Loop ensures equitable opportunities for input, enabling meaningful contributions from everyone involved. This capability is particularly valuable in hybrid work settings where employees may be dispersed across various time zones and adhere to different schedules. The platform's flexibility accommodates a range of working styles and preferences, thereby supporting equity and enhancing engagement.

Knowledge and Information Sharing

Furthermore, Microsoft Loop facilitates effective knowledge management and information sharing in a dynamic and sustainable manner. Conventional documents may become obsolete or difficult to locate within folders, hindering access to valuable insights. In contrast, Loop components function as dynamic content elements that can be updated and referenced in various contexts. This capability enables organizations to efficiently capture institutional knowledge, disseminate best practices, and foster a culture of continuous learning. Teams may develop Loop pages to serve as knowledge repositories, onboarding resources, or evolving FAQs, ensuring ongoing relevance and adaptability.

Compliance

Security and compliance are paramount factors, and Microsoft Loop leverages the comprehensive security framework provided by Microsoft 365. Organizations are able to control access permissions, track user activity, and maintain data protection standards with the familiar suite of Microsoft management tools. This uniform approach streamlines governance processes and mitigates the potential for data breaches or compliance infractions. For sectors operating under stringent regulatory regimes, such as healthcare and finance, this degree of oversight is indispensable.

Agile Workforce

In addition to its practical advantages, Microsoft Loop signifies a transformation in approaches to work and collaboration. The platform moves beyond static documents and isolated communication, promoting a more dynamic, interconnected, and human-centered methodology. By facilitating seamless content movement across various applications and teams, Loop enables a more agile and responsive workflow. This environment supports innovation, iterative development, and collective input—attributes that are increasingly vital in today's rapidly evolving professional landscape.

In summary, Microsoft Loop delivers numerous benefits that position it as an essential resource for contemporary teams and organizations. Its capabilities for real-time collaboration, modular content creation, smooth integration, and intuitive design contribute to enhanced productivity, efficient project management, and the cultivation of an inclusive and adaptive workplace culture. By breaking down silos between applications and allowing content to be shared and updated across multiple contexts, Loop empowers users to work with greater intelligence, speed, and cooperation. As the workplace continues to change, tools such as Microsoft Loop will be integral in maintaining connection, alignment, and operational effectiveness. Whether managing complex initiatives, leading brainstorming sessions, or organizing team activities, Microsoft Loop offers the versatility and capability required to achieve your objectives and ensure team success.

This chapter concludes with a review of the main topics covered: an introduction to Microsoft Loop, an overview of elements such as Loop components, pages, and workspaces, details on the three core elements of Microsoft Loop, potential uses for Loop, typical use cases, managing tasks using Loop Task lists, utilizing Copilot in Loop to draft and add content, keyboard shortcuts for Microsoft Loop, the importance of knowing these shortcuts, and the benefits provided by Microsoft Loop. In the upcoming chapter, we will take a deep dive into Microsoft Loop by exploring in detail Loop pages, components, and workspaces and their working with M365 applications and hence this will give us getting Started with Microsoft Loop.

CHAPTER 2

Getting Started with Microsoft Loop

The previous chapter covered an introduction to Microsoft Loop, including an overview of elements such as Loop components, pages, and workspaces. It also outlined the three core elements of Microsoft Loop, described possible applications and common use cases, explained task management with Loop Task lists, discussed the use of Copilot in Loop for drafting and adding content, presented keyboard shortcuts for Microsoft Loop, and addressed the relevance and benefits associated with these features. In the upcoming chapter, we will take a deep dive into Microsoft Loop by exploring topics such as creating a new loop workspace, creating pages and subpages within a loop workspace, favoriting a workspace, adding and removing loop workspace members, renaming and restyling a workspace, managing page versions, printing and exporting workspace pages, and deleting loop workspaces

Introduction

The Microsoft Loop app is accessible as a web application at loop.cloud.microsoft and through the Microsoft 365 App Launcher. A desktop version is also available, offering similar layout and interface to the web version. Additionally, Microsoft Loop can be used on Android and iOS mobile devices, enabling content creation and viewing from various locations.

    The initial page of the web app, referred to as the landing page, is located in the Workspaces tab. If no workspaces are currently set up or if there are none where membership has been assigned, a getting-started workspace may be available, containing informational content to assist new users.

Within a workspace, the navigation area is situated on the left side, which can be expanded or collapsed to display tool names alongside their icons. This section allows for efficient navigation between different areas, such as notifications, ongoing work, and recently accessed sections across multiple workspaces.

Navigation within a specific workspace occurs using the panel to the right of the navigation area. Content here is typically organized by hierarchy, including links to documents and pages. When establishing a new workspace, an untitled page is provided for initial use, with the option to add further pages and materials.

Returning to the main landing page can be done via the icon in the upper left corner. The page also includes sections for recent components and pages. Components refer to portable pieces of content usable across Microsoft 365 platforms and are accessible from this area regardless of whether they reside in a workspace. Pages from the workspace can be accessed similarly.

An ideas area is provided to store notes or concepts temporarily until they can be appropriately categorized into workspaces. Account information is located in the upper right corner, enabling account management or sign out. Next to this, the settings menu contains theme preferences, page order configuration, accessibility, privacy, language proofing, and editing options.

Creating a New Loop Workspace

Loop workspaces provide an effective environment for collaborative efforts on various initiatives, including projects and programs. Each workspace is structured with pages and subpages, offering organizational features similar to those found in OneNote notebooks—facilitating the management of related content.

A workspace enables collaboration on diverse materials such as textual content, meeting notes, videos, files, images, and Loop components within a unified platform. To establish a new workspace in the Loop application, select the plus symbol in the navigation area, choose "Create New," and then select "New Workspace" from the menu, as shown in Figure 2-1.

CHAPTER 2 GETTING STARTED WITH MICROSOFT LOOP

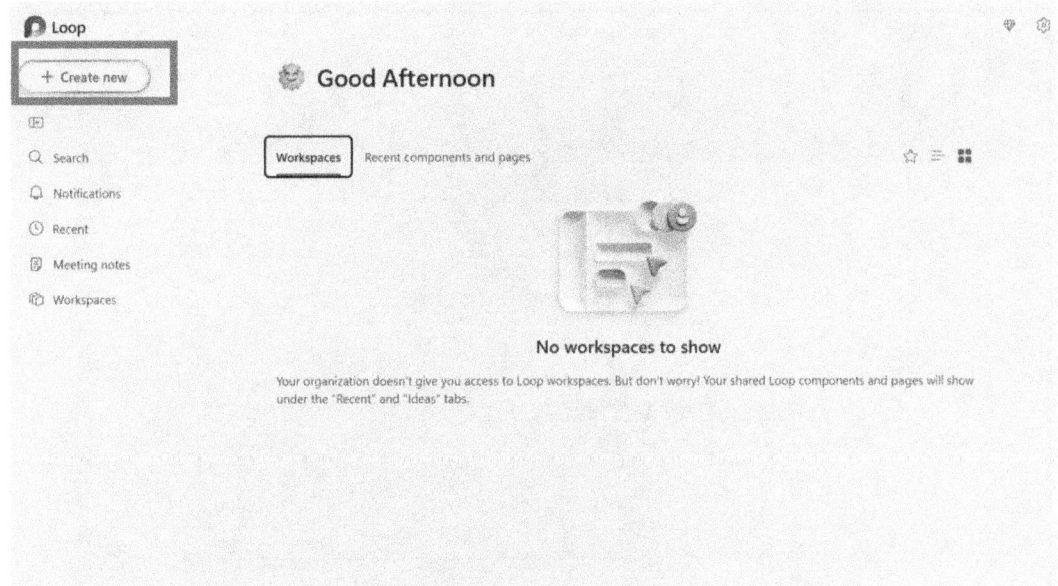

Figure 2-1. *Option to create a new Workspace*

Assign a suitable name to the workspace, as shown in Figure 2-2, and select an appropriate icon by browsing or searching through available emojis and categories, as shown in Figure 2-3.

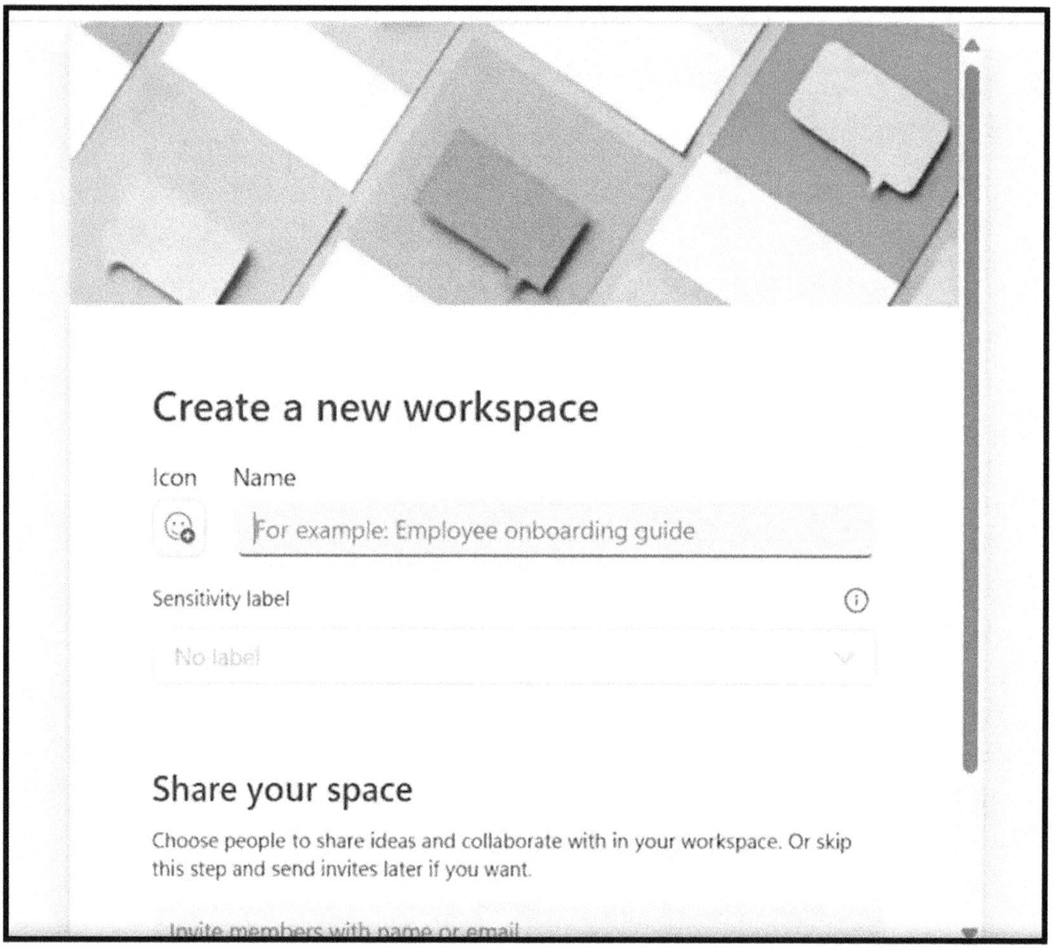

CHAPTER 2 GETTING STARTED WITH MICROSOFT LOOP

Figure 2-2. *Give a name to the Workspace*

CHAPTER 2 GETTING STARTED WITH MICROSOFT LOOP

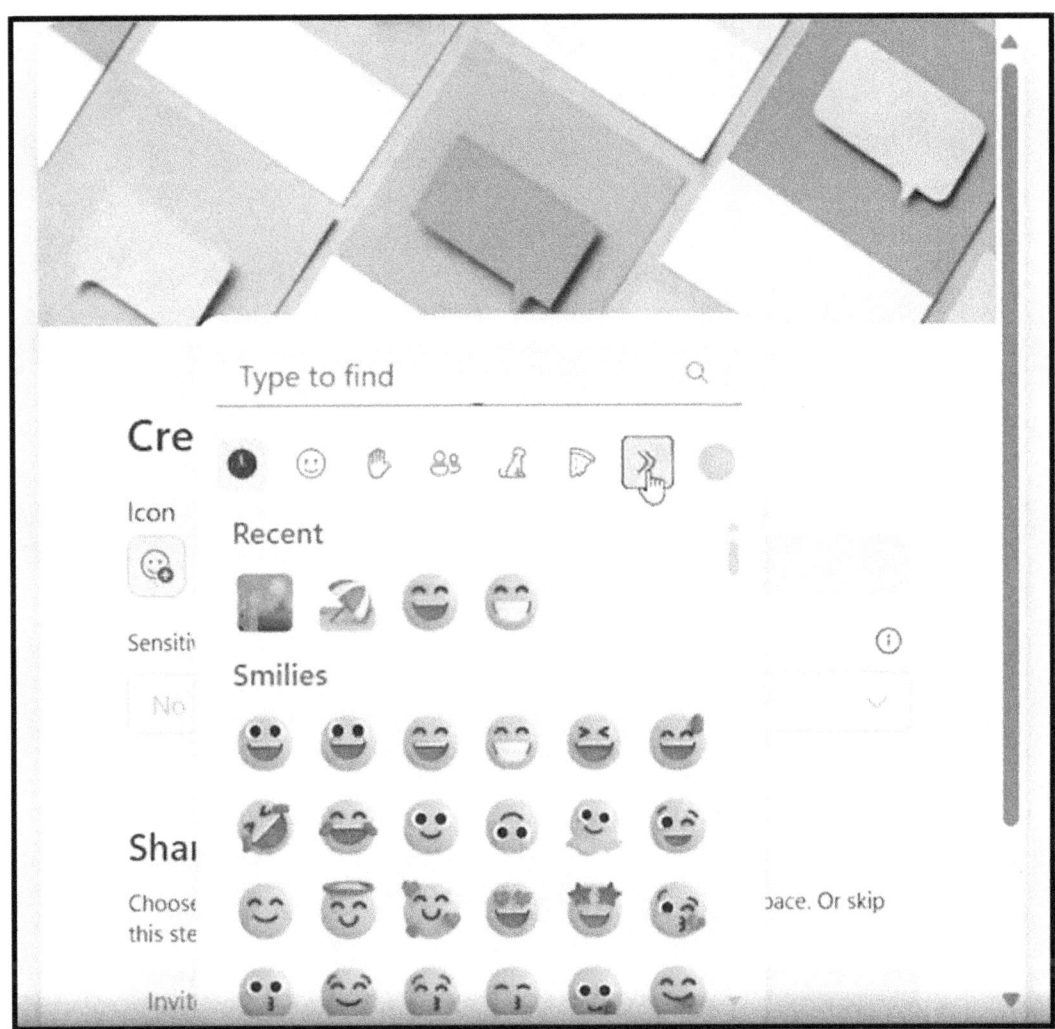

Figure 2-3. *Choose your Icon*

The option to invite colleagues to join the workspace is provided during setup, either by entering their names or email addresses, as shown in Figure 2-4. However, invitations may also be extended after configuring and organizing the workspace, depending on preferred workflow.

CHAPTER 2 GETTING STARTED WITH MICROSOFT LOOP

Figure 2-4. Invite your colleagues to your workspace

Then click on continue button, as shown in Figure 2-5, to proceed to next step of workspace creation.

CHAPTER 2   GETTING STARTED WITH MICROSOFT LOOP

Figure 2-5. *Continue option to proceed for workspace creation*

The system will display suggested files in the "All Files" area based on the workspace name, making it possible to link relevant documents—such as Events—to the workspace as needed, as shown in Figure 2-6. Additionally, it is advisable to include a brief description specifying the workspace's purpose, which further refines file suggestions, as shown in Figure 2-6.

CHAPTER 2 GETTING STARTED WITH MICROSOFT LOOP

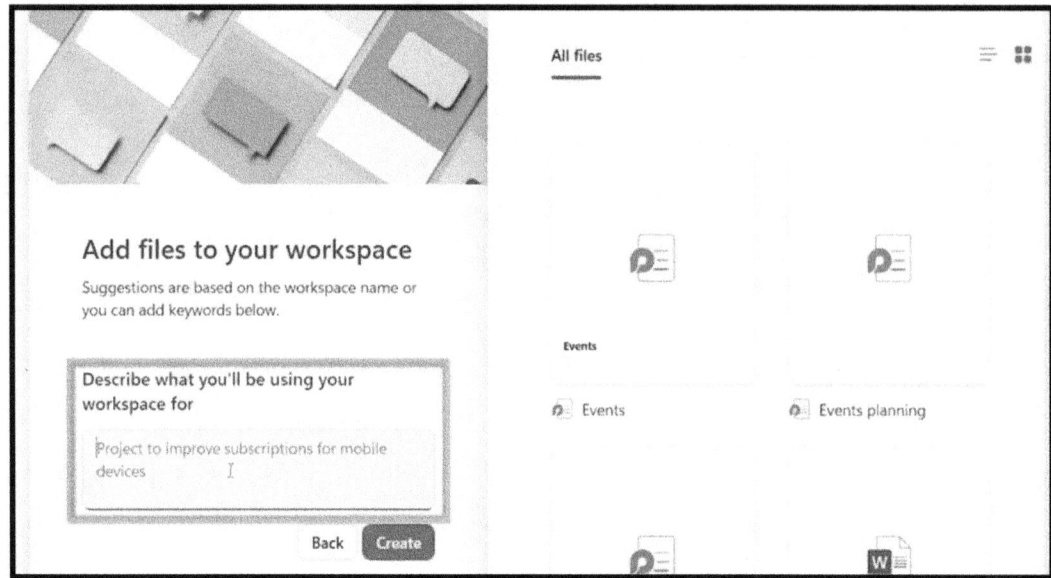

Figure 2-6. *Add workspace description and files to workspace*

Upon entering the workspace, its name appears at the top of the navigation pane, alongside a section displaying any linked documents added during setup, as shown in Figure 2-7. These documents remain linked to external files—in this case, for example, opening in Word for the web if using the Loop web application. Access permissions are required for all workspace members to view linked files. This integration facilitates streamlined access to supporting materials directly within the workspace context.

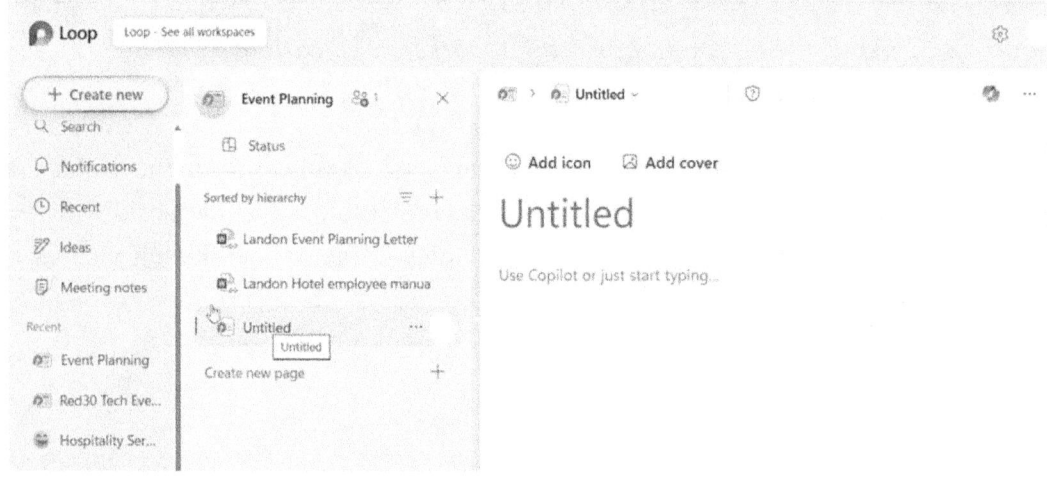

Figure 2-7. *Successful creation of workspace with files attached during setup*

An initial, untitled page is provided, serving as a canvas for adding content. Subsequent sections will address the best practices for creating, managing, and locating workspace content. This concludes the setup overview, ensuring users are prepared to effectively utilize Loop workspaces for collaborative engagement.

Creating Pages and Subpages Within a Loop Workspace

A well-structured book is essential, and this principle equally applies here. Prior to addressing content creation, it is beneficial to consider and establish the page layout. There are multiple methods available for adding a new page to your workspace. By hovering your cursor over the page area, as shown in Figure 2-8, you will see an option labeled "Create New Page," as shown in Figure 2-9. Alternatively, you may click on the plus sign at the top left, as shown in Figure 2-10 and select "Page" from the menu. Upon doing so, a new, entitled page will be generated, as shown in Figure 2-11.

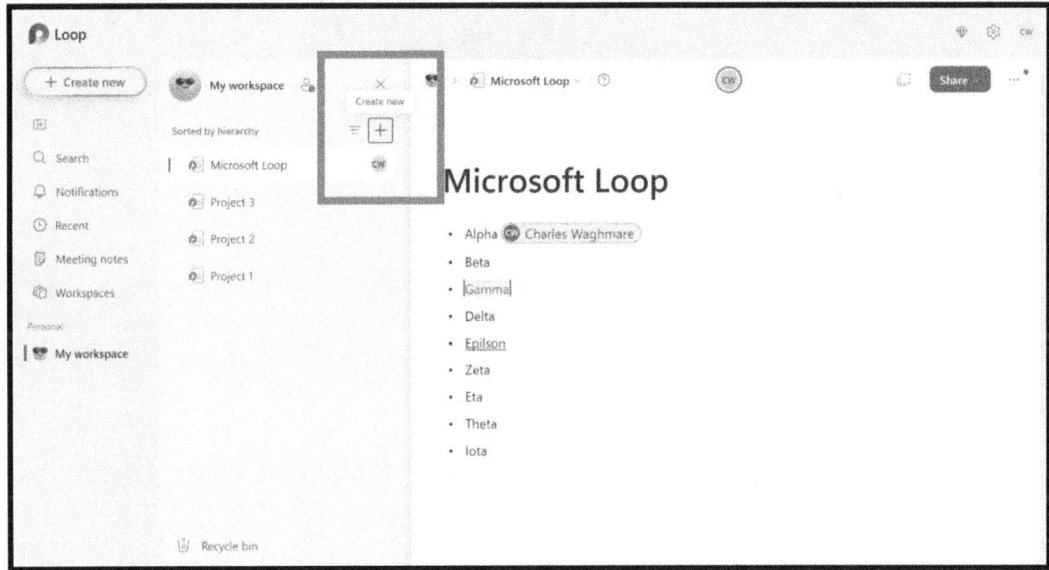

Figure 2-8. Hovering your cursor over the page area for a new page creation

CHAPTER 2 GETTING STARTED WITH MICROSOFT LOOP

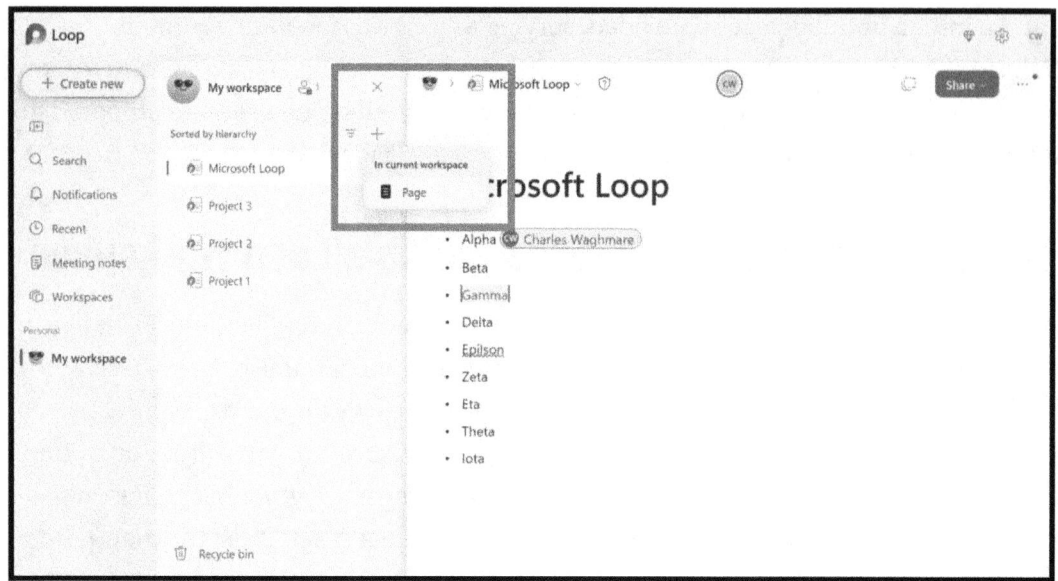

Figure 2-9. *Image to create a new page*

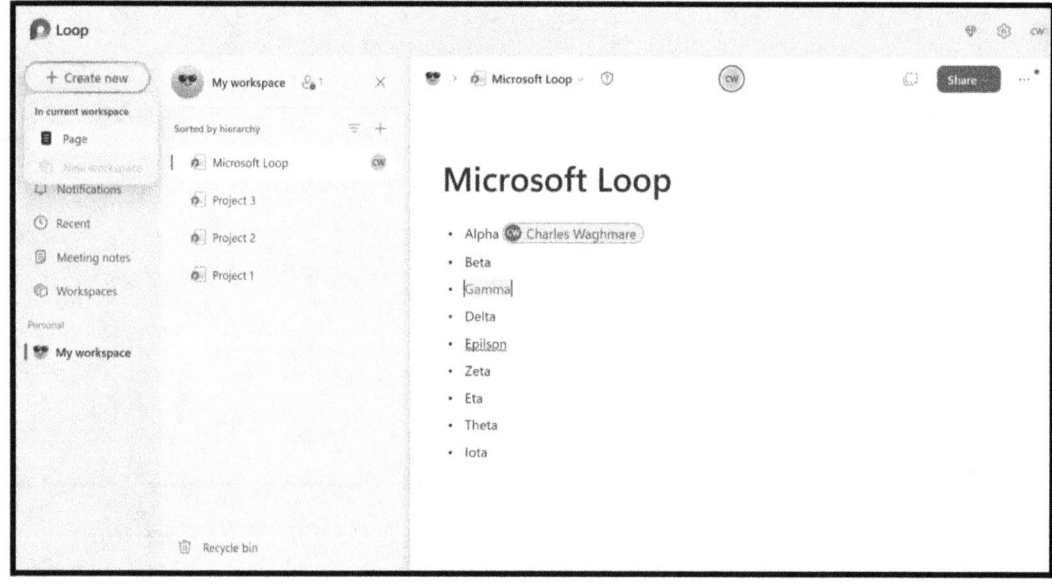

Figure 2-10. *Create a new page from Create option*

CHAPTER 2 GETTING STARTED WITH MICROSOFT LOOP

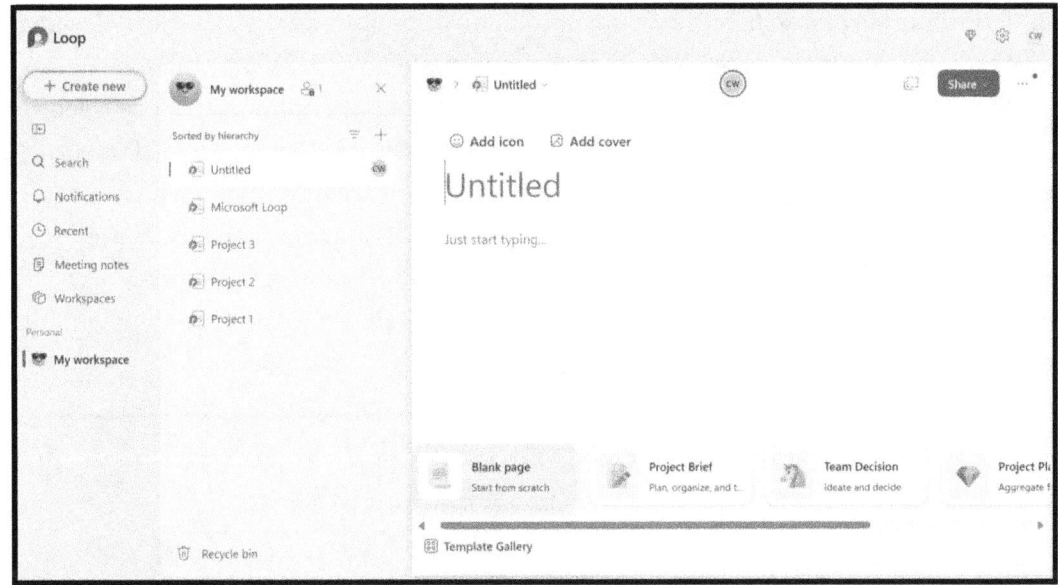

Figure 2-11. *Creation of a new untitled page*

For instance, assign appropriate titles to your pages—such as "Human Resources" and "Information Technology"—to ensure clarity and organization, as shown in Figure 2-12.

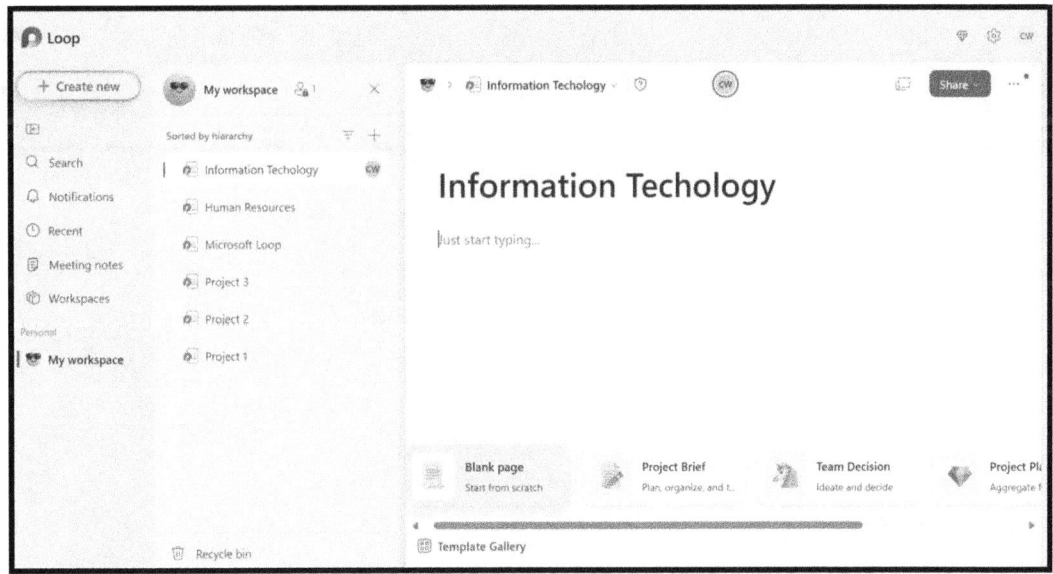

Figure 2-12. *Creation of new pages in workspace*

To establish a hierarchical structure or relationships among pages, you can designate subpages beneath main pages. For example, by hovering over the "Information Technology" page and selecting the three ellipses (more page options), choose "New Sub Page" from the menu, as shown in Figure 2-13. This new subpage, once named (e.g., "Software Engineering"), will appear indented beneath its parent page, as shown in Figure 2-14, indicating its subordinate status. The arrow icon beside the main page enables you to collapse, as shown in Figure 2-15, or expand subpages as needed, as shown in Figure 2-16, facilitating effective focus on relevant content without unnecessary distraction.

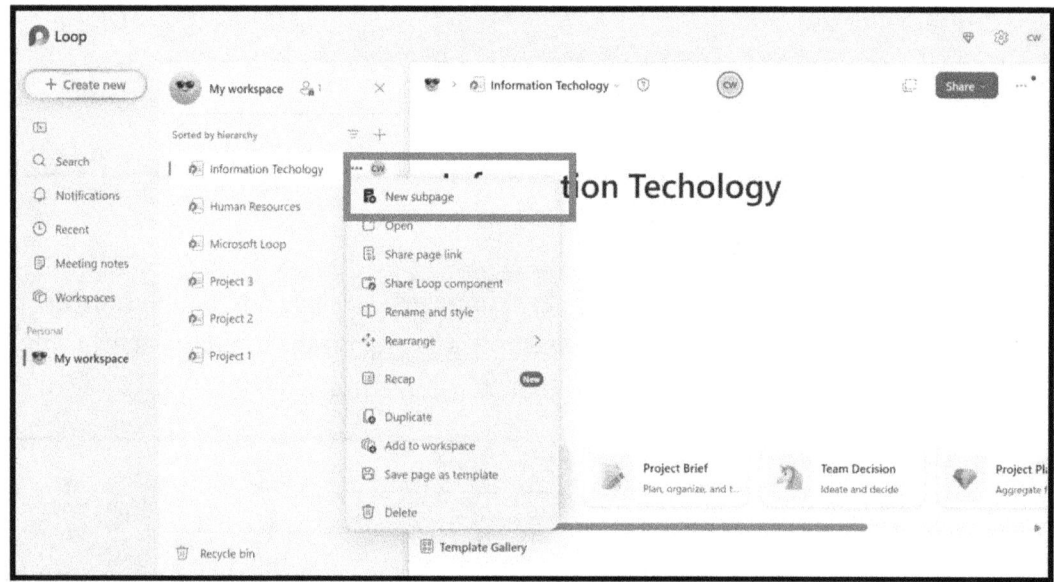

Figure 2-13. Option to create a New subpage

CHAPTER 2 GETTING STARTED WITH MICROSOFT LOOP

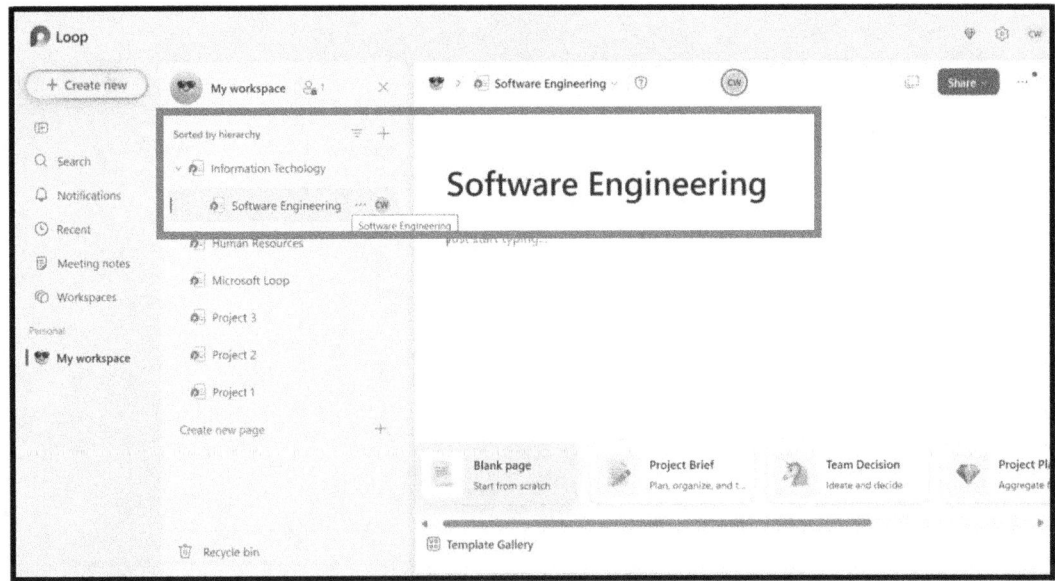

Figure 2-14. *Creation of a subpage*

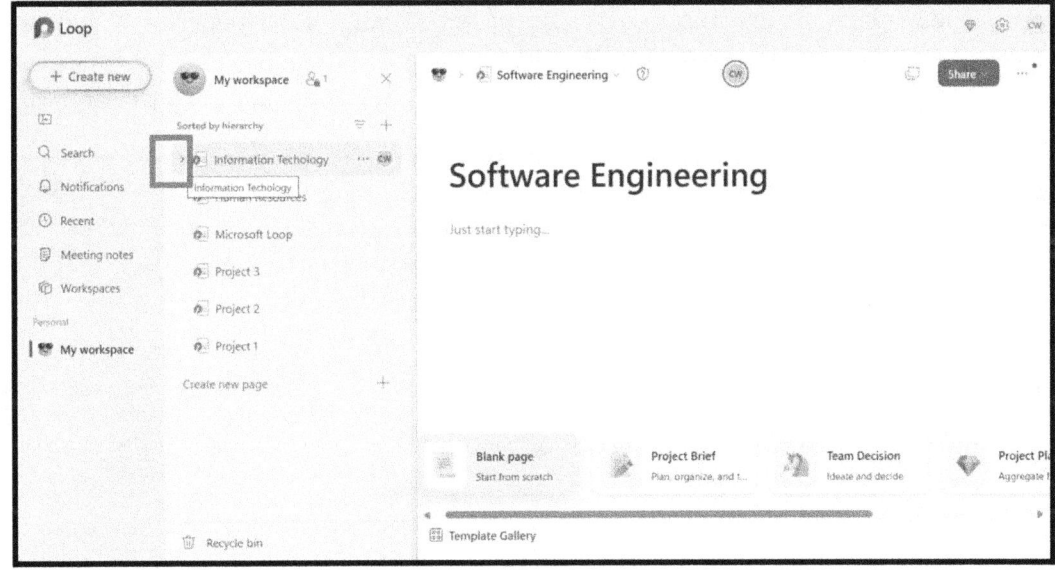

Figure 2-15. *Collapse of a subpage*

43

CHAPTER 2   GETTING STARTED WITH MICROSOFT LOOP

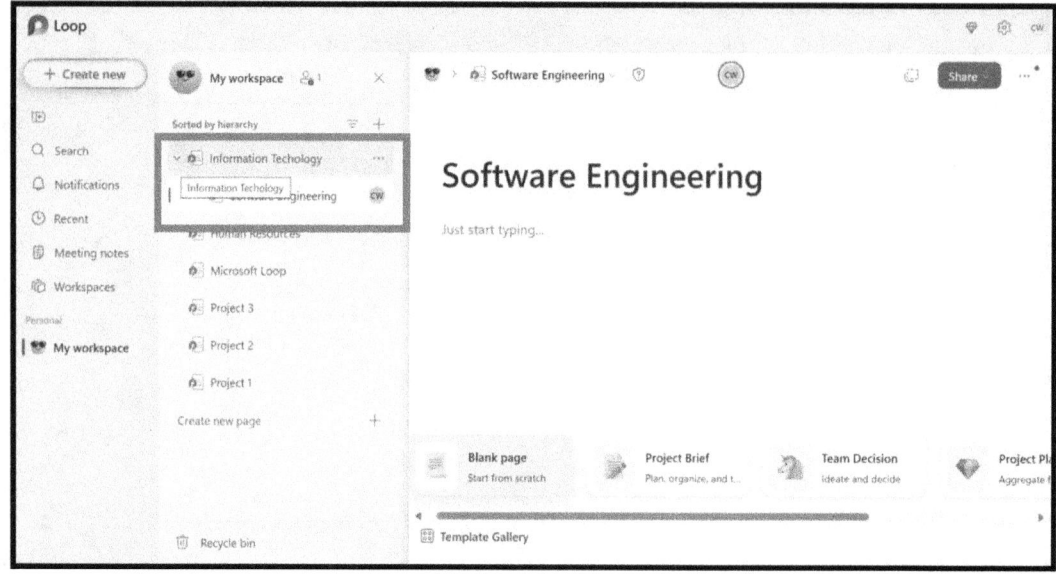

Figure 2-16. *Expanding a subpage*

Pages and subpages within your workspace can be rearranged using several approaches. Selecting the ellipses next to a page and clicking "Rearrange," as shown in Figure 2-17, allows you to move pages up or down or adjust them between main and subpage status. Additionally, you may manually drag and drop pages to reorder them.

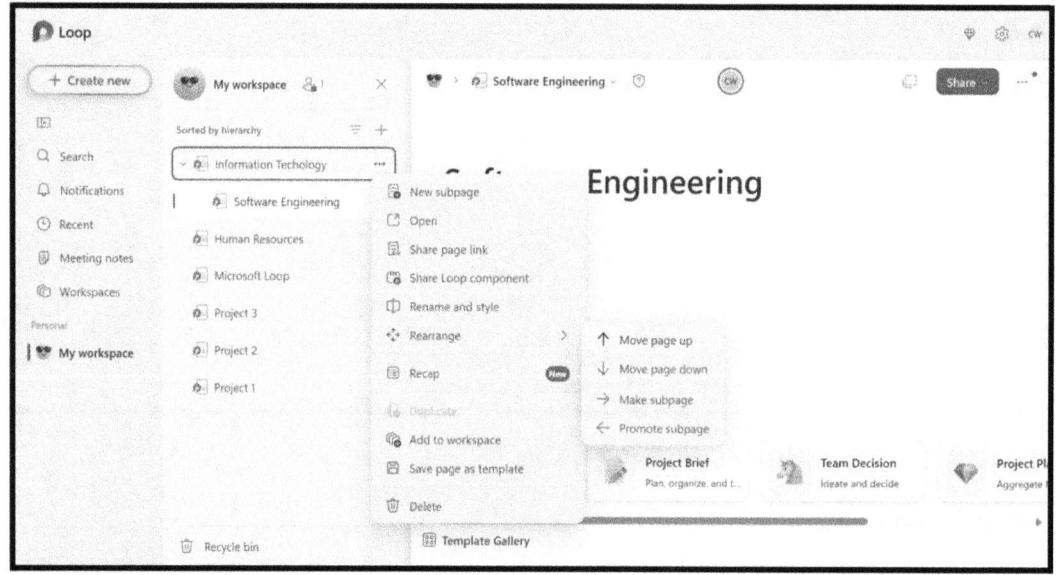

Figure 2-17. *Option to rearrange pages*

44

CHAPTER 2 GETTING STARTED WITH MICROSOFT LOOP

By default, new pages are added to the top of the page list; however, this setting is configurable. To modify the default positioning, navigate to Settings via the cog icon in the upper right corner, as shown in Figure 2-18, access the "Create New Pages" option, and select your preferred placement, as shown in Figure 2-19. Exit settings to save your changes. These steps will assist you in establishing a clear and systematic structure within your workspace, making it easier to organize and manage both pages and subpages according to your requirements.

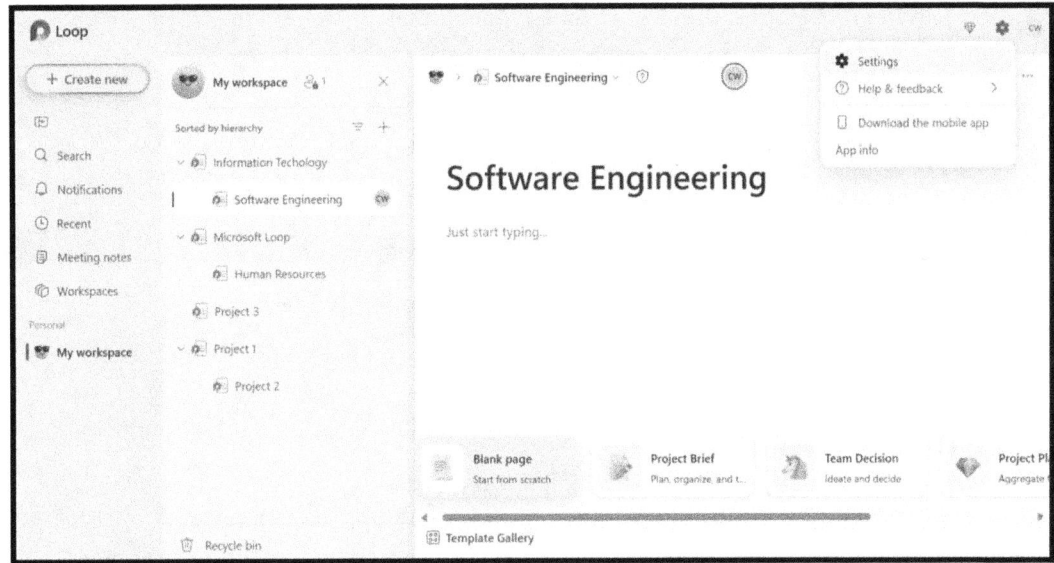

Figure 2-18. *Navigate to settings*

Figure 2-19. Option to manage the position of new page creation

Favoriting a Workspace

You may be a member of multiple workspaces. To efficiently access a specific workspace for viewing or editing content, you can add it to your favorites. The following steps outline how to choose your favorite workspace:

- Navigate from within any workspace to the landing page by selecting "Loop" in the upper-left corner, as shown in Figure 2-20.

- On the landing page, locate the workspace you wish to favorite—such as the "My workspace" and select start option to select "Favorite" from the More Menu, as shown in Figure 2-21.

CHAPTER 2   GETTING STARTED WITH MICROSOFT LOOP

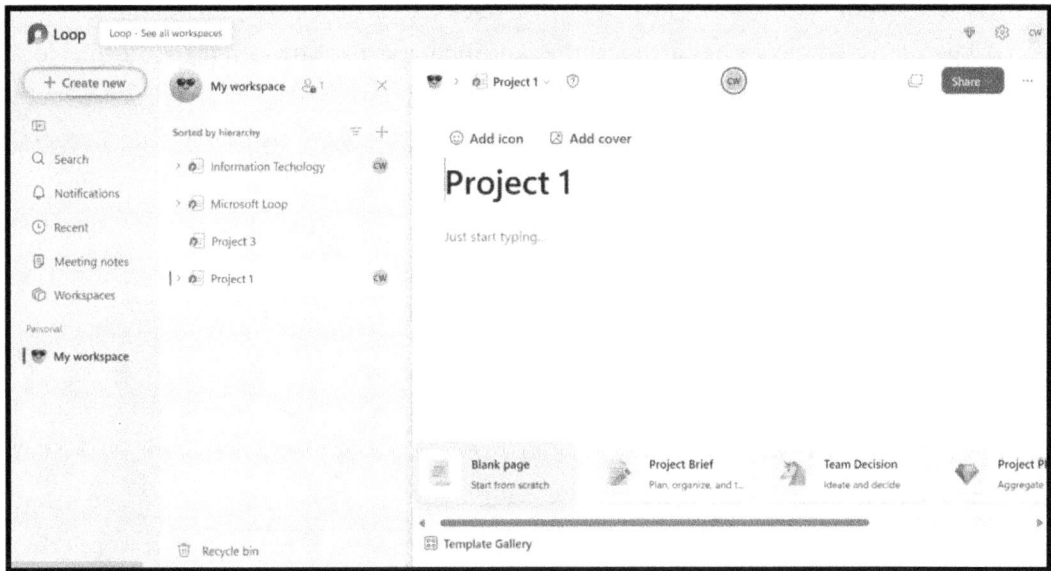

Figure 2-20. *Navigating to Loop landing page*

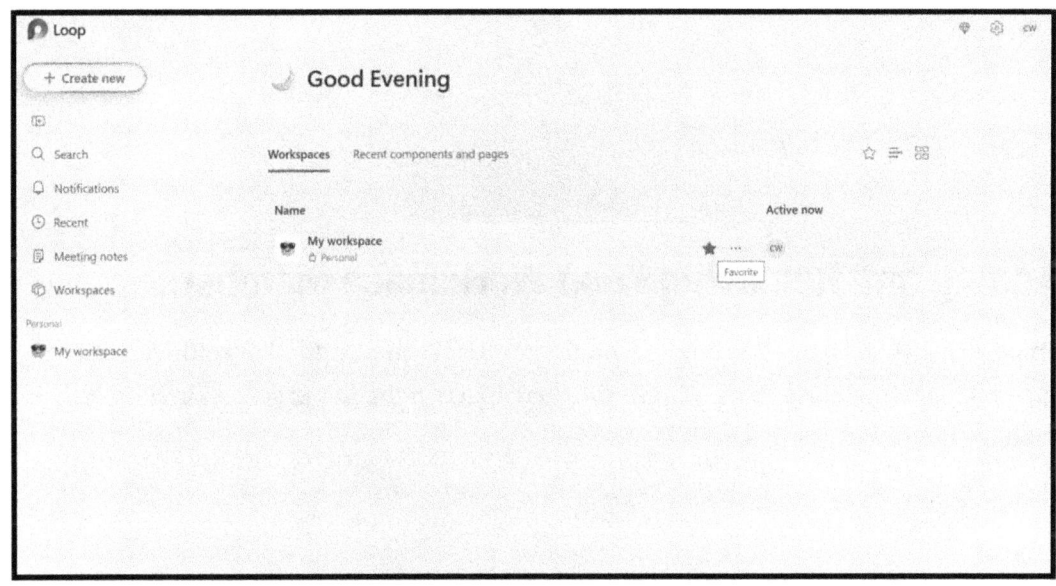

Figure 2-21. *Select "My workspace as favorite" through start selection*

47

CHAPTER 2   GETTING STARTED WITH MICROSOFT LOOP

To access your collection of favorite workspaces, select the star icon labeled "Favorites" in the upper-right corner of the landing page, as shown in Figure 2-22. Here, you will find all workspaces you have marked as favorites, and you can navigate directly to any of them from this list. This process enables you to efficiently manage and access your preferred workspaces.

Figure 2-22. *Access favorites*

Adding and Removing Loop Workspace Members

Once a Loop workspace has been created, members can be added or removed at any time by following these steps. Within the workspace in the Loop, select "Invite and manage members," as shown in Figure 2-23.

CHAPTER 2 GETTING STARTED WITH MICROSOFT LOOP

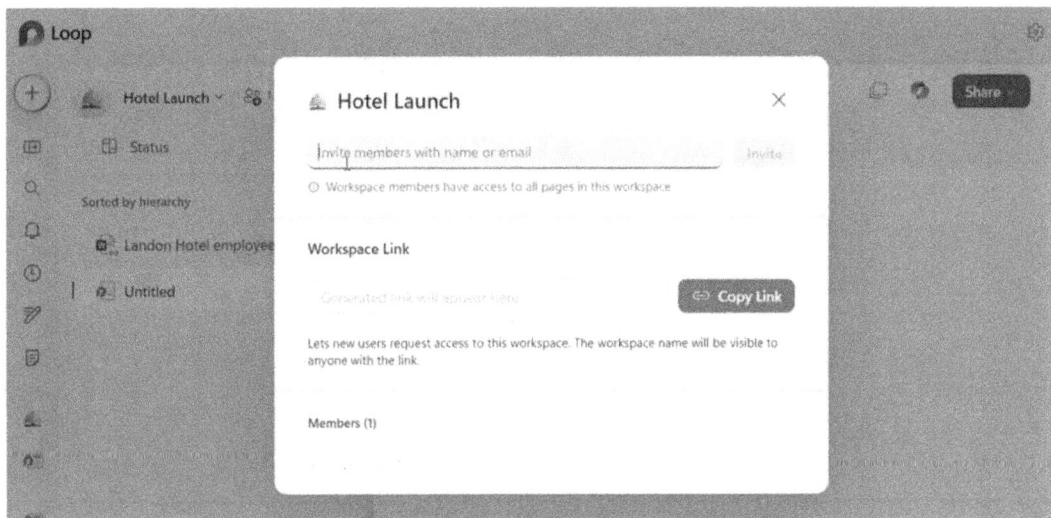

Figure 2-23. *Select "Invite and manage members"*

To invite new members, choose "Invite members with name or email" and enter the colleague's name or email address, as shown in Figure 2-24. When they appear in the list, they select their name. Multiple individuals may be invited simultaneously if required.

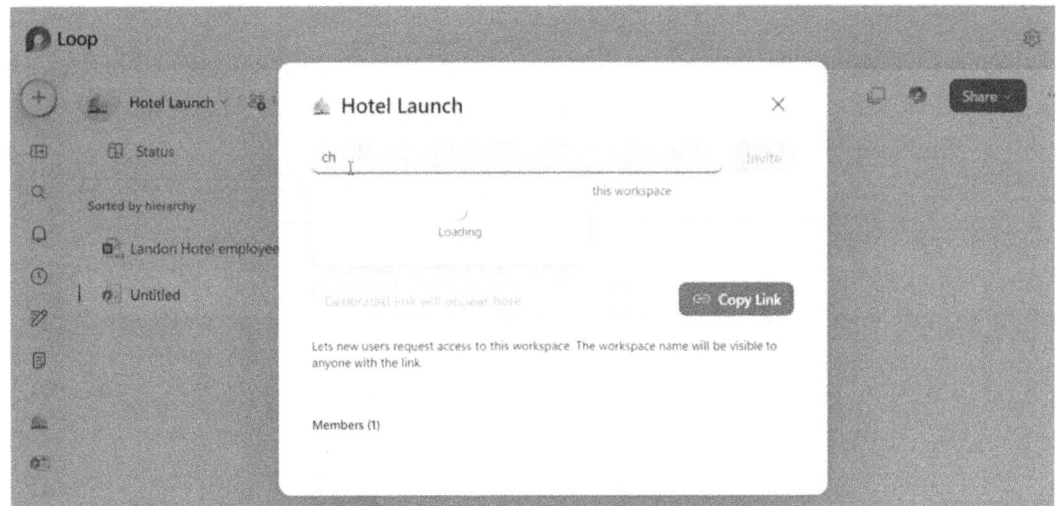

Figure 2-24. *Add an email address to send invitation*

CHAPTER 2   GETTING STARTED WITH MICROSOFT LOOP

Prior to sending invitations, you have the option to generate a workspace link by selecting "Copy Link", as shown in Figure 2-25. This link can then be shared via chat, presentation, or email, enabling recipients to request access to the workspace. Membership requests are subject to approval by the workspace owner.

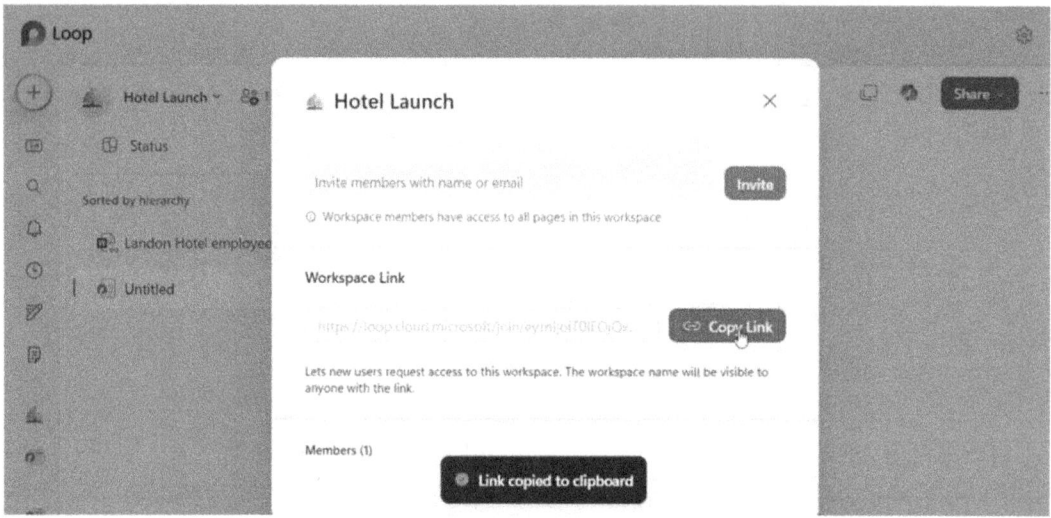

Figure 2-25. *"Copy link" to share workspace by link*

After clicking "Invite," you will receive a notification confirming that the member has been successfully added. The current members are listed below, including both newly added individuals and those who originally set up the workspace.

To remove a member, navigate again to "Invite and manage members," click on the relevant individual's name, and select the "X" next to it, as shown in Figure 2-26. This action revokes their access to the workspace and its contents. These procedures allow you to manage membership and control access within your Loop workspace efficiently.

CHAPTER 2 GETTING STARTED WITH MICROSOFT LOOP

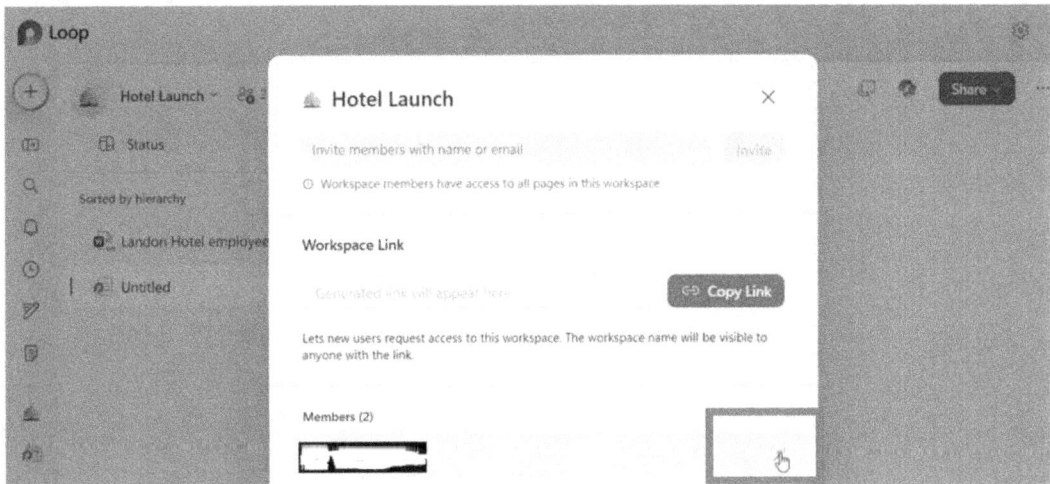

Figure 2-26. Remove user from workspace

Renaming and Restyling a Workspace

After creating a Loop workspace or page inside it, you may wish to update its name and adjust the cover style. To do this, navigate to the Workspaces list view, hover over the desired workspace or the page, and select "More" (represented by the ellipses in the upper right corner). From the menu, choose "Rename and style", as shown in Figure 2-27.

CHAPTER 2 GETTING STARTED WITH MICROSOFT LOOP

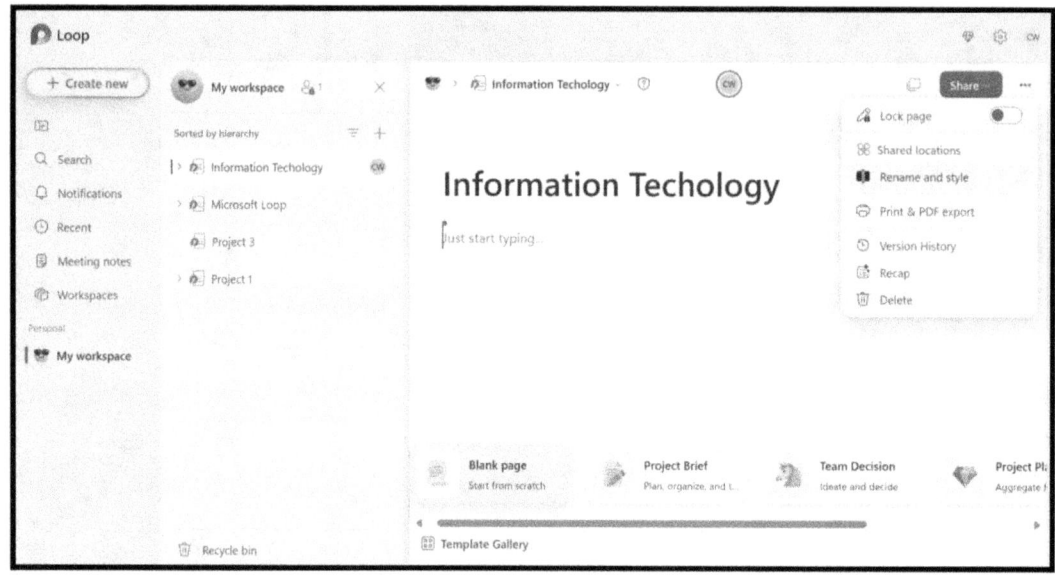

Figure 2-27. *Rename workspace or page*

To change the title, place the cursor in the Title field; all text will be selected automatically, as shown in Figure 2-28. Enter the new page name, such as "Information and Data," as shown in Figure 2-29.

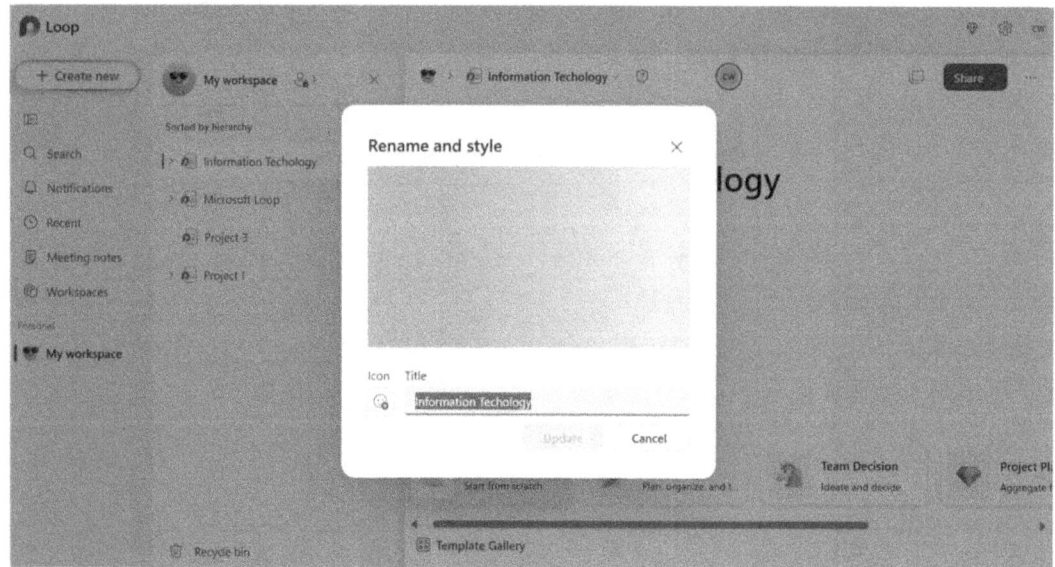

Figure 2-28. *Existing Title chosen by default*

CHAPTER 2 GETTING STARTED WITH MICROSOFT LOOP

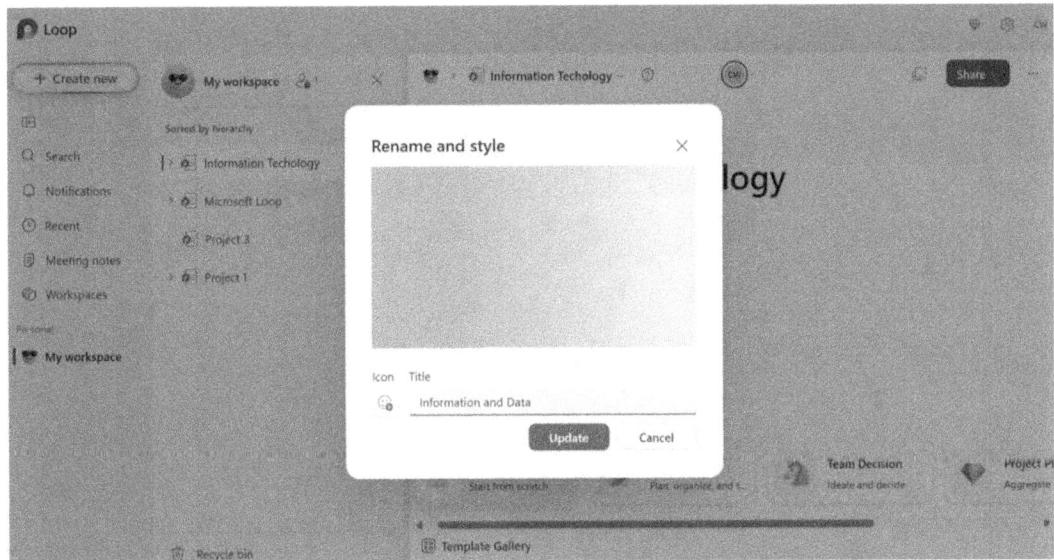

Figure 2-29. *Title changed to a new one called "Information and Data"*

To modify the icon, select the icon area to the left of the title, as shown in Figure 2-30. You may browse available categories or search by entering a keyword, for example, "information," and then select an appropriate icon, such as a bed, as shown in Figure 2-31.

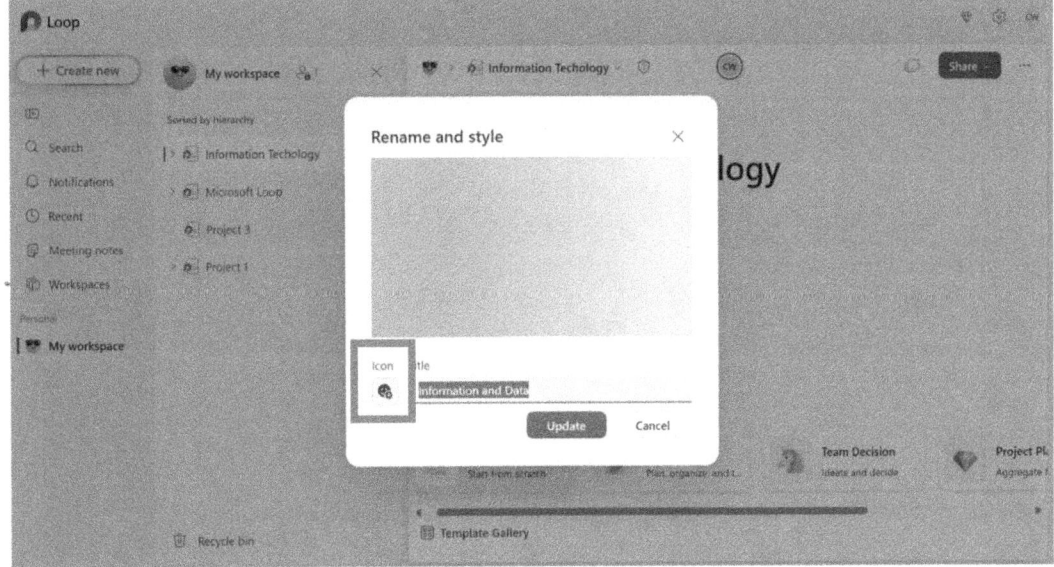

Figure 2-30. *Browse list of icons*

53

CHAPTER 2   GETTING STARTED WITH MICROSOFT LOOP

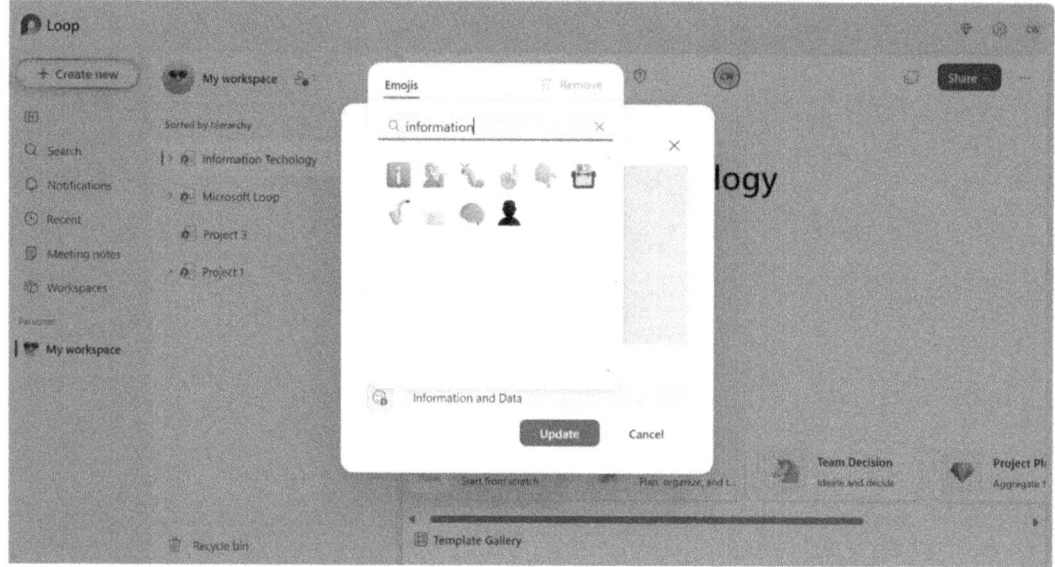

Figure 2-31. *Selection icon related to information*

For updating the cover image, position your cursor over the existing cover and choose the option to update it, as shown in Figure 2-32. This will open a menu where you can scroll through various categories, including Landscape and Workflow, as shown in Figure 2-33, or search by keyword. For instance, typing "Information" will display relevant options, as shown in Figure 2-34. You also have the option to select a random cover, as shown in Figure 2-35.

CHAPTER 2　GETTING STARTED WITH MICROSOFT LOOP

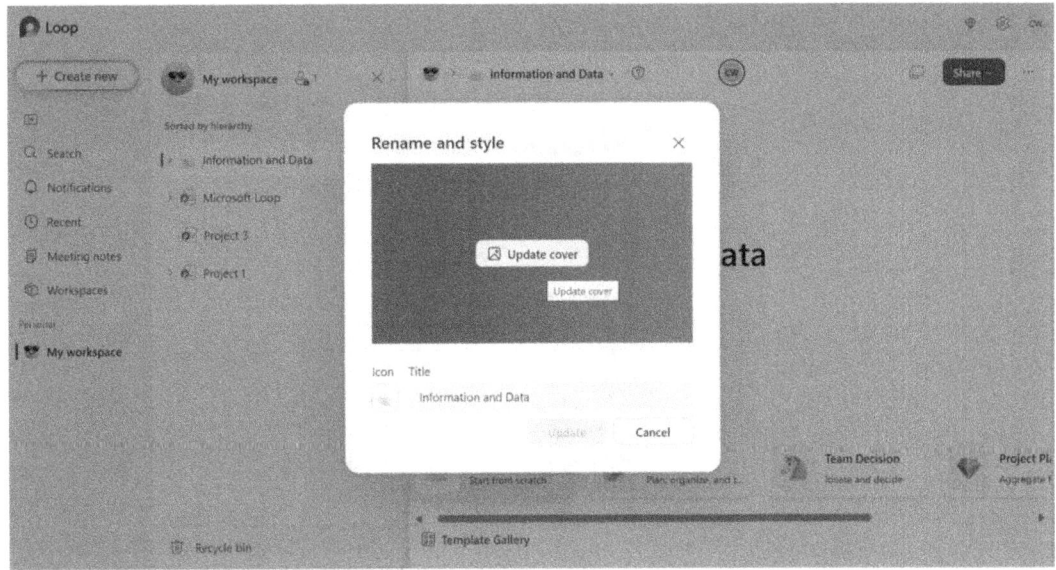

Figure 2-32. *Access "Update cover option"*

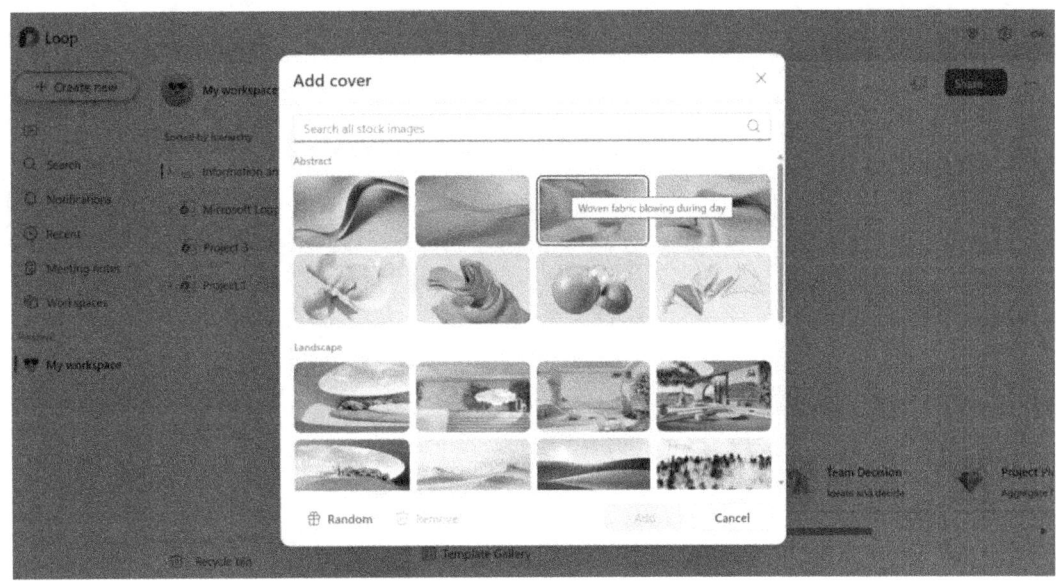

Figure 2-33. *Availability of different types of cover*

CHAPTER 2 GETTING STARTED WITH MICROSOFT LOOP

Figure 2-34. *Choosing information-related cover*

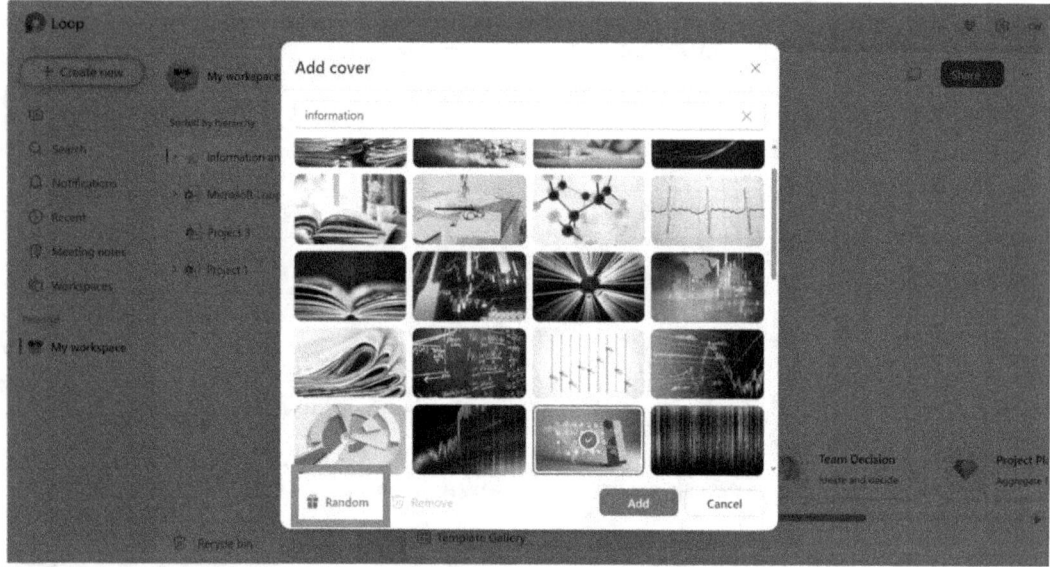

Figure 2-35. *Option to a random cover*

Upon selecting a new cover, such as the "stack of files" in Figure 2-36, confirm your choice by selecting "Update." The workspace will now reflect the revised title, icon, and cover design, as shown in Figure 2-37. These steps outline how to professionally restore your workspace's name, icon, and cover.

56

CHAPTER 2 GETTING STARTED WITH MICROSOFT LOOP

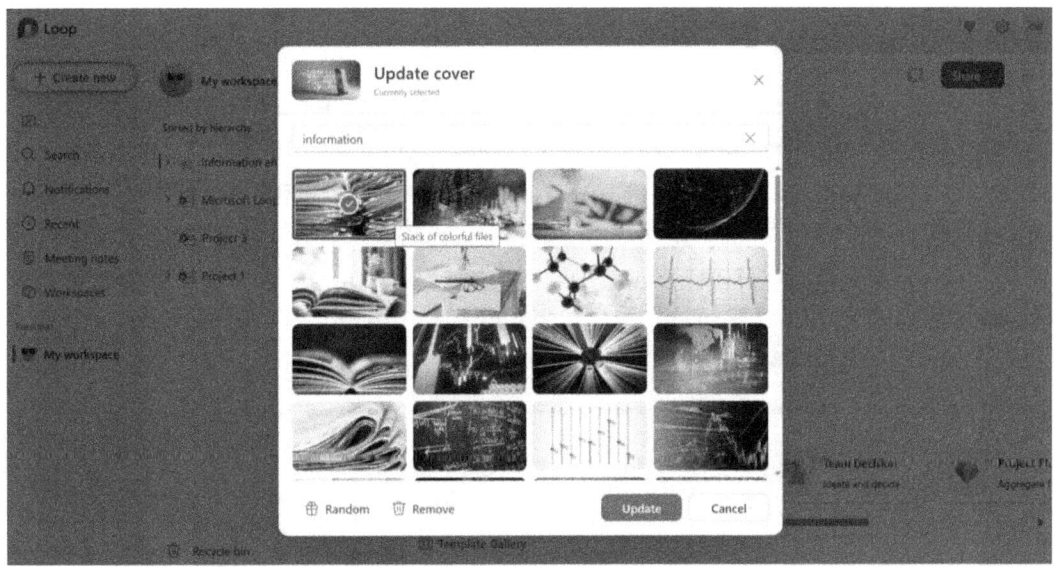

Figure 2-36. *Choose "stack of files" cover*

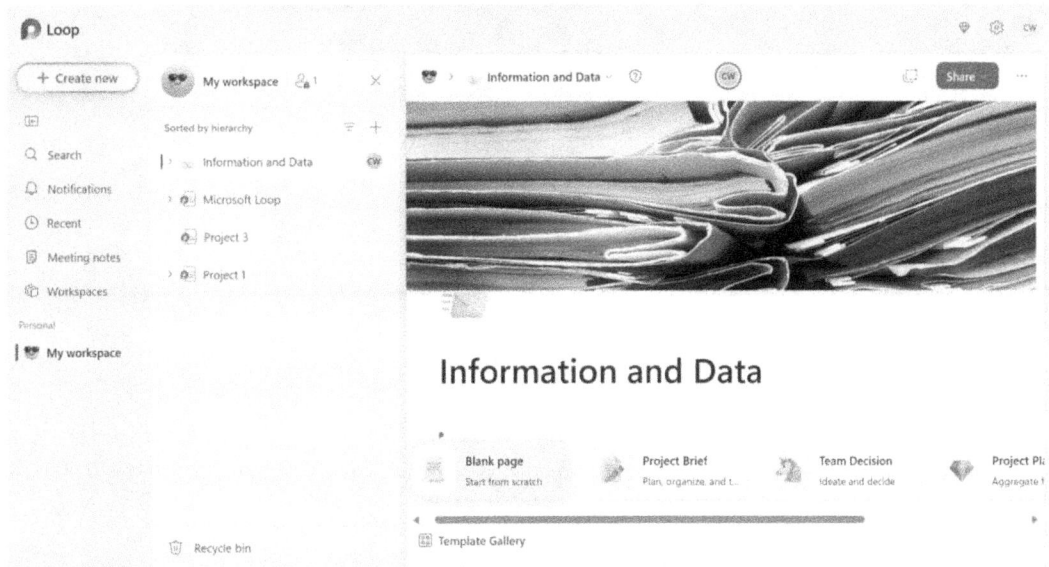

Figure 2-37. *Publishing of page with new icon, title, and cover*

Managing Page Versions

As content is continuously added or edited within a workspace page, all changes are automatically saved as versions. To access a page's version history, select the More Options menu in the upper right corner and choose Version History, as shown in Figure 2-38. The pane on the right will display the history of edits in chronological order, with the newest version at the top and the original version at the bottom, as shown in Figure 2-39. The version history feature also identifies the individuals responsible for each modification, as shown in Figure 2-39.

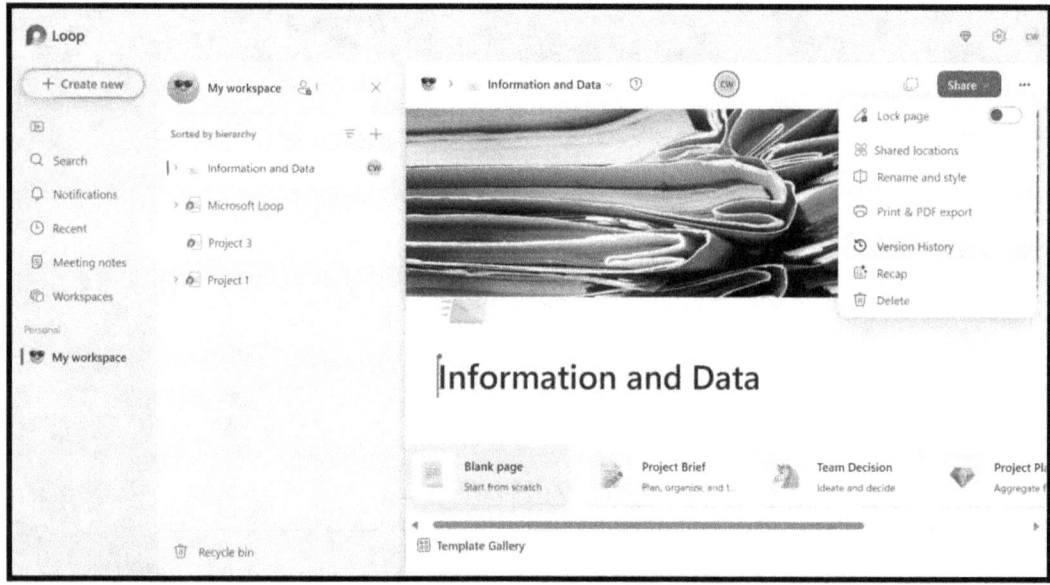

Figure 2-38. Access "More" option

CHAPTER 2   GETTING STARTED WITH MICROSOFT LOOP

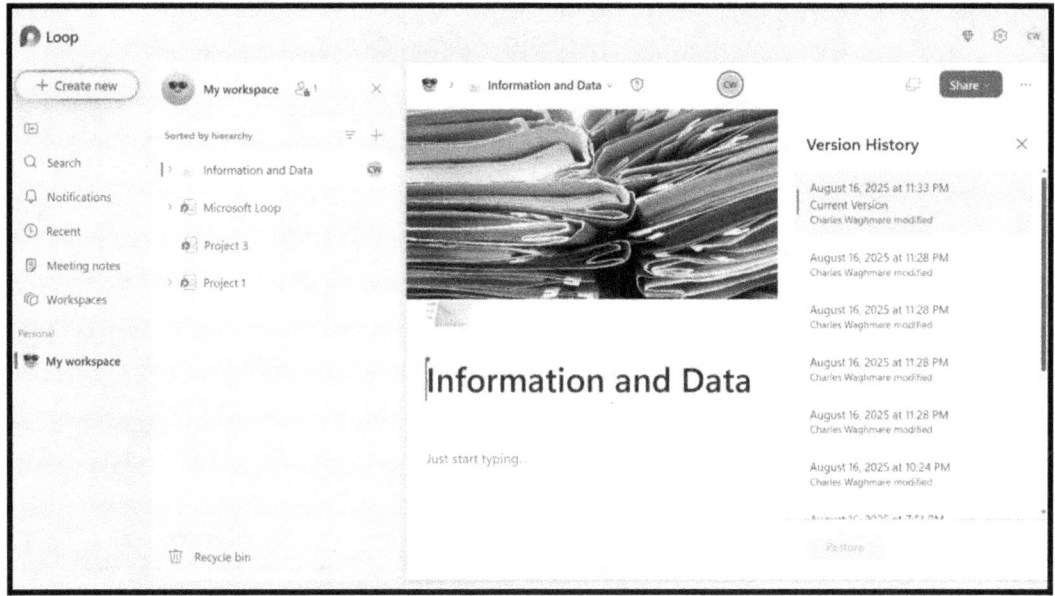

Figure 2-39. *List of all previous versions of a page*

If errors occur or there is a need to revert to a previous state, you can restore an earlier version from this history. By selecting the desired version from the list, the Restore button becomes available, as shown in Figure 2-40. Upon selection, a confirmation message will prompt you to proceed, as shown in Figure 2-41. The system may require refreshing the page to apply the change as instructed in the message. After confirming, the restoration process completes, and the selected version becomes active.

CHAPTER 2   GETTING STARTED WITH MICROSOFT LOOP

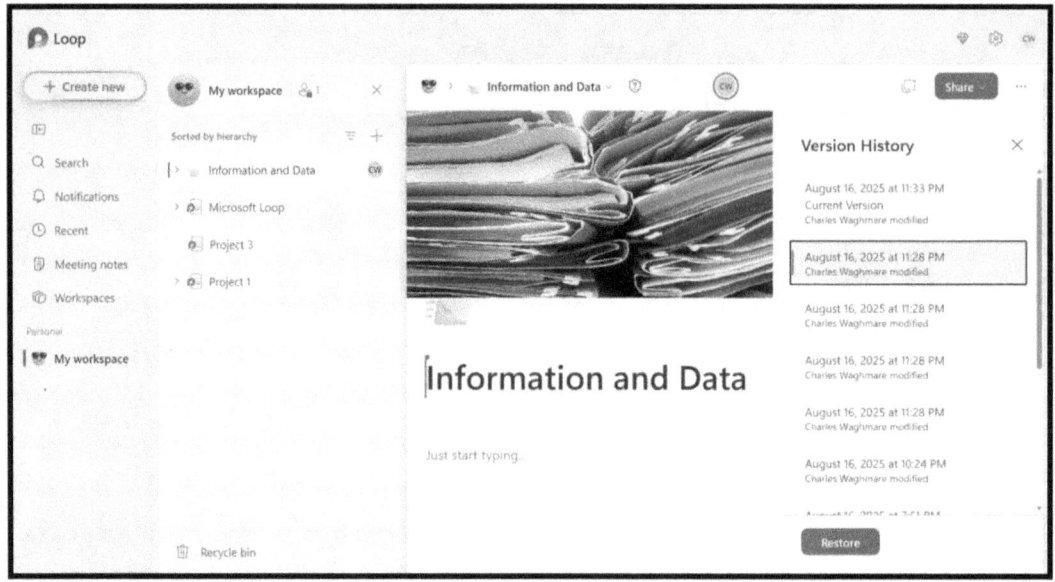

Figure 2-40. *Activation of restore button with selection of previous version*

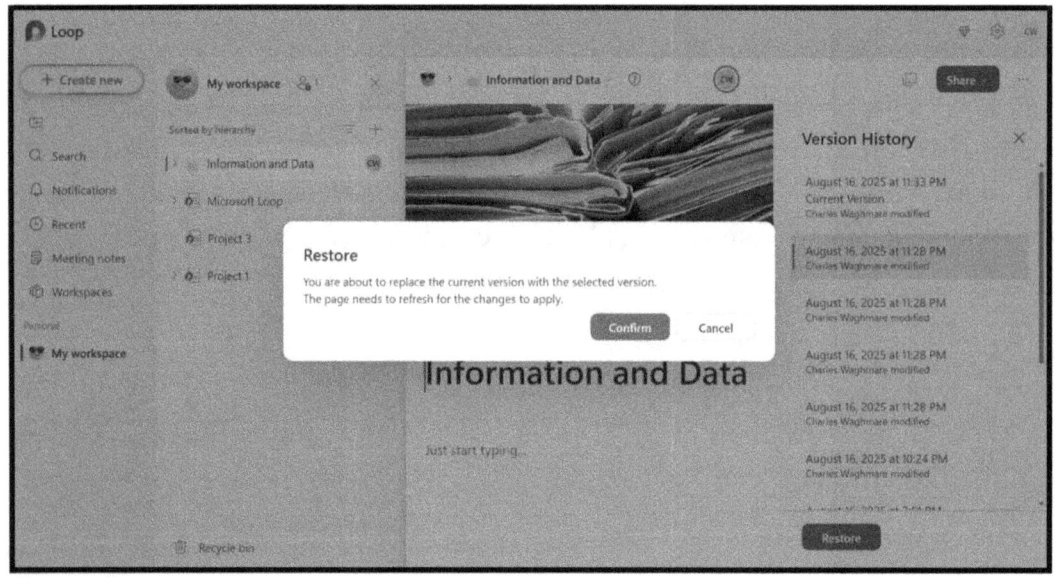

Figure 2-41. *Confirmation to restore previous version*

Returning to Version History will show that the restored version is now current, while previous iterations remain accessible. This process effectively promotes a prior version

CHAPTER 2   GETTING STARTED WITH MICROSOFT LOOP

to the latest, enabling further editing by all users. Utilizing version history allows you to track modifications and efficiently revert pages when necessary.

Printing and Exporting Workspace Pages

You can print or export a workspace page from both the Loop desktop application and the Loop web application. To begin, navigate to the relevant workspace page—here, we are using a catering page as an example. Select the three ellipses located in the upper right corner to access additional options, then choose "Print and PDF Export", as shown in Figure 2-42.

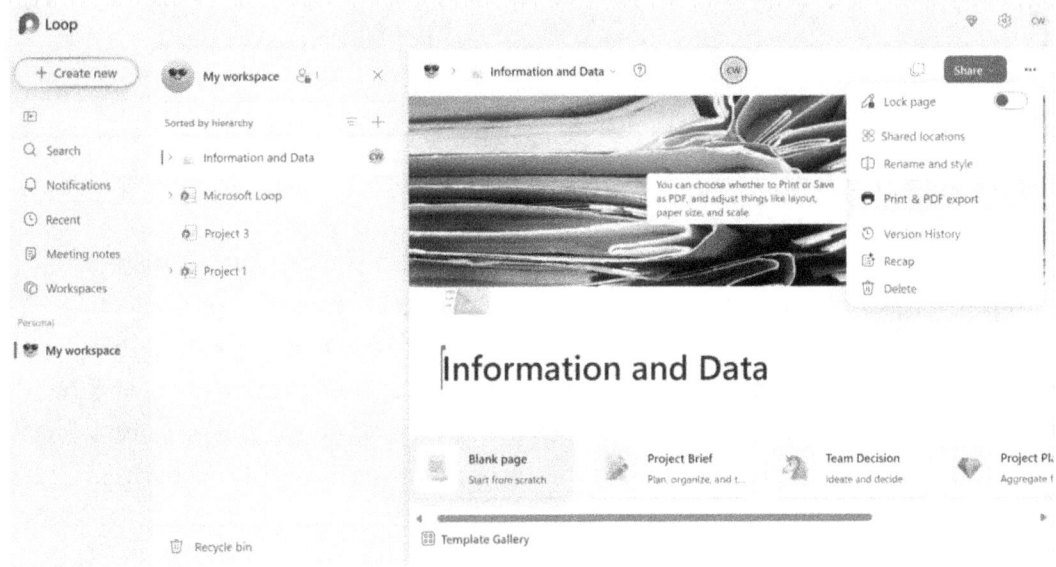

Figure 2-42. *Access Print and PDF option*

A new browser tab will open, displaying a preview of the page for printing or exporting. You may review the content by scrolling through the preview window. On the left side, you will find the option to select your desired printer, as shown in Figure 2-43. Available choices will depend on your device's configuration and installed software. For instance, you may have the ability to save as an Adobe PDF, export to OneNote, create an XPS document, or use the default Print to PDF function included with Microsoft applications, as shown in Figure 2-43.

CHAPTER 2   GETTING STARTED WITH MICROSOFT LOOP

Figure 2-43. *Print your loop page in different formats*

After selecting your preferred printer or print distiller, you can further customize settings such as the number of copies, page layout, pages to include, color selection, and additional preferences. If converting or exporting to a PDF file, clicking "Print," as shown in Figure 2-43, will prompt you to specify a destination location for saving the file. Choose your preferred folder, enter a file name (e.g., "Catering Notes"), and select "Save." This completes the process for printing or exporting a specific page within a Loop workspace.

Deleting Loop Workspaces

As with loop components or pages, it is possible to delete an entire loop workspace. Please note that once a workspace is deleted, end users can restore it independently from "Recyle" bin.

To delete a workspace, navigate to the list of workspaces or pages and locate the desired workspace (e.g., "Information and data"). Hover over the workspace, select the three-dot menu, and choose "Delete," as shown in Figure 2-44. You will be prompted to confirm your decision, as shown in Figure 2-45. Deleting a workspace permanently removes all associated pages and their content. After deletion, the workspace will no longer appear in the list.

CHAPTER 2 GETTING STARTED WITH MICROSOFT LOOP

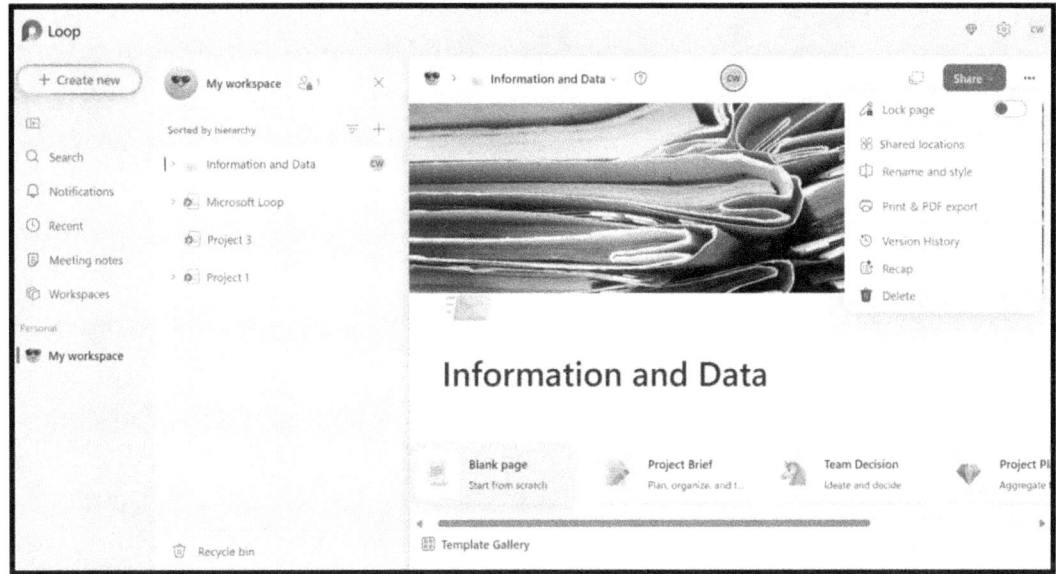

Figure 2-44. *Delete option to delete a Workspace*

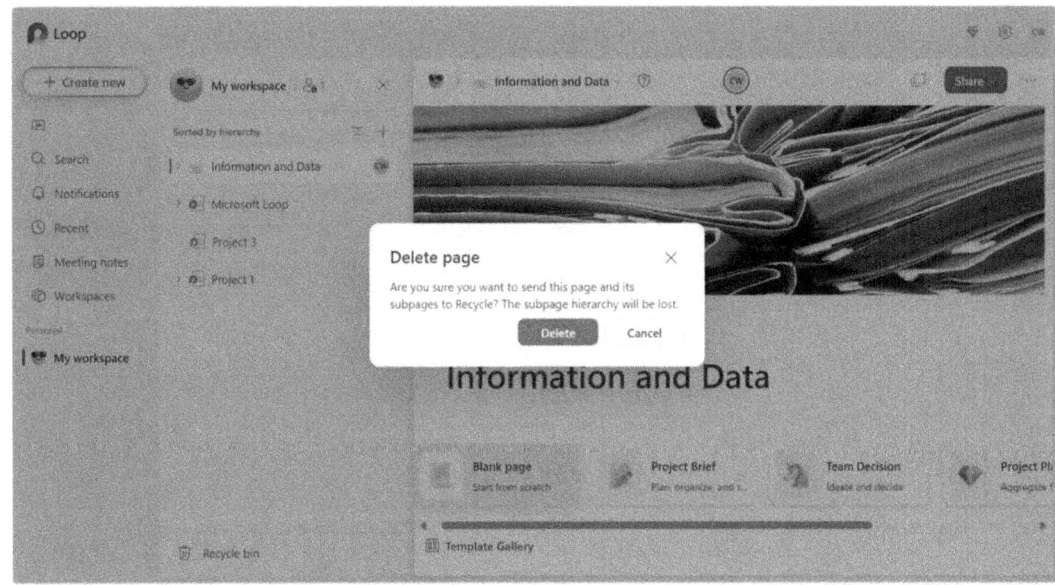

Figure 2-45. *Confirmation to delete*

To restore, access "Recycle" bin, as shown in Figure 2-46. From this "Recycle" bin console, you can restore the content, as shown in Figure 2-47. Further, from same console, you can permanently delete, and empty "Recycle" bin, as shown in Figure 2-48.

63

CHAPTER 2   GETTING STARTED WITH MICROSOFT LOOP

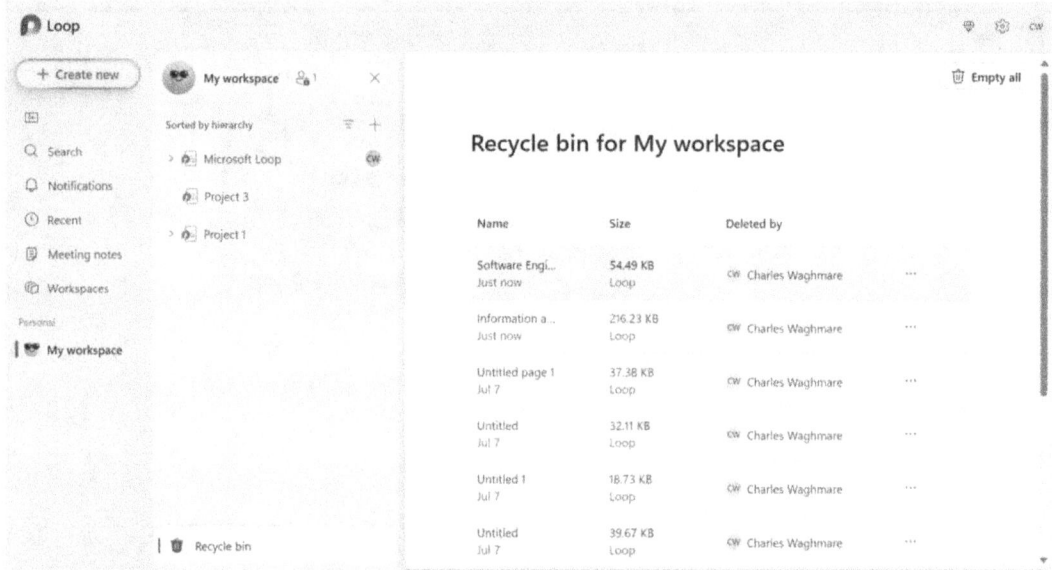

Figure 2-46.   *Access Recycle bin Console*

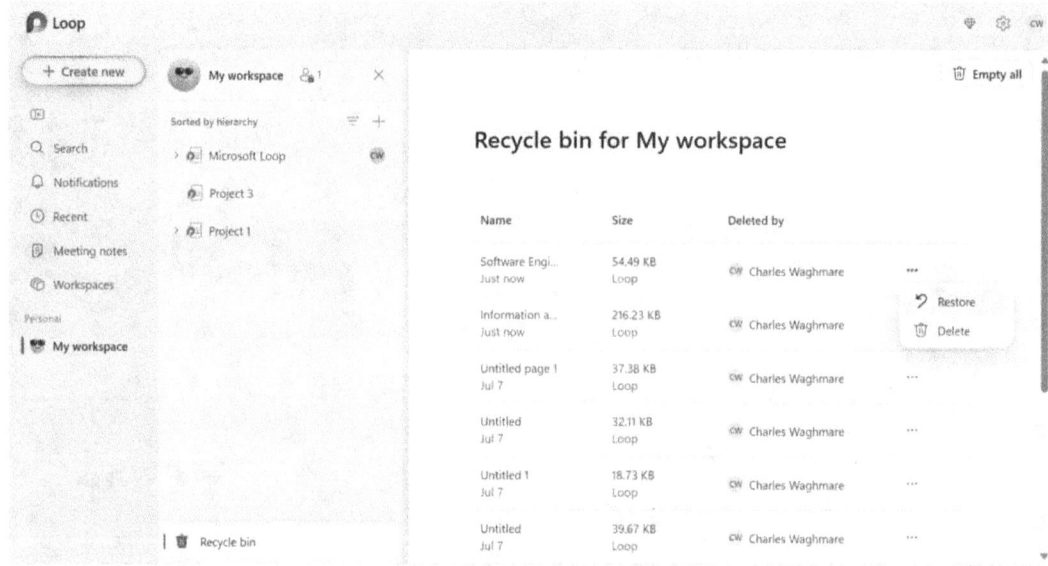

Figure 2-47.   *Option to restore content*

CHAPTER 2 GETTING STARTED WITH MICROSOFT LOOP

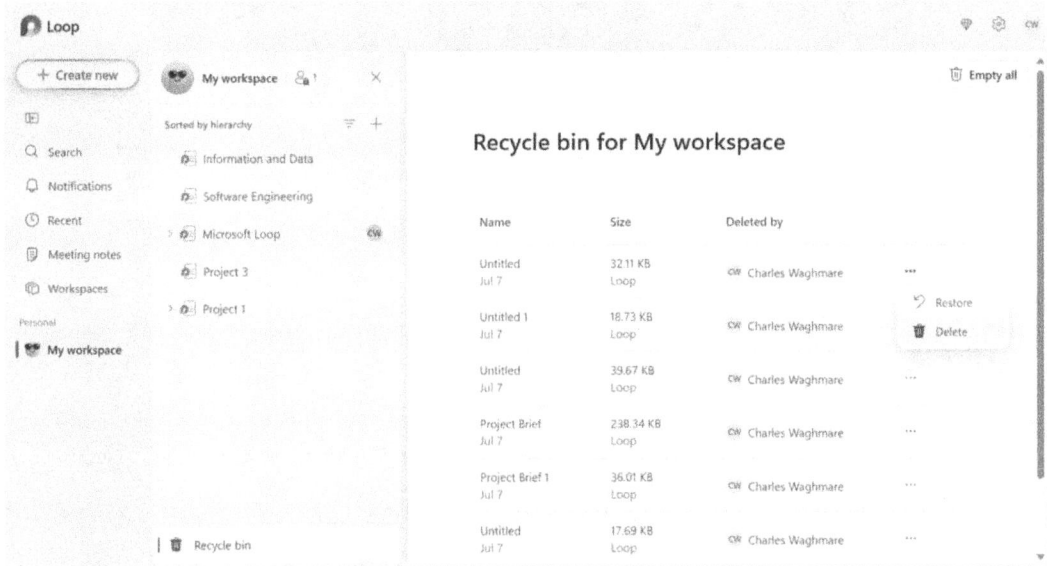

Figure 2-48. *Permament delete and Empty all recycle bin*

With this we have come to the end of this chapter. In this chapter, we have learnt to create a new loop workspace, creating pages and subpages within a loop workspace, favoriting a workspace, adding and removing loop workspace members, renaming and restyling a workspace, managing page versions, printing and exporting workspace pages, and deleting loop workspaces. In the upcoming chapter, we will take a look into Cocreation and managing Loop components by describing different types of Loop components and explain creation and customization process.

CHAPTER 3

Co-creation and Managing Loop Components

Let's learn how to cocreate in Loop workspaces and components. There are many different Microsoft 365 apps that you likely work in every day, for communicating and collaborating with other people. If you're not familiar with Microsoft Loop, it's a collaborative app that is part of Microsoft 365. With Microsoft Loop components, you can cocreate content across many Microsoft 365 communications and files, or within an organized Loop workspace.

Microsoft Loop is a transformative co-creation and collaboration platform within the Microsoft 365 ecosystem, designed to empower teams to ideate, plan, and execute together in real time. At its core, Loop introduces a new way of working through Loop components, Loop pages, and Loop workspaces, which together create a dynamic, fluid environment for managing content, tasks, and ideas across multiple applications like Teams, Outlook, Word, OneNote, and Whiteboard. In this chapter, we will cover introduction on co-creation of content using Microsoft loop, send a loop voting table component in a Teams communication, create a Teams meeting agenda loop component, set up a loop task list component in an outlook message, share a loop component across Microsoft 365 apps, find loop components, coauthor a loop component, and manage access for a loop component, what to know about Microsoft loop before getting started, and cocreation challenges using Microsoft loop.

Introduction

Loop Components are the Building Blocks of Co-Creation. Loop components are portable, interactive content blocks—such as tables, task lists, paragraphs, or checklists—that can be embedded directly into chats, emails, or documents. These components are not static; they are live and editable, meaning any changes made by one user are instantly visible to all collaborators, regardless of where the component is accessed. This real-time synchronization eliminates version control issues and fosters a seamless collaborative experience.

Each Loop component is saved as a .loop file in the creator's OneDrive, making it discoverable and manageable like any other Office document. These files can be restored to previous versions, searched across Office.com and OneDrive, and shared with specific permissions. However, moving a .loop file to a SharePoint site can break its functionality in Teams or Outlook, so careful management of file locations is essential.

Loop Pages and Workspaces are organizing Collaboration. Beyond components, Loop offers Loop pages, which are flexible canvases where users can gather components, links, tasks, and data. These pages can be expanded and adapted as ideas evolve, serving as a centralized hub for project-related content. Pages can be shared across Microsoft 365 apps either as links or embedded components, maintaining their dynamic nature. Loop workspaces are shared environments that provide a bird's-eye view of all project-related activities. They help teams track progress, monitor contributions, and stay aligned. Workspaces are particularly useful for managing complex projects, as they consolidate all relevant Loop pages and components into a single, navigable space.

Practical Applications and Productivity Gains exist through loop. Professional across industries are leveraging Loop to streamline workflows. For instance, consultants use Loop to build reusable databases of knowledge, storing frequently used content like classification schemes or best practices as Loop components. These can be dropped into reports or proposals, saving time and ensuring consistency. Loop also excels in content development, allowing marketers and writers to manage drafts, research notes, and feedback in one place. Components can be embedded in emails or documents for collaborative editing without switching apps. In project management, Loop supports task lists, timelines, and checklists that update in real time, keeping teams aligned and informed

There are many ways for managing Loop Components effectively. To manage Loop components efficiently, organizations must ensure proper configuration of OneDrive and SharePoint services, as these underpin the storage and sharing of .loop files. Admins can control Loop functionality via Microsoft 365 settings, including permissions, sharing policies, and retention rules. If Loop is disabled, users lose the ability to create new components, and existing ones render as static hyperlinks. Known issues include limitations in federated environments, where external recipients may not be able to view or edit Loop components unless sharing is explicitly enabled. Additionally, default tenant permissions set to "Specific people" can complicate sharing in large group chats, requiring manual adjustments.

Loop has become a Game-Changer. Loop's strength lies in its flexibility, integration, and real-time collaboration. It adapts to solo and team workflows, integrates seamlessly with Microsoft 365 apps, and ensures that updates are instantly reflected across all instances of a component. This reduces redundancy, enhances transparency, and accelerates decision-making. Whether you're brainstorming in Teams, drafting a report in Word, or planning a project in Outlook, Loop keeps your content synchronized and accessible. It breaks down silos, fosters creativity, and transforms how teams collaborate in the digital age.

Send a Loop Voting Table Component in a Teams Communication

Content organization does not have to be limited to traditional paragraphs. Loop components offer an effective way to structure information within a designated layout. To set up a Loop component, begin by opening a drafted channel or chat post and selecting Loop components, as shown in Figure 3-1. Scroll down to view available components such as Tables, Bulleted list, Checklist, Task list, Voting table, and others. In Figure 3-2, a paragraph-formatted component has been created, allowing the inclusion of a title and supporting text. Once the post is published, all users with access to the channel can collaborate, making further modifications and edits as needed.

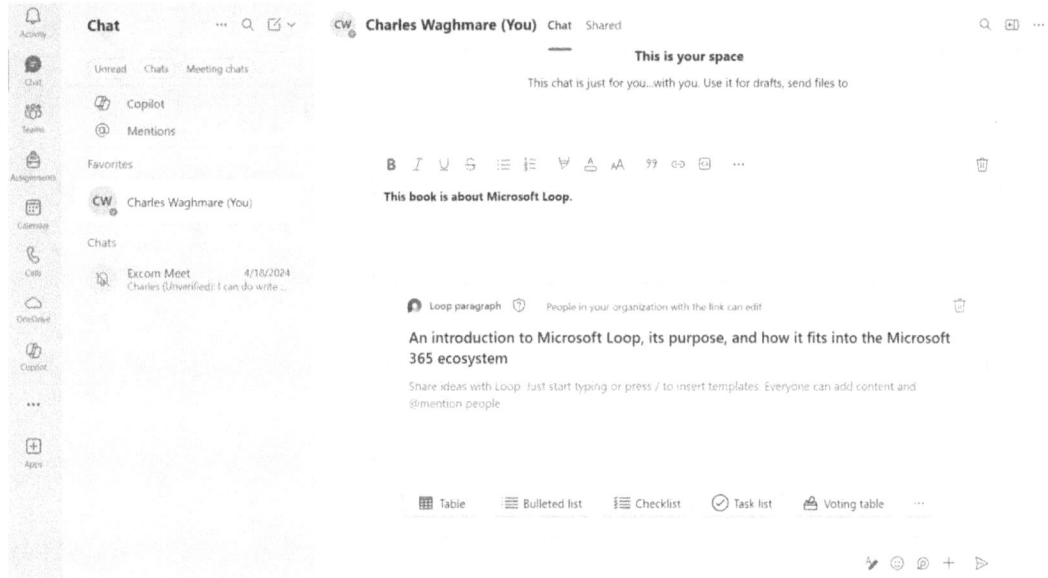

Figure 3-1. *Loop component in a Teams Chat*

CHAPTER 3   CO-CREATION AND MANAGING LOOP COMPONENTS

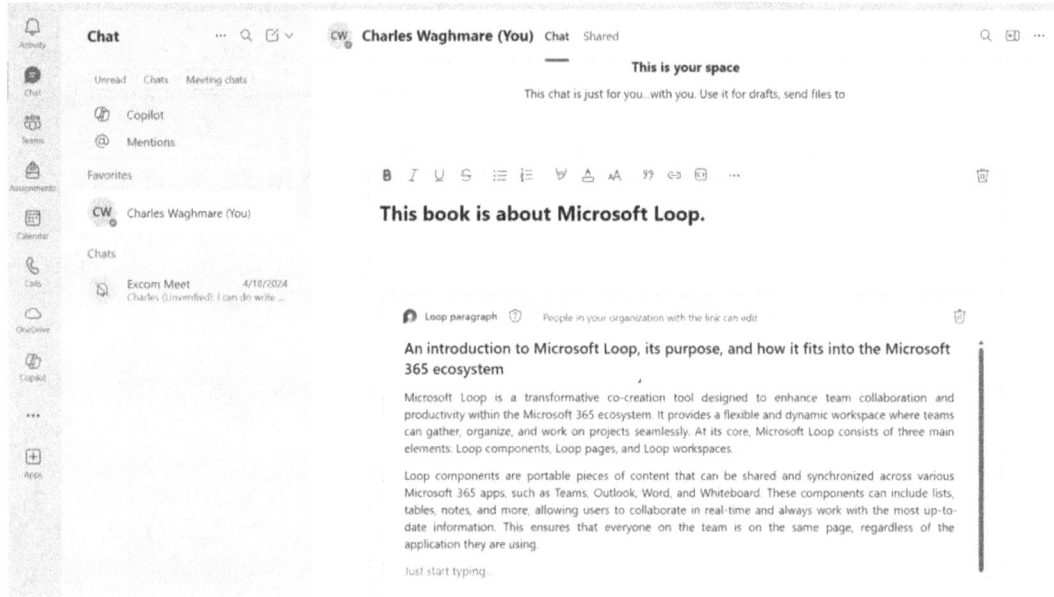

Figure 3-2. *Paragraph-formatted component*

To change the component type, select the "+" option, as shown in Figure 3-3, at the bottom of the component. Various options are available, such as General (containing Table, Checklist, and others), as shown in Figure 3-3-1, Text Styles, as shown in Figure 3-3-2, Templates, as shown in Figure 3-3-3, Communication, as shown in Figure 3-3-4, and Media, as shown in Figure 3-3-5.

CHAPTER 3   CO-CREATION AND MANAGING LOOP COMPONENTS

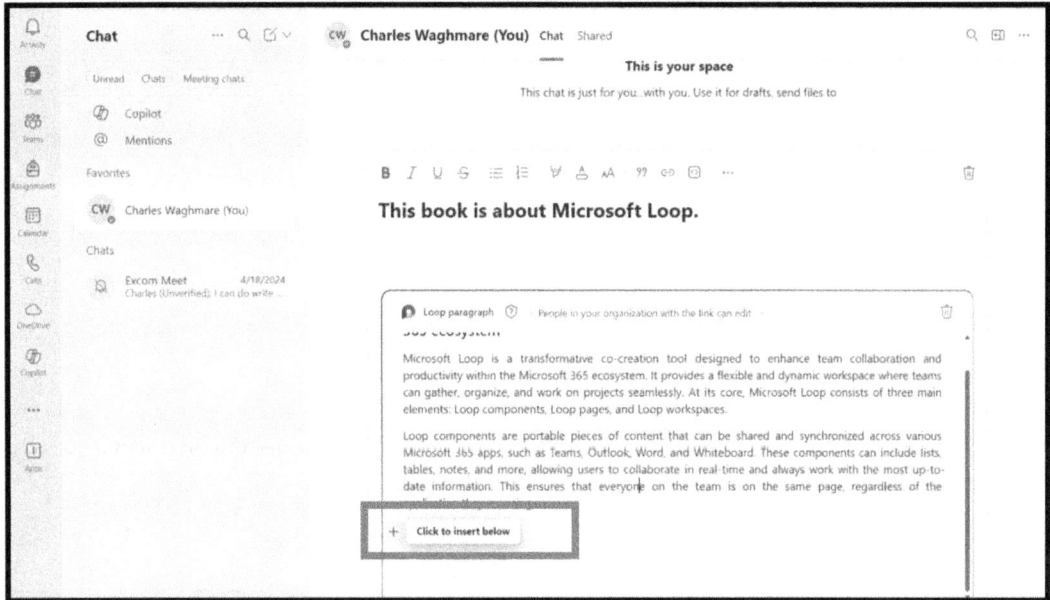

Figure 3-3. *"+" option to add components*

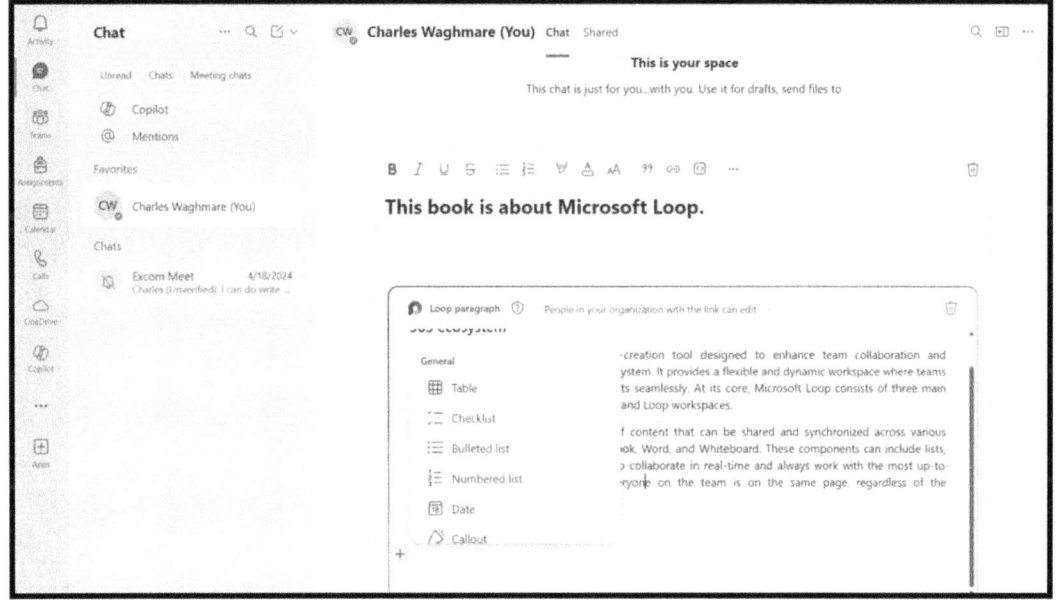

Figure 3-3-1. *General Loop Components*

71

CHAPTER 3   CO-CREATION AND MANAGING LOOP COMPONENTS

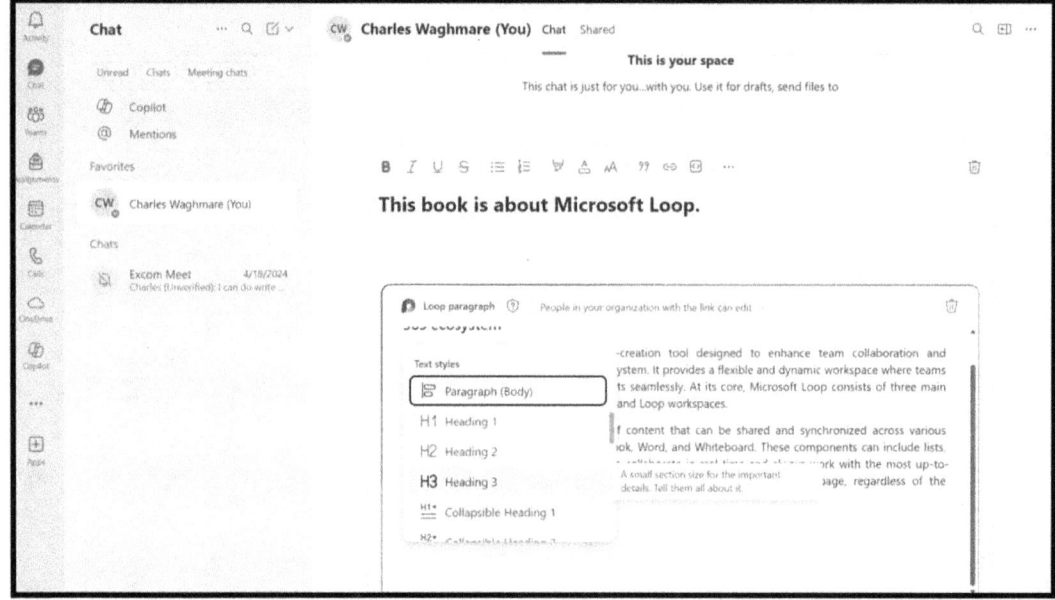

Figure 3-3-2. *Text Style Loop Components*

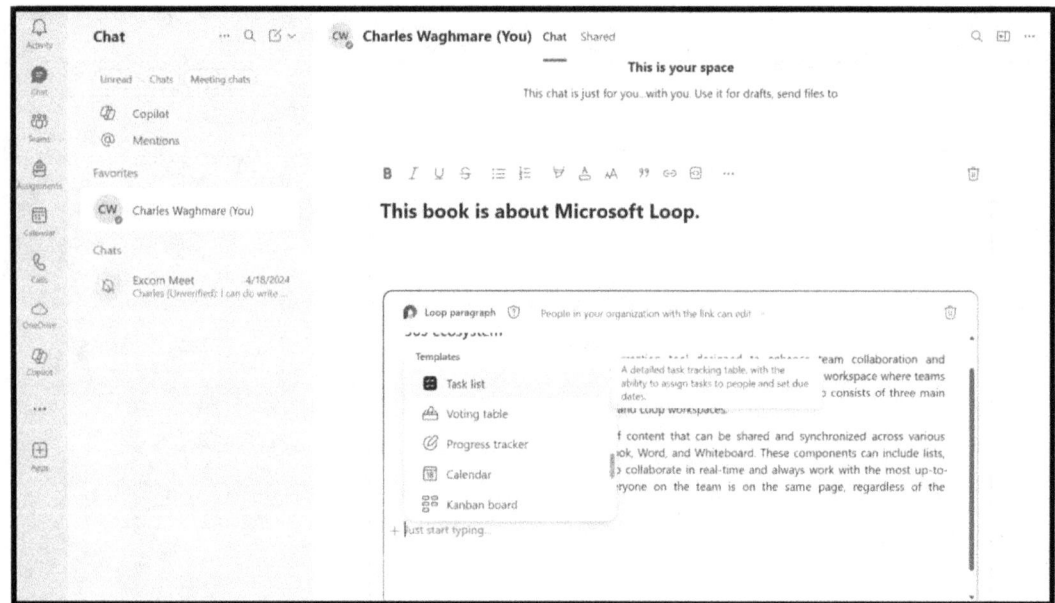

Figure 3-3-3. *Templates Loop Component*

CHAPTER 3   CO-CREATION AND MANAGING LOOP COMPONENTS

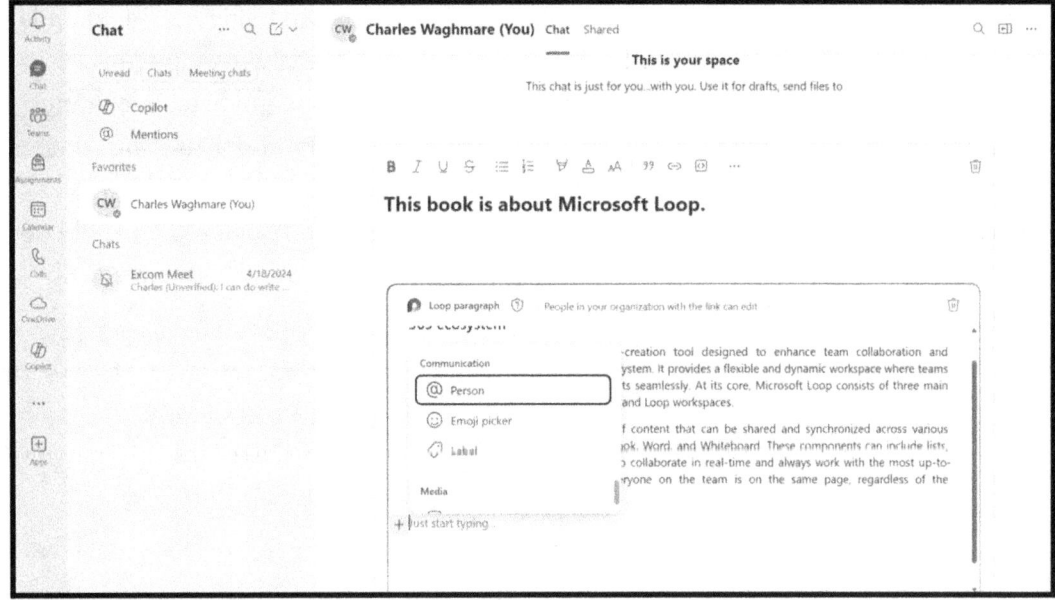

Figure 3-3-4. *Communication Loop Components*

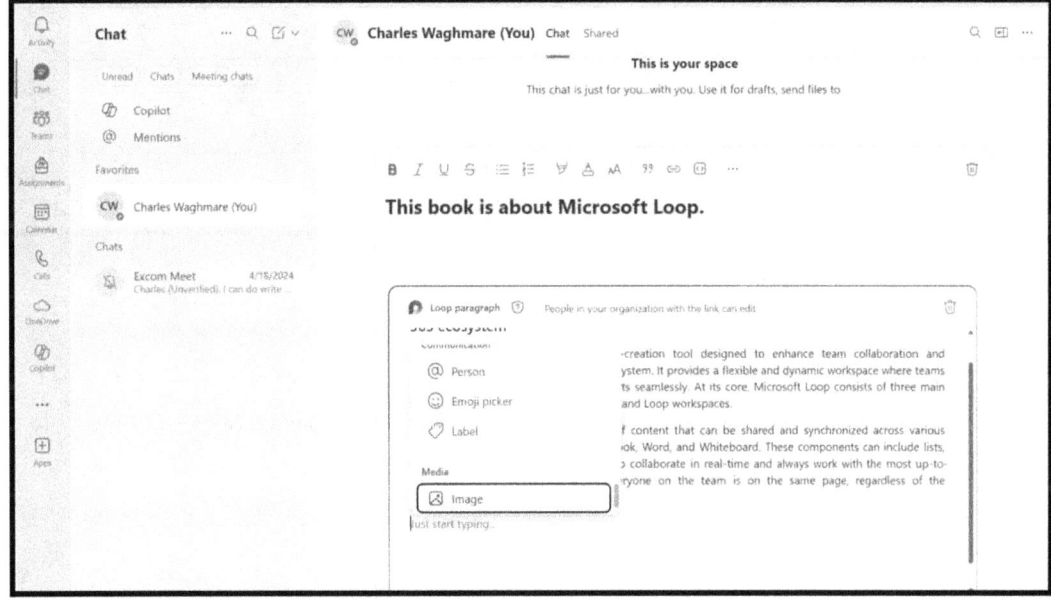

Figure 3-3-5. *Media Loop Component*

73

CHAPTER 3 CO-CREATION AND MANAGING LOOP COMPONENTS

From Templates components, select "Voting table," as shown in Figure 3-4, to update the component format to a table with predefined headings: Ideas, Pros, Cons, and Votes, as shown in Figure 3-5. Add an idea to provide context and guide team channel collaborators on their contributions, as shown in Figure 3-6. After finalizing the content, scroll down and publish the conversation, as shown in Figure 3-7. This enables real-time collaboration on the voting table within the team channel. The newly created Loop component will be stored in the Channel folder of the SharePoint site associated with the team.

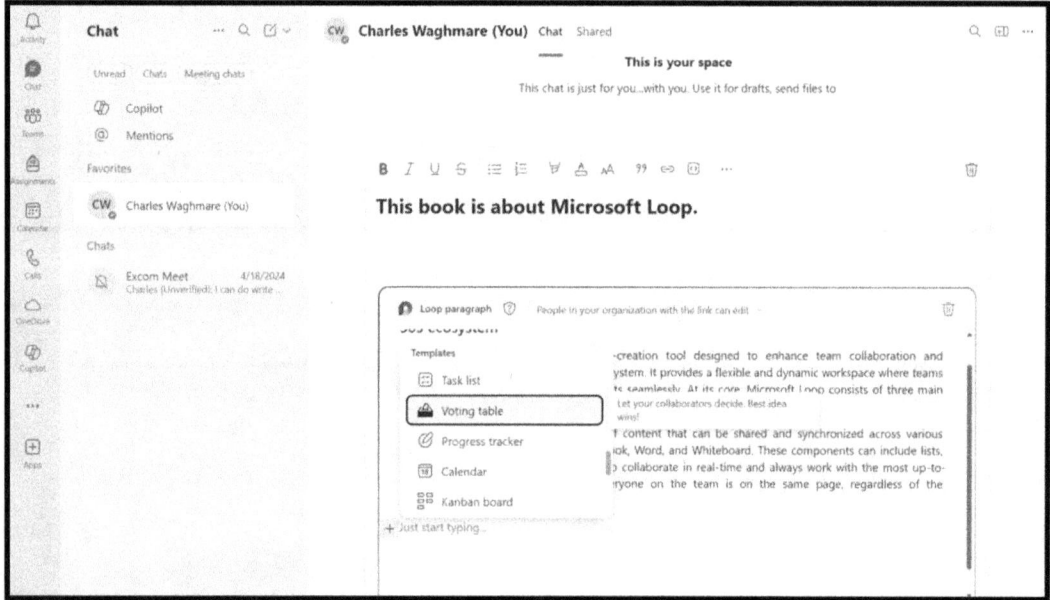

Figure 3-4. Selection of Voting table

CHAPTER 3   CO-CREATION AND MANAGING LOOP COMPONENTS

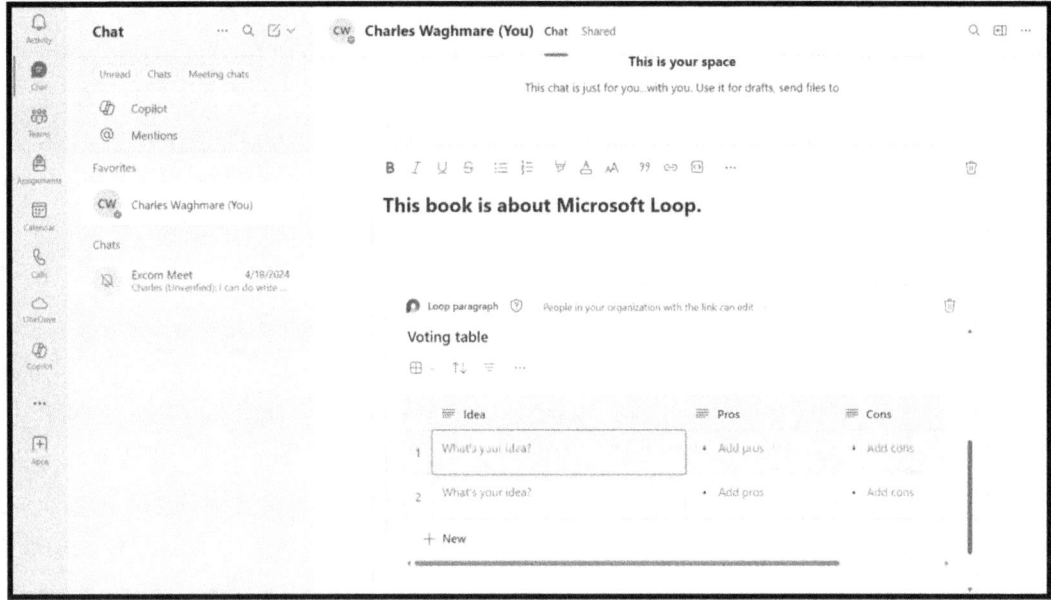

Figure 3-5. *Voting table with predefined columns*

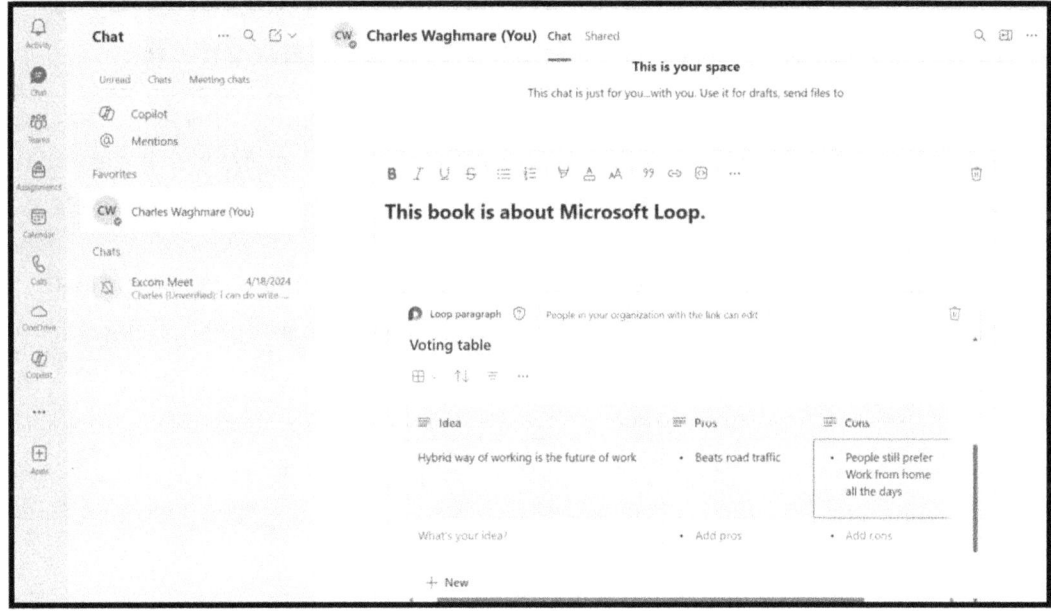

Figure 3-6. *An idea on Hybrid way of working added*

75

CHAPTER 3   CO-CREATION AND MANAGING LOOP COMPONENTS

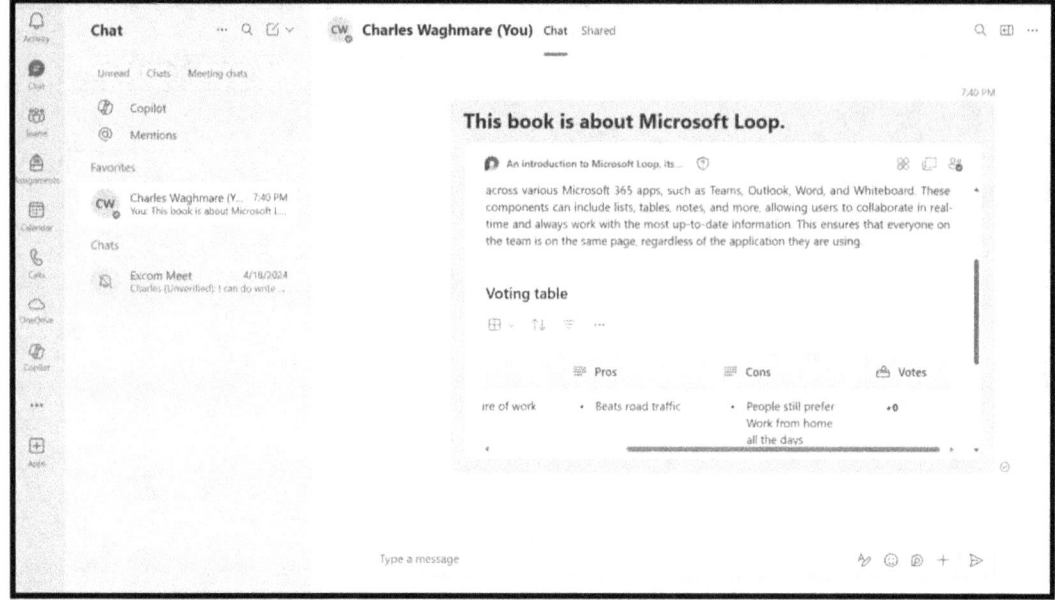

Figure 3-7.   *Voting table is published for collaboration*

Create a Teams Meeting Agenda Loop Component

Establishing an effective Microsoft Teams meeting begins with preparing a clear agenda. Microsoft Loop offers a versatile component that enables users to organize the agenda within the meeting invite and collaboratively document notes and action items before, during, and after the meeting.

To utilize this feature, start by drafting your team's meeting, then click on "Add an Agenda," as shown in Figure 3-8 and the agenda component gets added, as shown in Figure 3-9.

CHAPTER 3   CO-CREATION AND MANAGING LOOP COMPONENTS

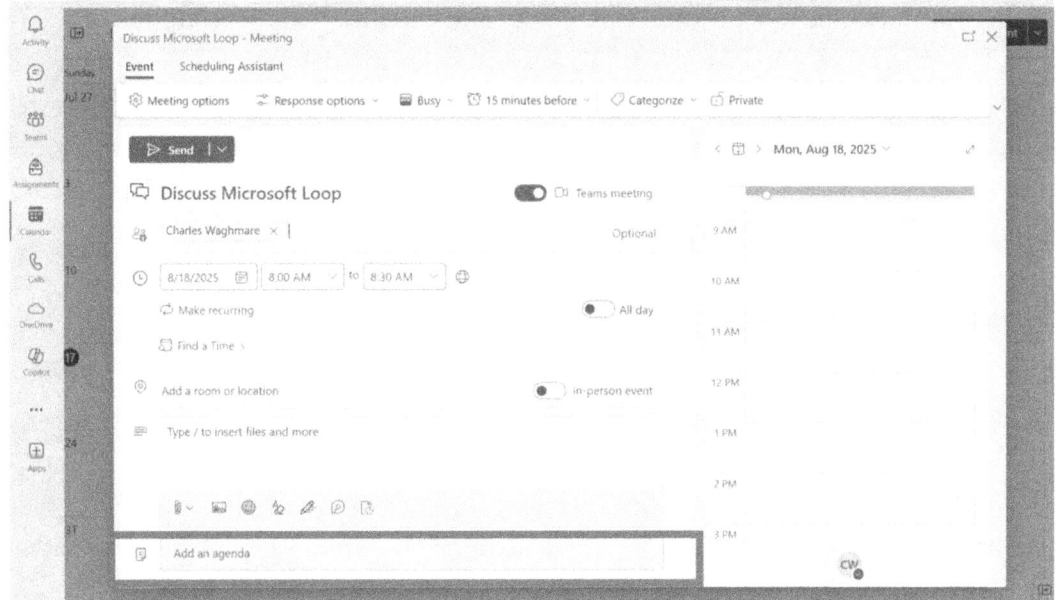

Figure 3-8. *Set up Teams meeting invitation and click "Add an agenda"*

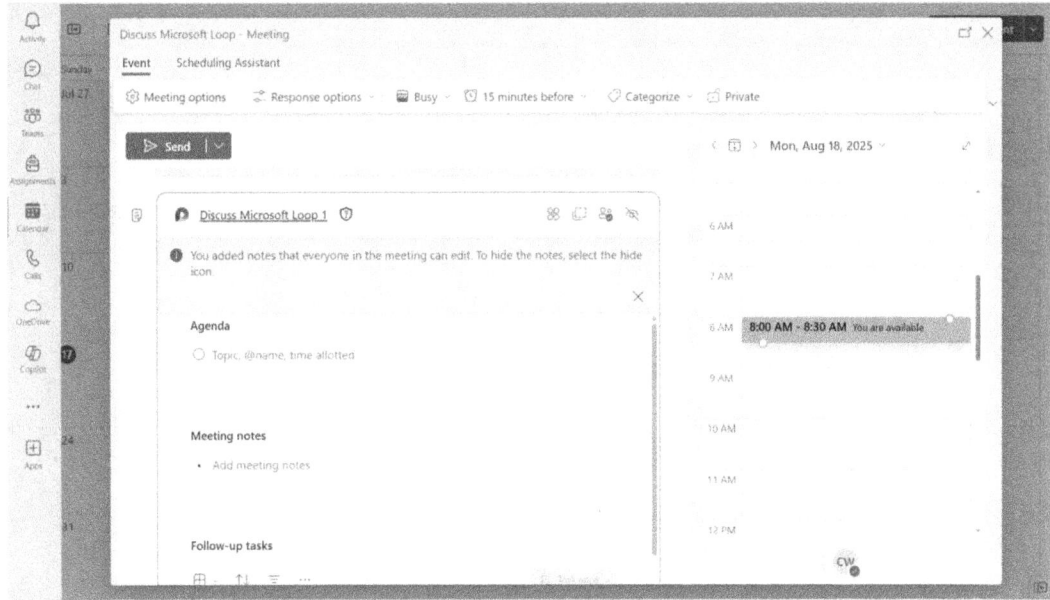

Figure 3-9. *Agenda components gets added*

CHAPTER 3   CO-CREATION AND MANAGING LOOP COMPONENTS

In the agenda section, position your cursor and enter a concise description of each agenda item, as shown in Figure 3-10. To assign responsibilities, use the "@" symbol followed by a colleague's name, selecting from the people list as appropriate, as shown in Figure 3-11. Further, you can also tag a link to a file using @mention, as shown in Figure 3-12.

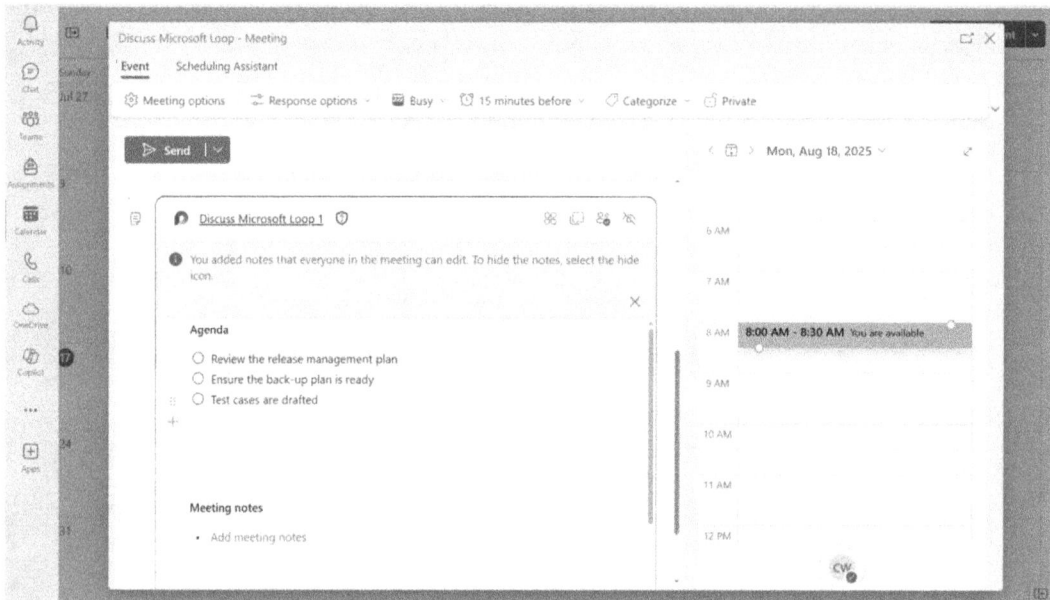

Figure 3-10. *Agenda in section is updated*

CHAPTER 3 CO-CREATION AND MANAGING LOOP COMPONENTS

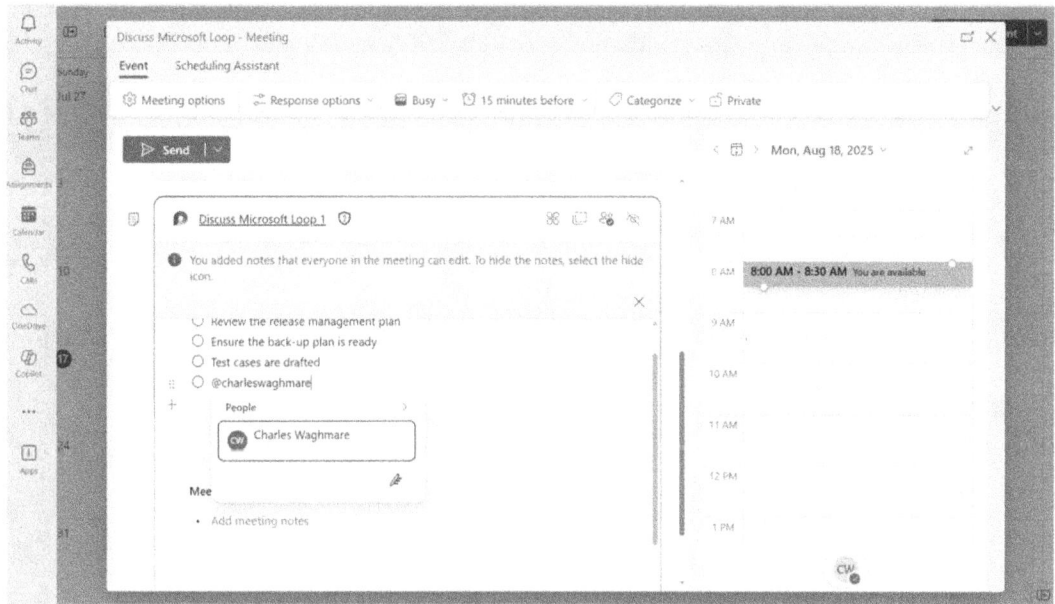

Figure 3-11. *Allocate actions to specific person using @-mention*

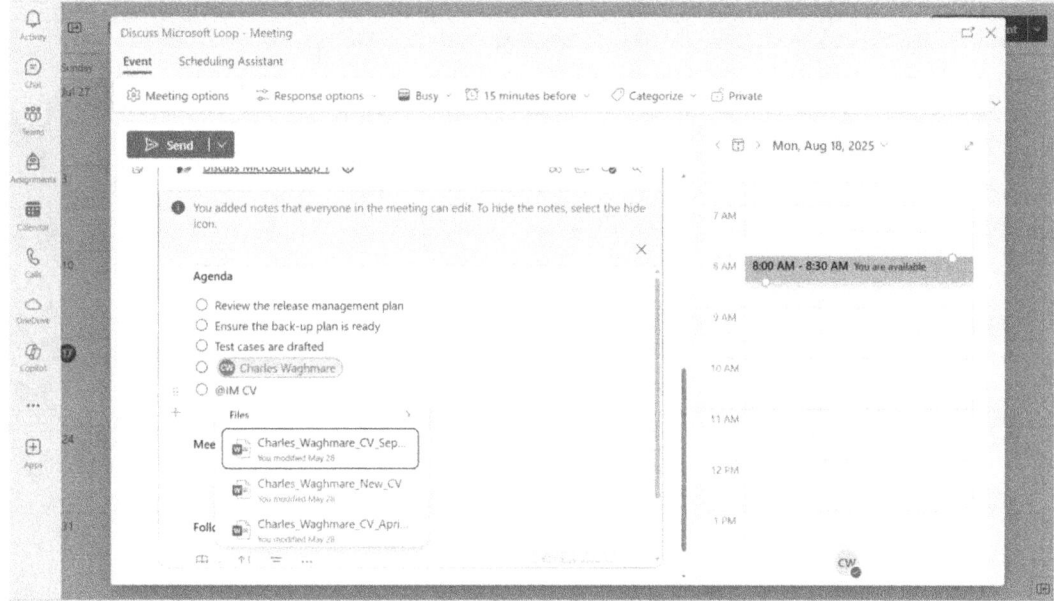

Figure 3-12. *@mention to tag file URL*

CHAPTER 3   CO-CREATION AND MANAGING LOOP COMPONENTS

Finally, one can add Meeting notes, as shown in Figure 3-13. Follow up tasks using Add task component, as shown in Figure 3-14.

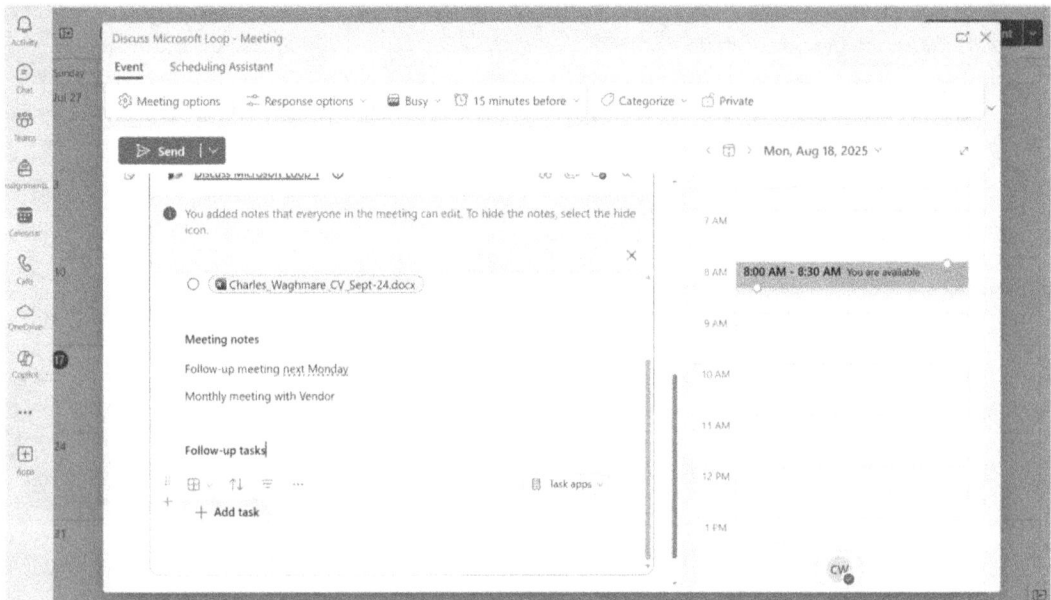

Figure 3-13. Update Meeting notes, follow-up tasks using task components

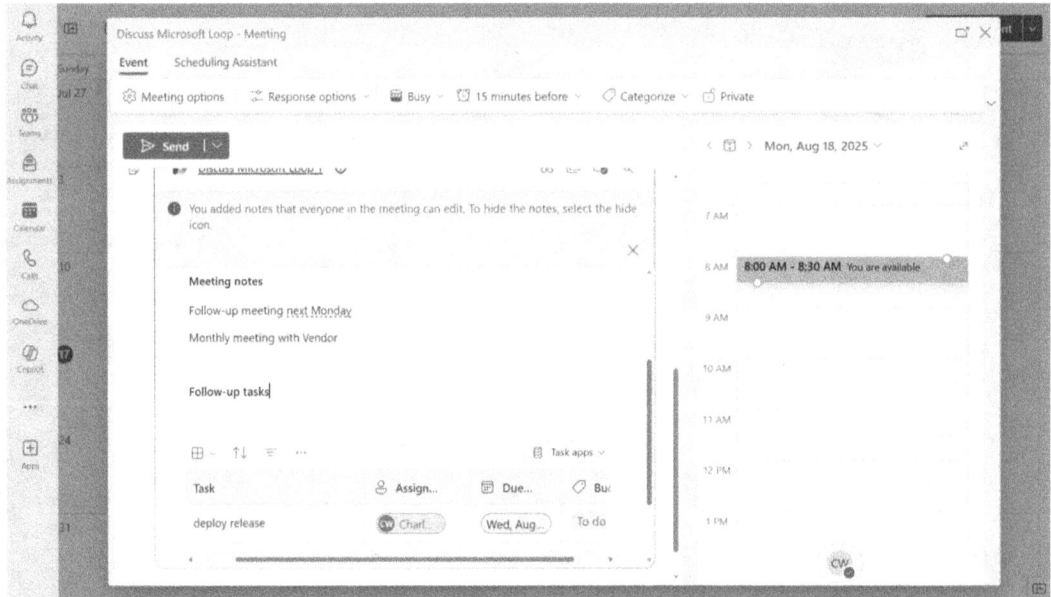

Figure 3-14. Create follow-up tasks using task components

CHAPTER 3   CO-CREATION AND MANAGING LOOP COMPONENTS

Once the invitation is sent, all invited participants can contribute to and edit the agenda, as well as record pertinent notes and tasks throughout the meeting life cycle. This process ensures a structured and collaborative approach to managing meeting objectives using the Loop component.

Set Up a Loop Task List Component in an Outlook Message

Microsoft 365 offers a variety of tools for task management, and the choice often depends on your team's preferred collaboration platform. For those utilizing Outlook messages, the Loop Task List component can streamline task assignments and tracking.

To insert a Loop Task List into an Outlook message, begin by placing your cursor at the desired insertion point in your draft. Navigate to the ribbon above—note that depending on your Outlook version and where the message is open, Loop Components may be located under Insert, as shown in Figure 3-15, or Message ribbons, as shown in Figure 3-16. Select "Loop Components" and then choose "Task List," as shown in Figure 3-17. The new task list component will appear within your message, as shown in Figure 3-18.

Figure 3-15. *Loop under Insert Menu*

CHAPTER 3   CO-CREATION AND MANAGING LOOP COMPONENTS

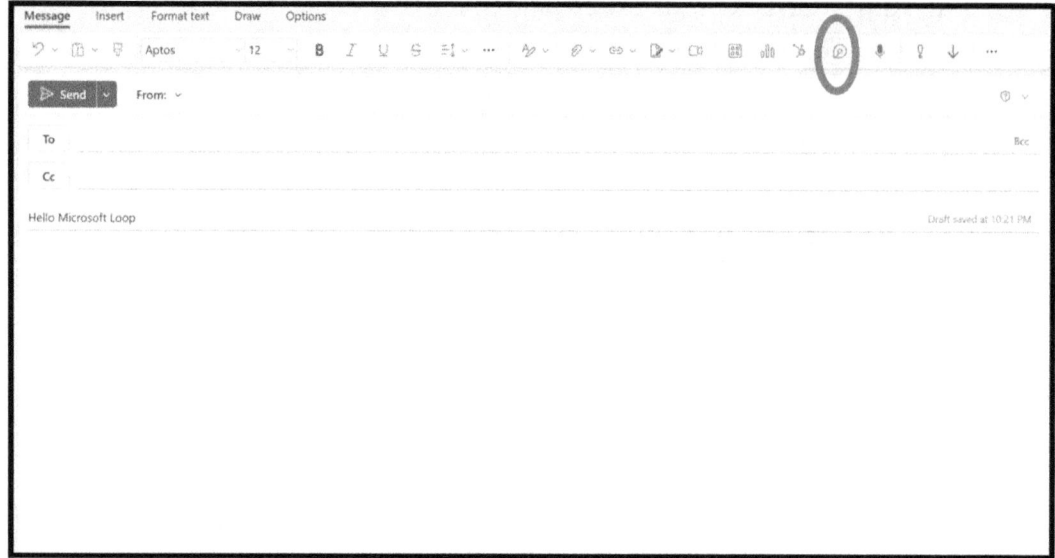

Figure 3-16. *Loop under Message Menu*

Figure 3-17. *Selecting Loop Component and Task List*

CHAPTER 3   CO-CREATION AND MANAGING LOOP COMPONENTS

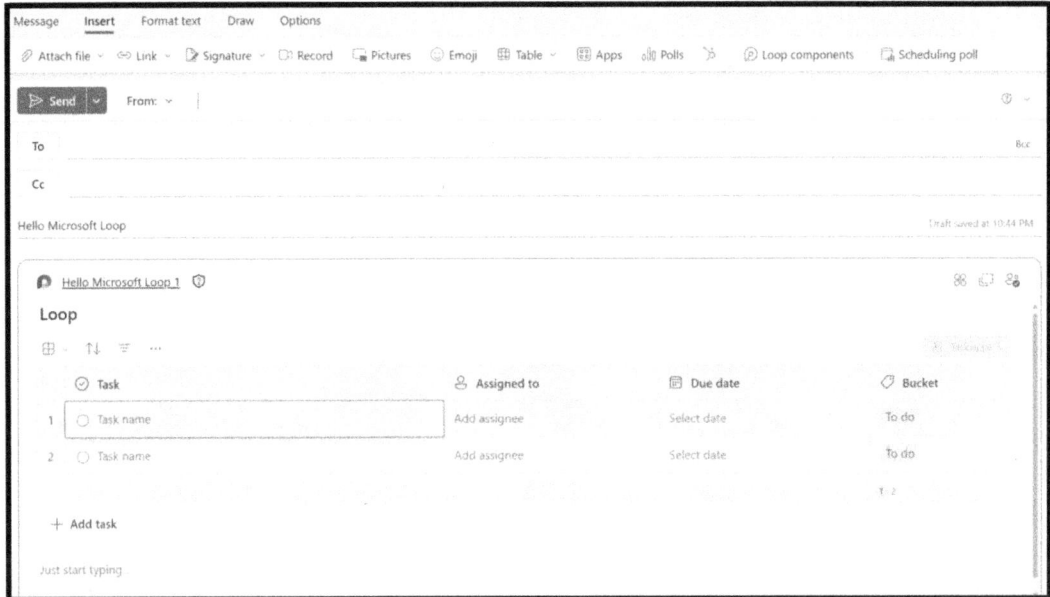

Figure 3-18. *Inserted New Task List Component*

Begin by entering the first task called as "Class Algebra" in the provided cell, as shown in Figure 3-19. You may use the Tab key or click the next cell to continue. When selecting the assignee cell, a dropdown menu will display colleagues, say "Charles Waghmare" whom you have recently collaborated with, as shown in Figure 3-19; if the desired individual is not listed, simply start typing their name. Once selected, assign a due date using the calendar popup, as shown in Figure 3-19, though this step is optional. Next, select the "Bucket" cell—by default, tasks are assigned to the "To Do" bucket, as shown in Figure 3-19, but you may create new buckets for better organization by choosing "Add Option," as shown in Figure 3-20, and called call it as "Not done," as shown in Figure 3-21, and naming the bucket accordingly, as shown in Figure 3-22.

CHAPTER 3   CO-CREATION AND MANAGING LOOP COMPONENTS

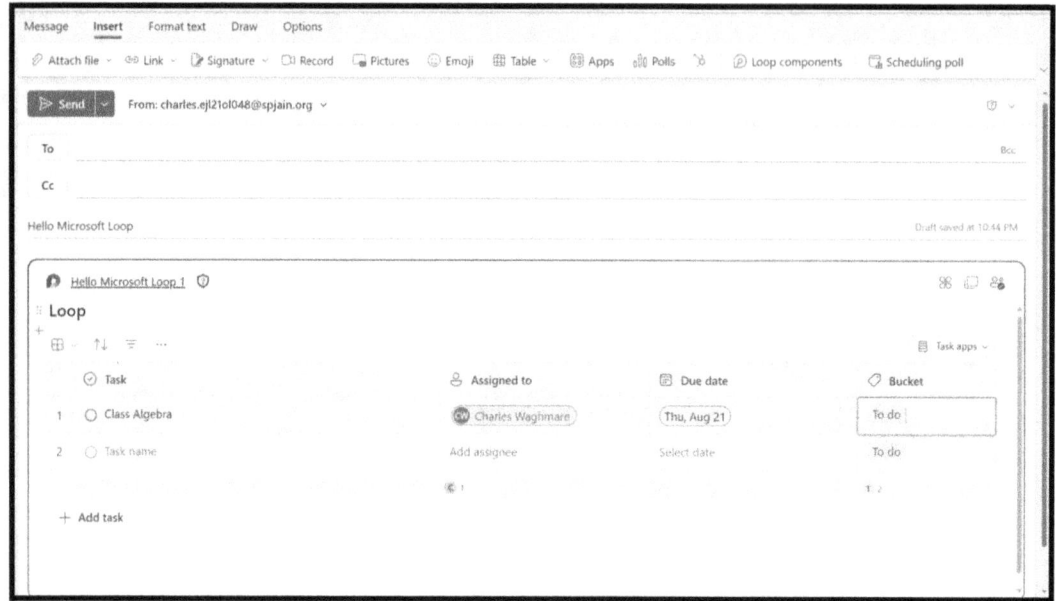

Figure 3-19. Update Task 1

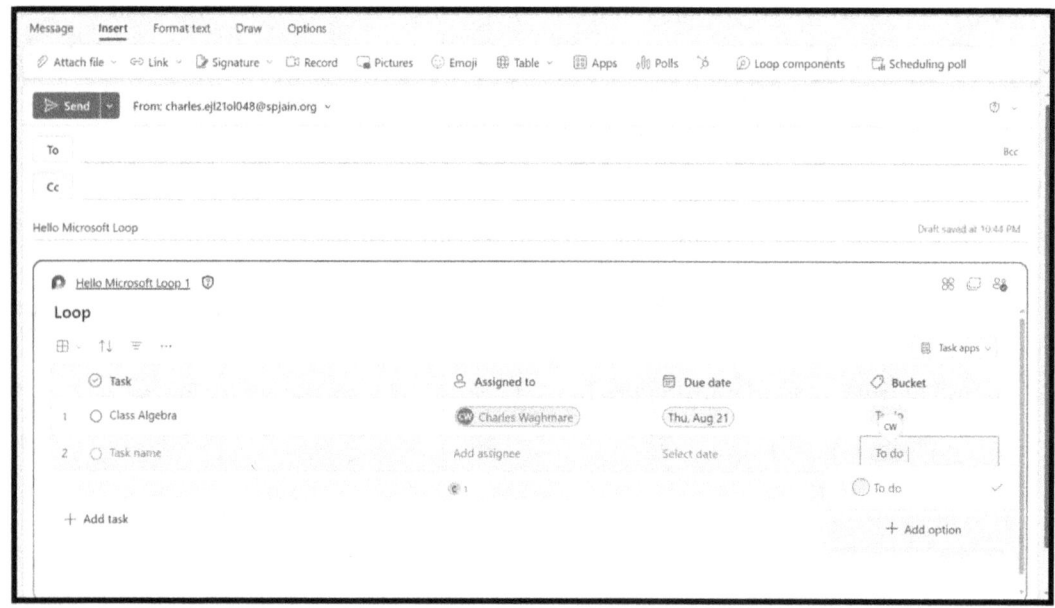

Figure 3-20. Access Add option to create another bucket

CHAPTER 3   CO-CREATION AND MANAGING LOOP COMPONENTS

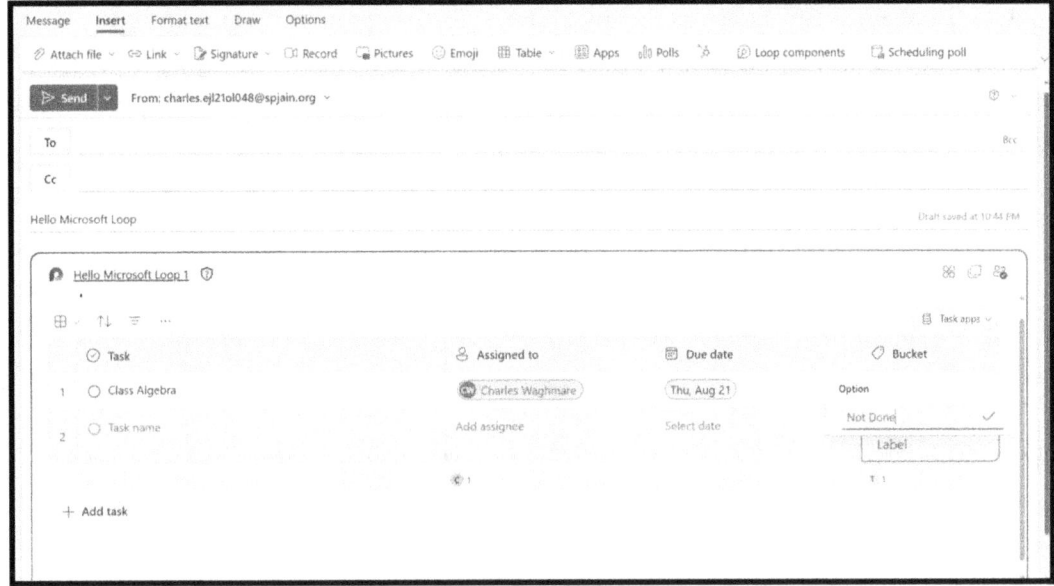

Figure 3-21. *Creation of bucket "Not done"*

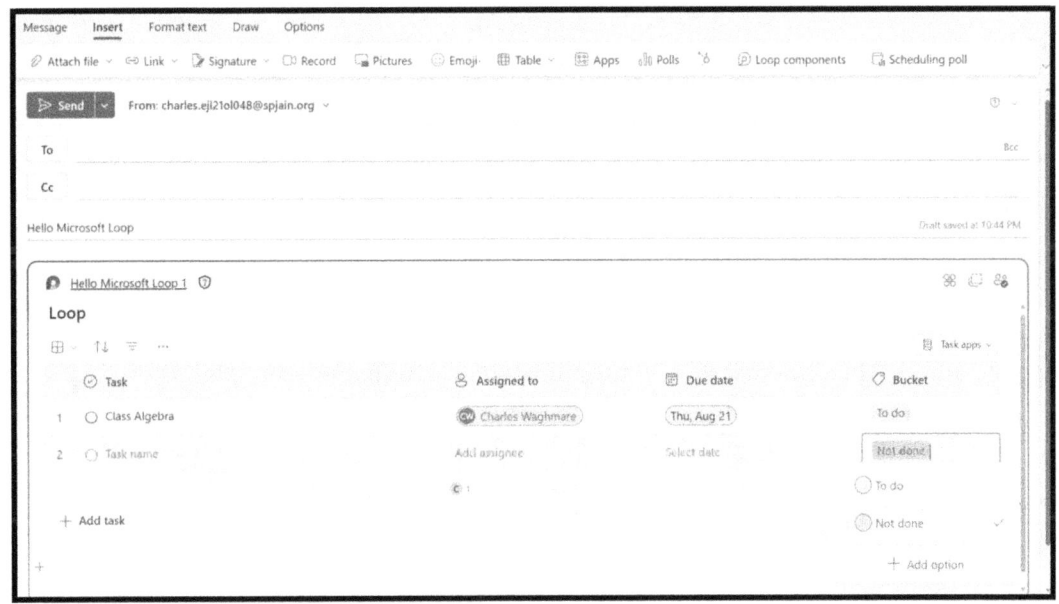

Figure 3-22. *Successful creation of bucket "Not done"*

Continue adding tasks as needed by filling out subsequent rows and adding additional rows via the "Add Task" button at the bottom, as shown in Figure 3-23. To provide context, select "Add a Title," as shown in Figure 3-23, and update it appropriately. When you are ready, send the message; recipients can then update tasks directly from email and integrated Microsoft 365 applications such as Planner and To-Do, along with any location where Loop components are shared.

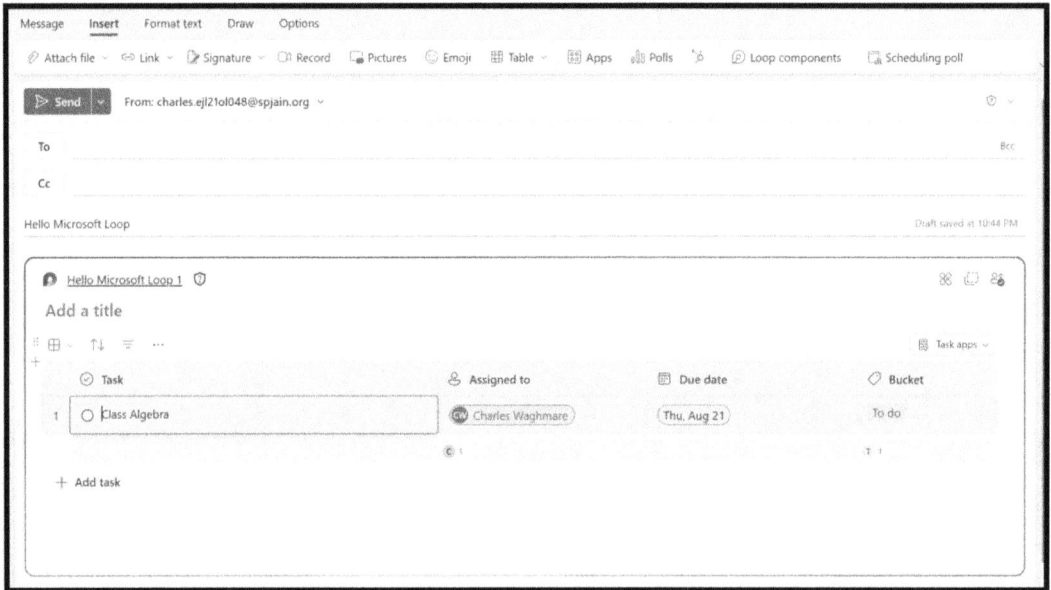

Figure 3-23. "Add a Title" and "Add Task" options

Please note that when a Loop component is created within an Outlook message addressed to specific individuals, it is saved in your OneDrive document library in a folder named "Attachments" with you as the owner. This ownership grants you full control over permissions, which will be discussed in detail later in the course.

Share a Loop Component Across Microsoft 365 Apps

A Loop component created within one application file or communication can be shared across other Microsoft 365 files and communications. To do so, locate the existing Loop component, then select "Copy Component," as shown in Figure 3-24. Next, navigate to the desired location where the component should be shared, for example, Microsoft Teams Chat, as shown in Figure 3-25.

CHAPTER 3 CO-CREATION AND MANAGING LOOP COMPONENTS

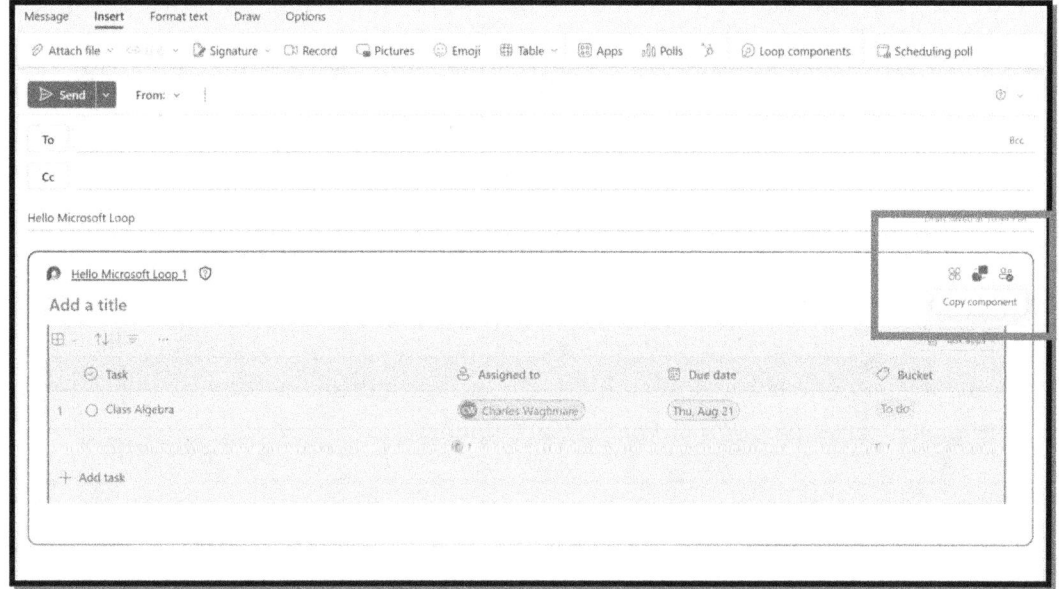

Figure 3-24. *Copy loop component*

Figure 3-25. *Copy loop component from Outlook to Teams*

To insert the copied Loop component, you may use the Home ribbon's Paste option, right-click and select Paste, or utilize the shortcut Control + V. Please note that, in some contexts, pasting the component will result in a link being inserted rather than displaying the original component format. This usually occurs when the destination does not support rendering the component natively. However, users can select the link to open and collaborate on the Loop component in a web browser.

As another example, if you paste the same Loop component into a OneNote notebook using Control + V, it will appear in its original format, retaining the formatting from the source email, as shown in Figure 3-26. Individuals with access can collaborate on the Loop component from any supported location, with all real-time changes synchronizing across all instances of the component.

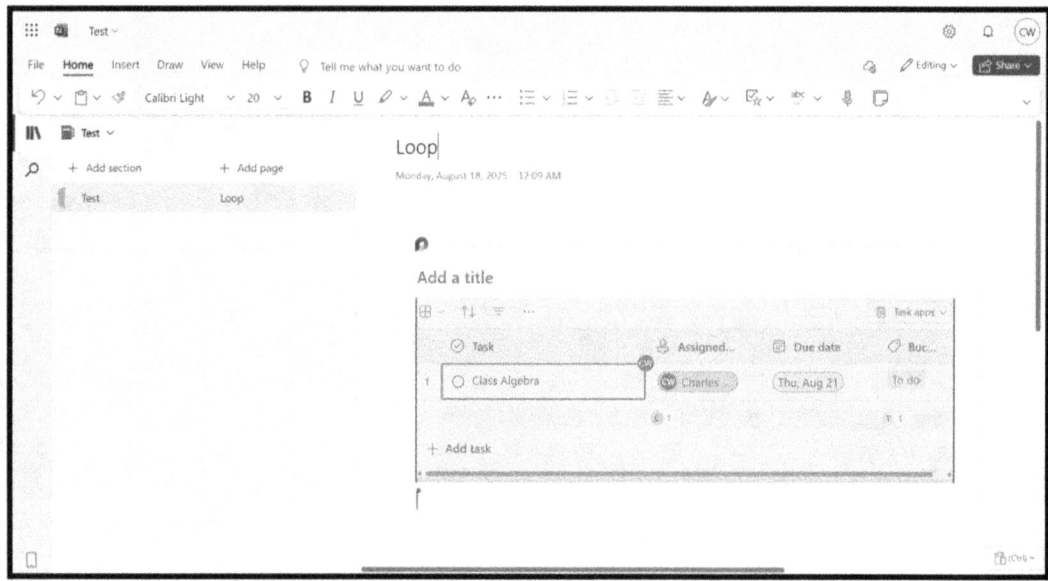

Figure 3-26. *Loop Component copied into OneNote*

Find Loop Components

Loop components are a distinct file type within the Microsoft ecosystem. Similar to searching for Word documents or Excel workbooks, users can locate loop components across document libraries, such as OneDrive in Microsoft Teams or directly from the Microsoft 365 homepage.

CHAPTER 3   CO-CREATION AND MANAGING LOOP COMPONENTS

To begin, navigate to the Microsoft 365 homepage and place your cursor in the search box. Enter ".loop" as the file type to retrieve all items associated with loop, as shown in Figure 3-27. Please note that this search may yield results beyond loop components, including unrelated files; these can be identified by their respective icons. Scrolling further will display additional loop-related items, including folders and loop components, which are marked by an icon featuring a white document background with a purple loop overlay. Selecting any of these items allows you to access them directly.

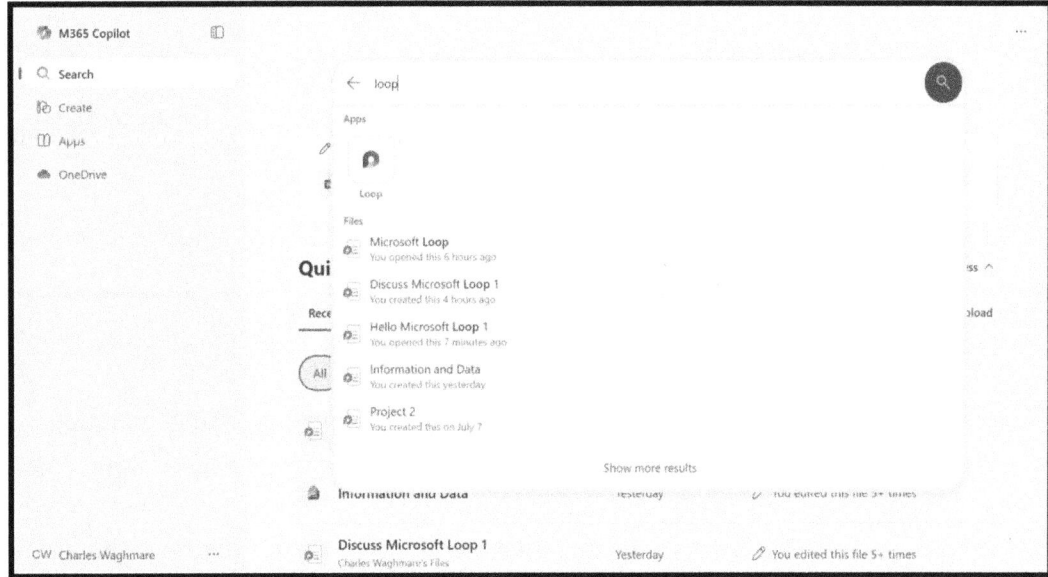

Figure 3-27. *Loop files across M365*

The same method applies within Teams—by searching for ".loop," you can identify loop references in messages, links to loop components, and, under the Files section, all available loop component files and possible workspace pages. (Figure 3-28)

CHAPTER 3   CO-CREATION AND MANAGING LOOP COMPONENTS

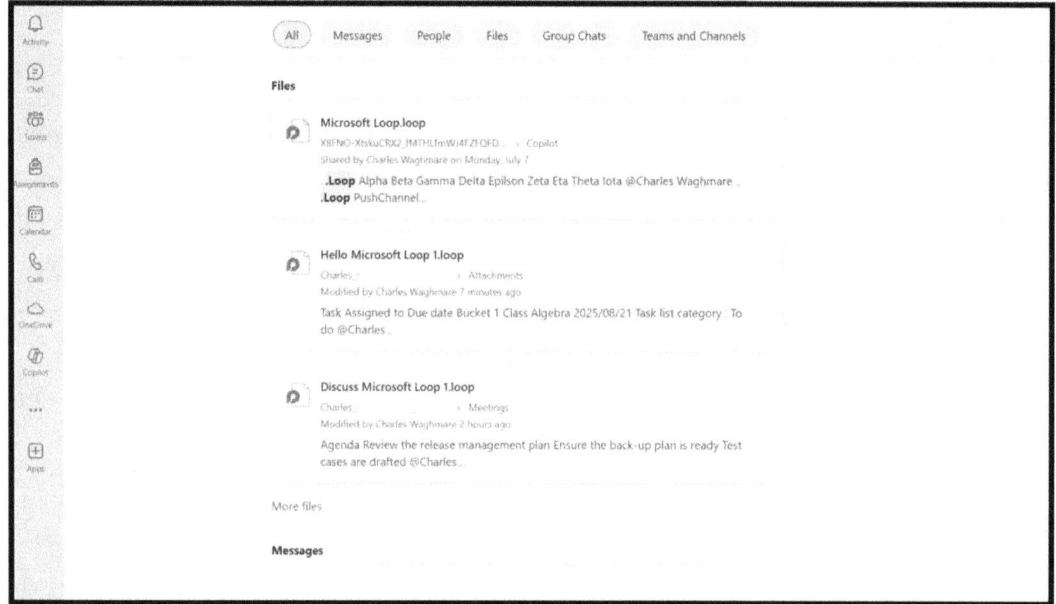

Figure 3-28.   *Loop files across Teams*

For more targeted results, enter the specific name of a loop component you wish to find. For instance, searching "website updates" will return any related files, such as "website updates needed," even if the match is not exact.

This process is also applicable in OneDrive; by using the search feature at the top and entering ".loop," you will see all corresponding loop components and folders linked to your account.

In summary, whether you are utilizing the Microsoft 365 homepage, Teams, or a cloud document library like OneDrive, these steps enable efficient discovery and management of loop components across platforms.

Coauthor a Loop Component

Similar to real-time co-editing available in Word documents or PowerPoint presentations, Loop components also support simultaneous collaboration. When multiple individuals are updating content within a Loop component, their initials and names will display, indicating their editing locations. The platform enables more than two users to coauthor a component concurrently, assigning a unique color to each collaborator.

At the top of the component, user profiles and initials are visible; hovering over them reveals the corresponding color outline and additional information about each participant, as shown in Figure 3-29. Within the component, this same color is used to outline cells, providing clear visual cues regarding who is making edits. Edits occur in real time and are automatically saved and synchronized across all instances where the component has been shared. This functionality ensures that teams are equipped to effectively coauthor Loop components.

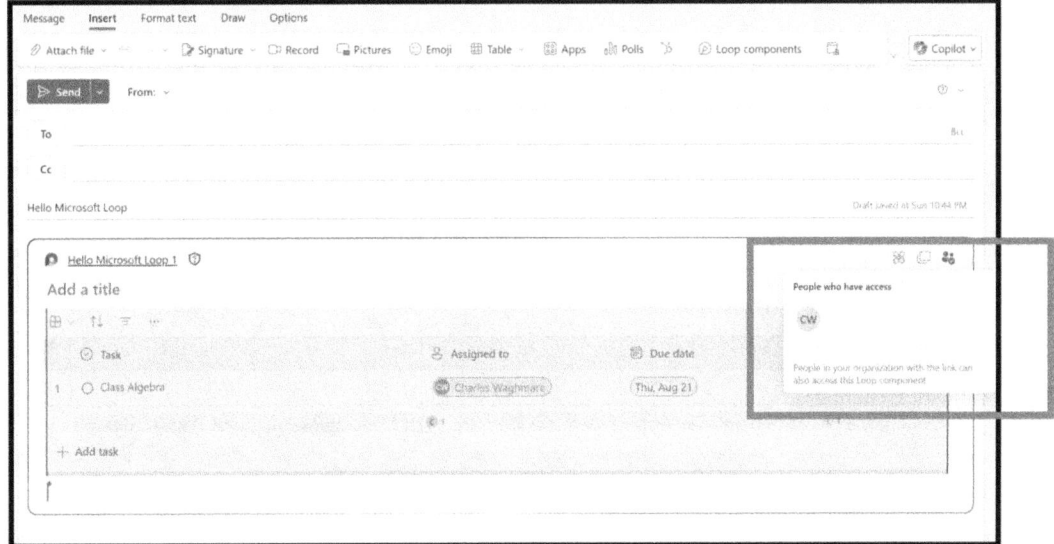

Figure 3-29. *Who has access to loop component*

Manage Access for a Loop Component

When a loop component is created, the creator becomes its owner and can manage access permissions. To view and manage access, open the loop component and select "see who has access" to display the list of users with current access rights, as shown in Figure 3-29.

To manage a loop component from OneDrive, locate the stored component, hover over it, and select "more actions," as shown in Figure 3-30. Choose "manage access" from the menu, as shown in Figure 3-31. Sharing can be initiated by selecting "share" in the top left corner, as shown in Figure 3-32, entering the intended recipient's name, and selecting it from the list, as shown in Figure 3-33. Optionally, a message can be included before sending the invitation, as shown in Figure 3-33.

CHAPTER 3　CO-CREATION AND MANAGING LOOP COMPONENTS

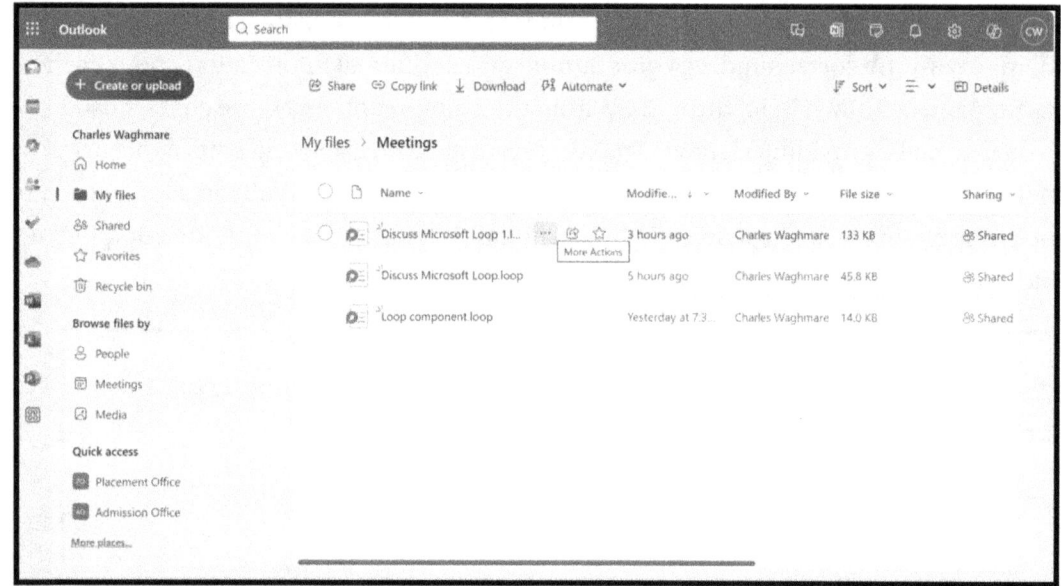

Figure 3-30. *Select "More Actions"*

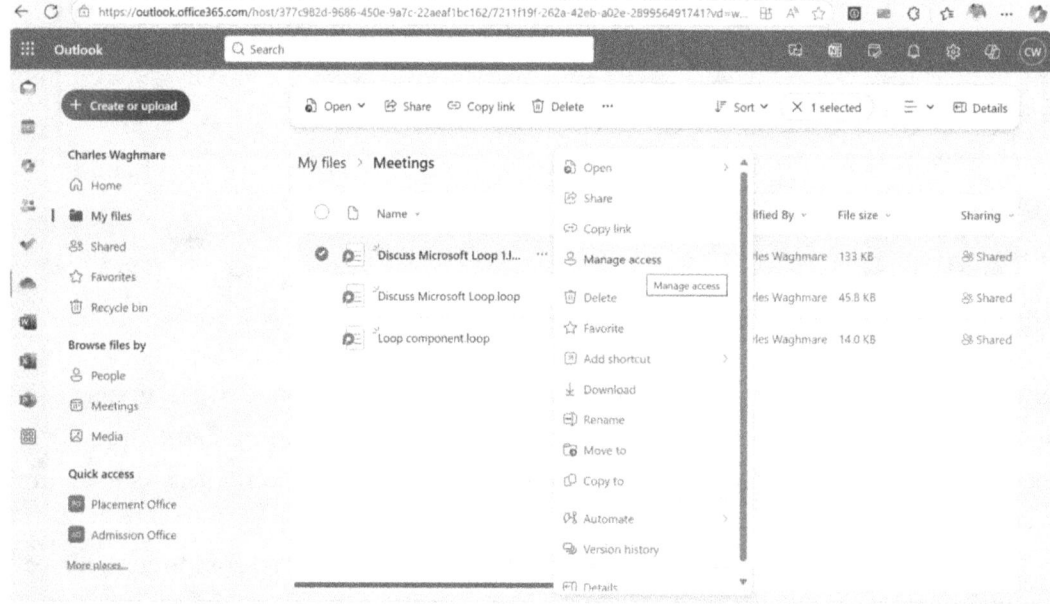

Figure 3-31. *Click on Manage access*

CHAPTER 3   CO-CREATION AND MANAGING LOOP COMPONENTS

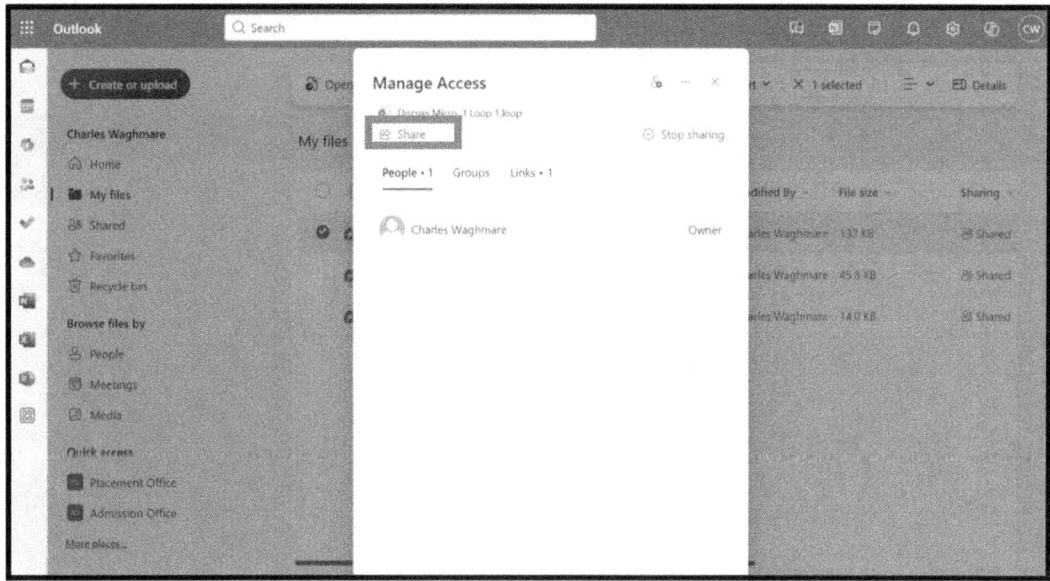

Figure 3-32. *Select "Share" option*

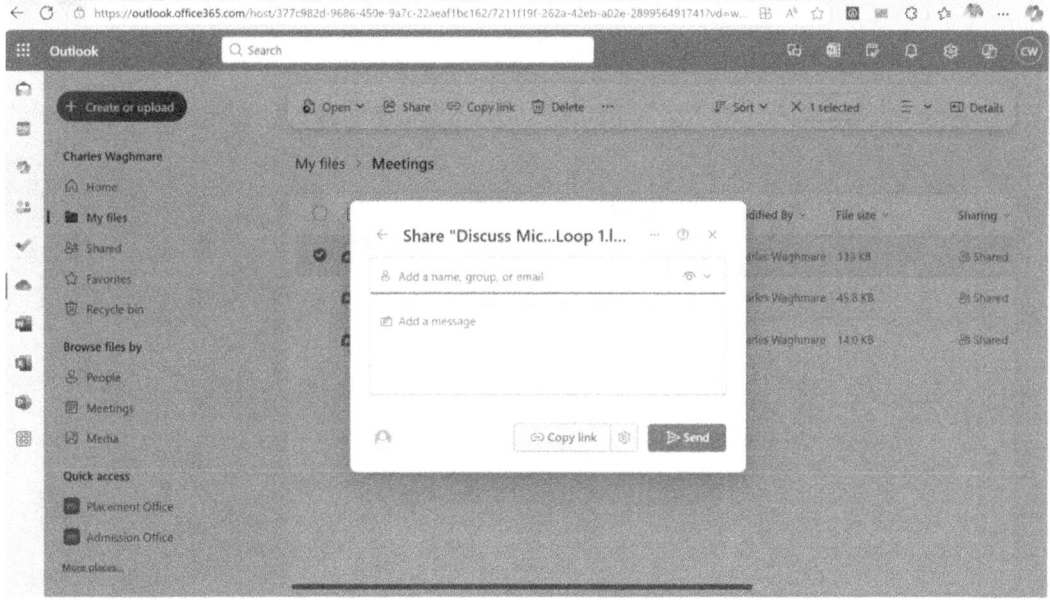

Figure 3-33. *Add reciepient name and message to grant access*

Notifications can be closed, and further management options are accessible via "more actions" and then "Manage Access." In the upper right corner, selecting "stop sharing" restricts access to only the owner after confirming the action, as shown in

93

CHAPTER 3   CO-CREATION AND MANAGING LOOP COMPONENTS

Figure 3-34. For example, only Charles Waghmare, owner of component, may have access after this step, as shown in Figure 3-35.

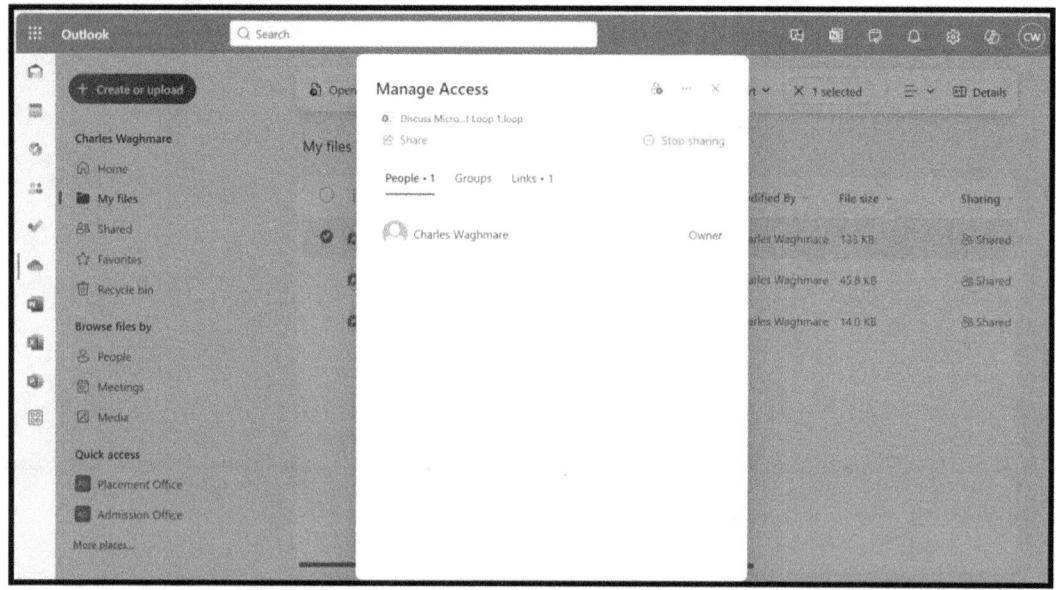

Figure 3-34. *Access stop sharing option*

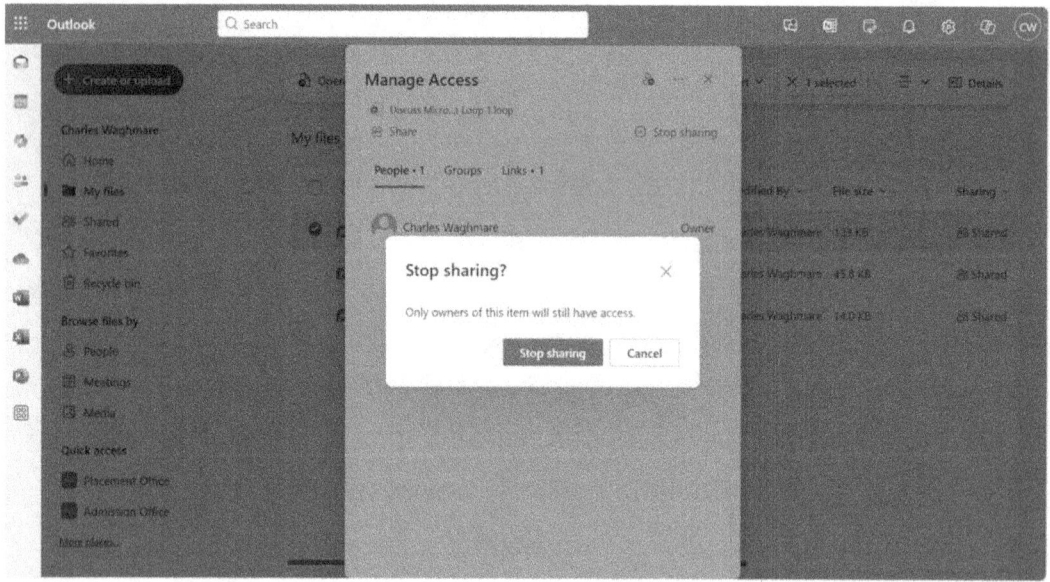

Figure 3-35. *Only Loop owner has access*

The interface includes three tabbed areas: "People," which lists individuals with access and their respective permissions (with the option to adjust individual access), "Groups," which shows group sharing status for the component, and "Links," where sharing links can be created or existing link permissions managed, as shown in Figure 3-36, respectively. These steps outline how to view and manage access permissions for a loop component.

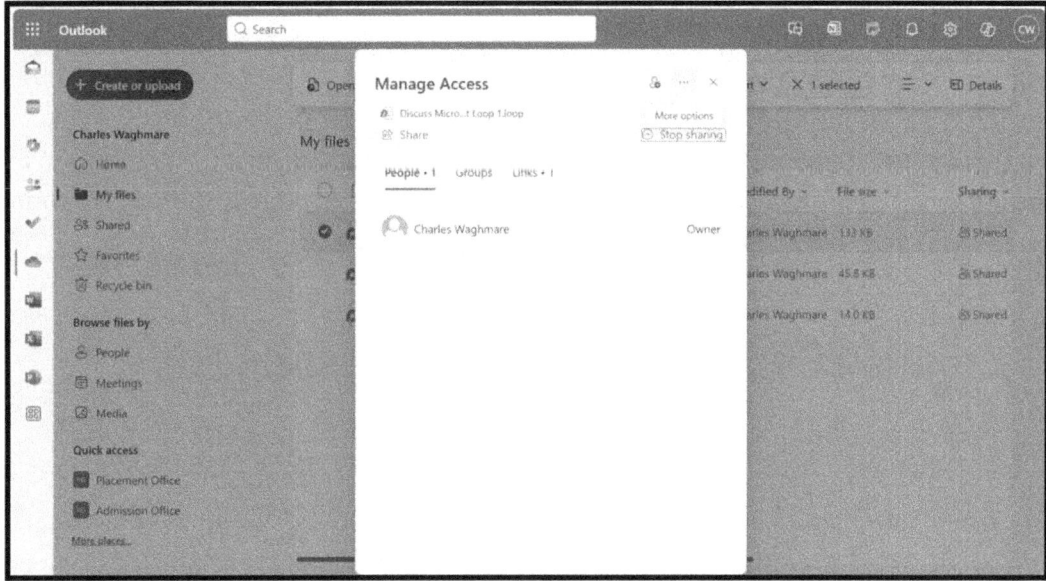

Figure 3-36. Interface showing access for people, groups and links

What to Know About Microsoft Loop Before Getting Started

Microsoft Loop powers components—portable blocks of content that can be configured and shared across multiple Microsoft 365 applications and communication platforms. Available component types include bulleted, check, and numbered lists; voting tables; progress trackers; Kanban boards; team retrospectives; Q&A sessions; and more. Loop components are supported in various Microsoft 365 applications such as Outlook, Teams, Word, OneNote, Whiteboard, and the Loop app. Please note that individuals using personal Microsoft accounts do not yet have access to Loop components within Teams, Outlook, or other Microsoft 365 apps.

Throughout this book, you will learn to build and share components within Microsoft 365 files and communications. While these components may appear simple, they enable robust collaboration and synchronization. There are several types of workspaces available in Microsoft Loop. Shared workspaces are managed via a roster system instead of a Microsoft 365 group and have designated owners and members. Personal workspaces, also roster-managed, are intended for single users. If a workspace creator departs the organization, their workspace becomes ownerless. Both Loop workspaces and pages count toward your individual Microsoft 365 storage quota.

Most Microsoft Loop features are accessible to users with a work or school account, specifically those using a Microsoft Entra account. If you encounter issues accessing the Loop app or specific features through your work account, please consult your IT department to ensure these options are enabled. Users with personal Microsoft accounts can access Loop through its iOS, Android, and web applications.

Cocreation Challenges Using Microsoft Loop

Microsoft Loop, while promising a revolutionary approach to collaboration within the Microsoft 365 ecosystem, presents a range of challenges that organizations must navigate to fully harness its potential. These challenges span technical, organizational, and strategic dimensions, and understanding them is crucial for successful adoption and integration.

Overlap with Existing Microsoft 365 Tools: One of the most frequently cited challenges is redundancy and confusion due to Loop's overlap with existing Microsoft 365 tools like OneNote, Planner, and Teams. Many users struggle to understand when to use Loop components vs. traditional tools. For instance, task lists in Loop may seem redundant when Planner or To Do already exist, and collaborative notes may duplicate OneNote's functionality. This overlap can lead to fragmented workflows, reduced productivity, and resistance from users who are already comfortable with existing tools.

Adoption and Change Management: Despite its innovative features, Loop faces adoption hurdles. Many organizations report low initial uptake due to a lack of awareness, training, or clear use cases. Employees may be hesitant to switch from familiar tools, especially if Loop is perceived as "just another app" in an already crowded digital workspace. Without a strong management strategy—including training, champions, and clear communication—Loop risks becoming underutilized or abandoned.

Storage and Data Management Complexity: Loop introduces new storage paradigms that can complicate data governance. Loop components created in Teams channels are stored in SharePoint, while those created in Outlook or OneNote are stored in the creator's OneDrive. This split storage model can lead to confusion, clutter, and difficulty in tracking content. Administrators must carefully manage storage quotas, retention policies, and access controls across multiple platforms to avoid performance issues and ensure compliance.

Compliance, Discovery, and Legal Risks: The dynamic and distributed nature of Loop content poses challenges for legal discovery, compliance, and data retention. Loop components are live, editable, and portable across apps, making it harder to capture a consistent snapshot of content for audits or investigations. Organizations must update their compliance frameworks to account for Loop's unique data structures and ensure that Loop content is included in eDiscovery and retention policies.

Security and Privacy Concerns

Loop's real-time collaboration features raise security and privacy concerns, especially in regulated industries. The ability to embed live components in emails or chats increases the risk of unintentional data exposure. Moreover, the integration of personal and work data—especially in hybrid work environments—can blur boundaries and complicate data classification. Organizations must implement robust data loss prevention (DLP) policies and educate users on secure sharing practices.

Integration and Ecosystem Maturity: Although Loop is designed to integrate seamlessly with Microsoft 365, its ecosystem is still maturing. Some users report inconsistent behavior when embedding components across apps, limited third-party integrations, and bugs in the Loop app itself. Additionally, the roadmap for Loop's development remains somewhat unclear, leading to uncertainty about its long-term viability and support. This lack of clarity can deter organizations from fully committing to Loop as a core collaboration tool.

Governance and Administrative Control: Administrators face challenges in governing Loop usage across the organization. Unlike traditional documents, Loop components are lightweight and easily shared, which can lead to sprawl and loss of control. Admins must configure sharing settings, monitor usage patterns, and enforce policies to prevent misuse or data leakage. However, the tools for managing Loop at scale are still evolving, and many organizations find the current admin controls insufficient.

User Experience and Learning Curve: While Loop offers a modern and intuitive interface, it introduces new paradigms that may confuse users. The distinction between Loop components, pages, and workspaces is not always clear, and users may struggle to understand how to organize their content effectively. Without proper onboarding, users may misuse Loop or revert to older tools, undermining its benefits.

Performance and Scalability Issues: As Loop adoption grows, some organizations report performance bottlenecks, especially when managing large numbers of components or pages. Syncing content across multiple apps in real time can strain network resources and lead to latency or data conflicts. Ensuring a smooth user experience at scale requires robust infrastructure and optimization, which may not be feasible for all organizations.

Strategic Alignment and ROI: Finally, organizations must assess whether Loop aligns with their strategic goals and collaboration culture. While Loop excels in agile, fast-paced environments, it may not suit all teams or workflows. Without a clear ROI or measurable productivity gains, decision-makers may hesitate to invest in training, support, or integration efforts. Loop's success depends on its ability to deliver tangible value beyond what existing tools offer.

In conclusion, Microsoft Loop represents a bold step toward fluid, real-time collaboration, but its adoption is not without significant challenges. From technical hurdles like storage management and compliance to cultural barriers like user resistance and tool fatigue, organizations must approach Loop with a well-defined strategy. By addressing these challenges proactively—through governance, training, and thoughtful integration—Loop can evolve from a promising innovation to a transformative force in the digital workplace.

This chapter concludes our discussion on the topics outlined. We explored the co-creation of content using Microsoft Loop, including how to send a Loop voting table component in Teams communications, create a Teams meeting agenda Loop component, set up a Loop task list component in Outlook messages, share Loop components across Microsoft 365 applications, locate and coauthor Loop components, manage access, as well as foundational knowledge and potential challenges associated with Microsoft Loop.

In the following chapter, we will undertake a detailed examination of Loop's real-time collaboration features, focusing on the communication process and the functionalities for real-time editing and teamwork within Microsoft Loop.

CHAPTER 4

Real-Time Collaboration Using Loop

The previous chapter discussed the co-creation of content with Microsoft Loop, including the process for sending a Loop voting table component in Teams communications, creating a Teams meeting agenda Loop component, setting up a Loop task list component in Outlook messages, sharing Loop components across Microsoft 365 applications, locating and coauthoring Loop components, managing access, and covering foundational knowledge and possible challenges related to Microsoft Loop.

The following chapter will provide a detailed analysis of Loop's real-time collaboration features, concentrating on the communication process and capabilities for real-time editing and teamwork within Microsoft Loop. With a focus on real-time collaboration and communication process we will cover real-time collaboration using loop, rewriting content with copilot assistance, instructing copilot to summarize a loop workspace page, asking copilot to brainstorm an idea in a loop workspace page, create loop workspace content with copilot, and finally, understanding the communication process by comparing Microsoft loop with Microsoft teams, Microsoft Outlook, and OneNote. To access **Microsoft Copilot for Microsoft Loop**, use the following steps:

- **Microsoft 365 Copilot License**: An active Microsoft 365 Copilot license is required to access Copilot features in Loop.

- **Microsoft Loop Access**: Confirm that Microsoft Loop has been enabled for your organization through the Microsoft 365 Admin Center.

CHAPTER 4 REAL-TIME COLLABORATION USING LOOP

Real-Time Collaboration Using Loop

If your Microsoft 365 subscription includes Copilot, you can utilize this AI assistant to help generate content within a new workspace page. To begin, navigate to an untitled page. If one is not available, open the workspace sidebar and select "Create New Page," as shown in Figure 4-1. Once on the new page, locate the section at the bottom labeled "Set up your page with Copilot" and expand it by selecting the double arrow icon called Expand Copilot Overlay, as shown in Figure 4-2.

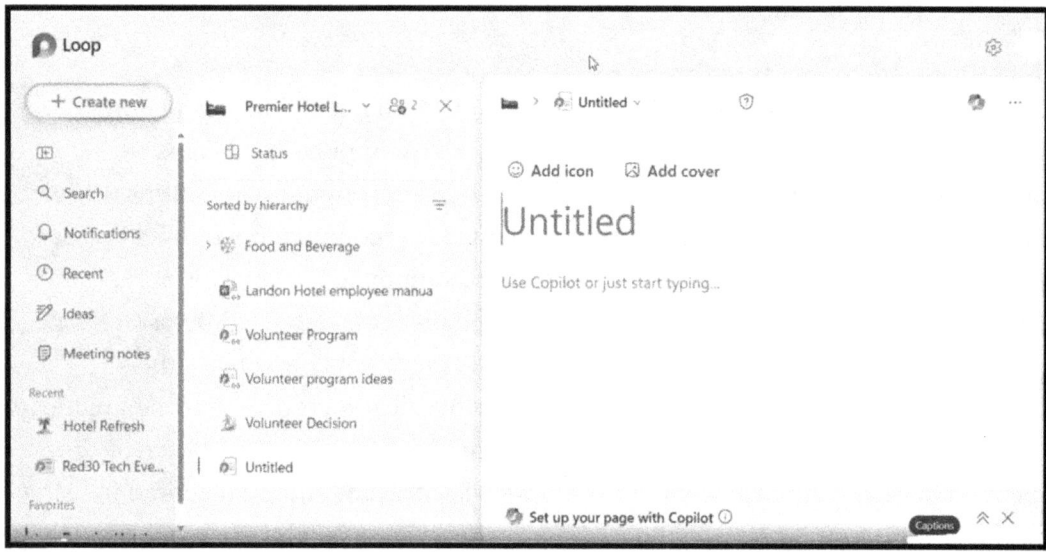

Figure 4-1. Create an untitled page to Copilot for content generation

CHAPTER 4 REAL-TIME COLLABORATION USING LOOP

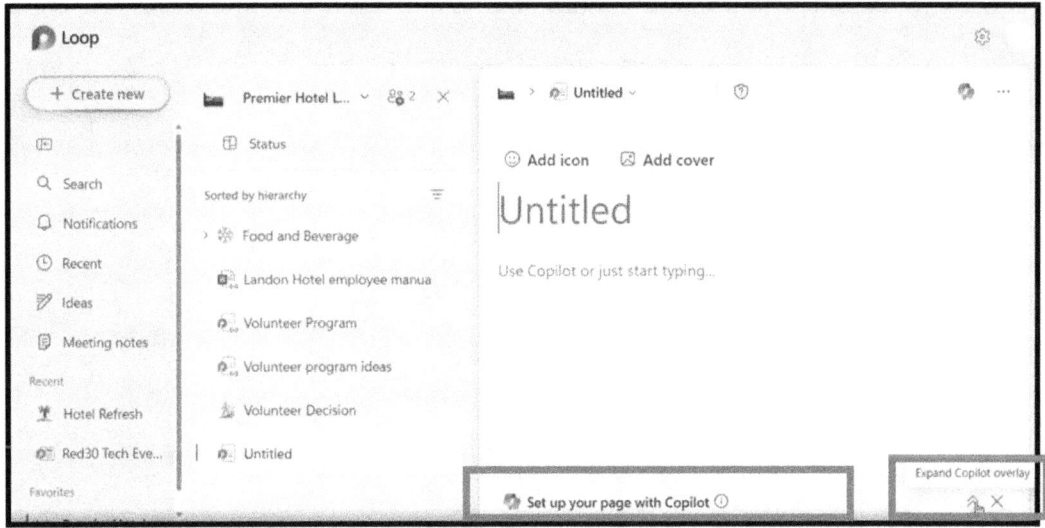

Figure 4-2. *Access "Set up your page with Copilot" and "Expand Copilot overlay"*

Within the instruction field that prompts you to describe your page, click to enter your description, as shown in Figure 4-3. For demonstration purposes, we will use a description related to a volunteer program for Landon Hotel employees and then submit this description to Copilot, as shown in Figure 4-4. Progress notifications will appear as the content is generated, as shown in Figure 4-5.

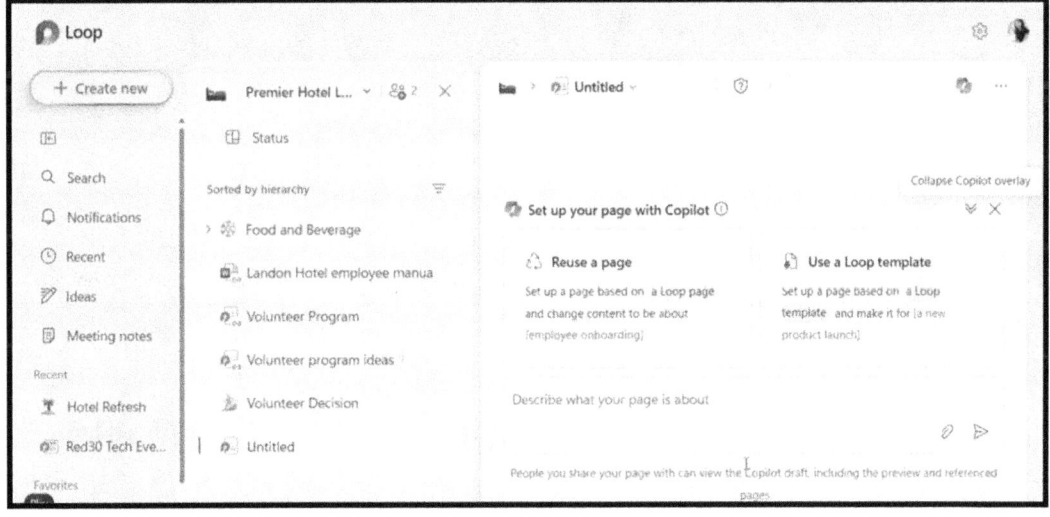

Figure 4-3. *Option to setup page using Copilot*

101

CHAPTER 4   REAL-TIME COLLABORATION USING LOOP

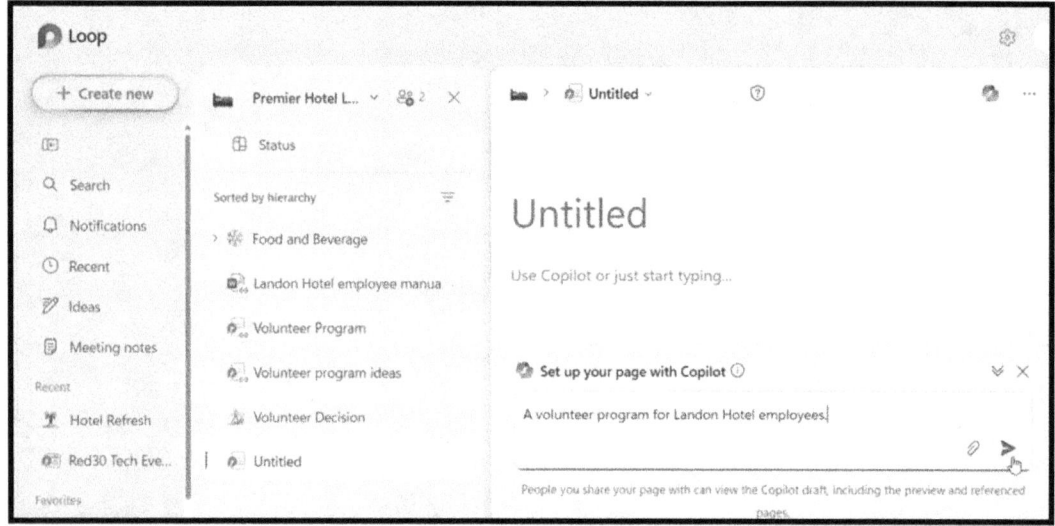

Figure 4-4.   Prompt for demonstration

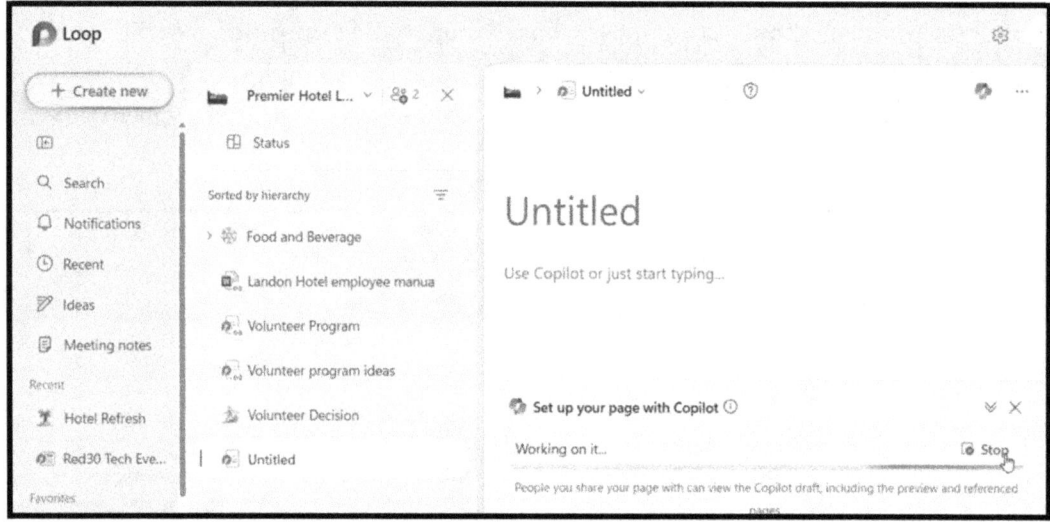

Figure 4-5.   Copilot Content generation is in progress

The resulting page will display the entered prompt, an automatically added icon, and the content created by Copilot, as shown in Figure 4-6. It is advisable to review the generated content to ensure it meets your requirements. If edits are needed, modify the instructions in the prompt area or start over as necessary. When satisfied, select "Keep Draft" or start over to save your work, as shown in Figure 4-7.

CHAPTER 4   REAL-TIME COLLABORATION USING LOOP

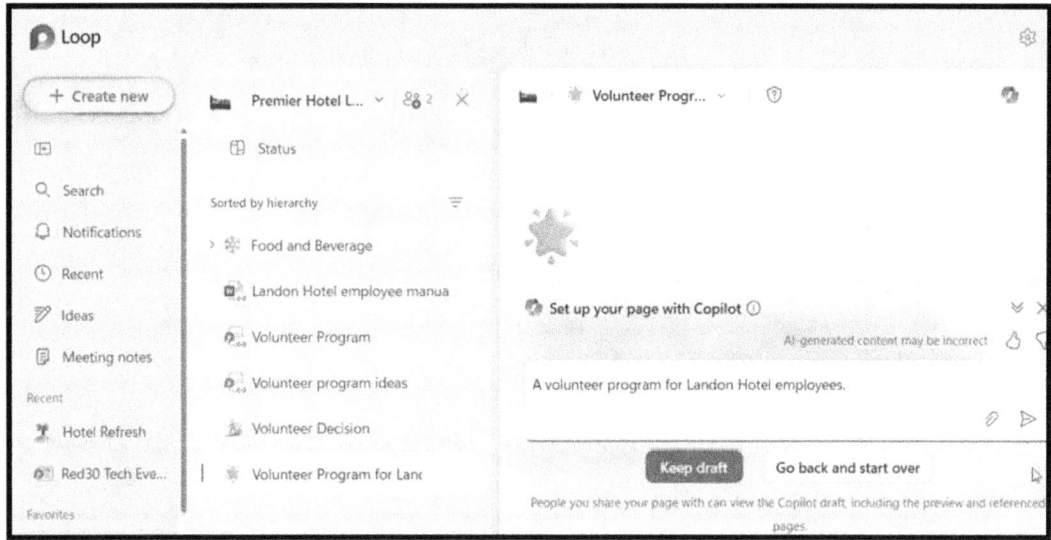

Figure 4-6. *Resulting page from Copilot*

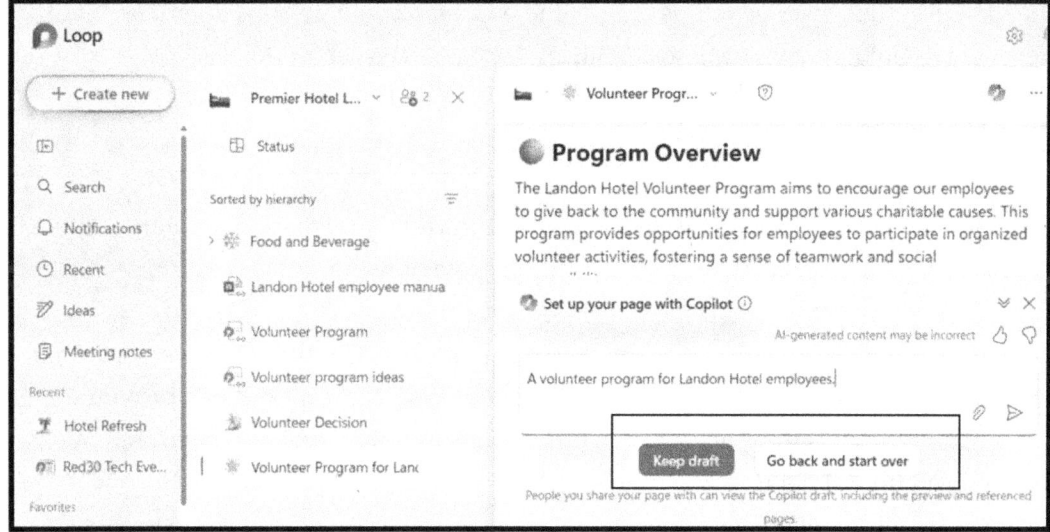

Figure 4-7. *Review content and use "Keep draft" or "Go back and start now" options*

Additionally, creating another new page reveals the option to include reference files by using the paperclip icon, allowing Copilot to tailor content based on those files, as shown in Figure 4-8. The prompt you provide serves as Copilot's instruction for content creation.

103

CHAPTER 4   REAL-TIME COLLABORATION USING LOOP

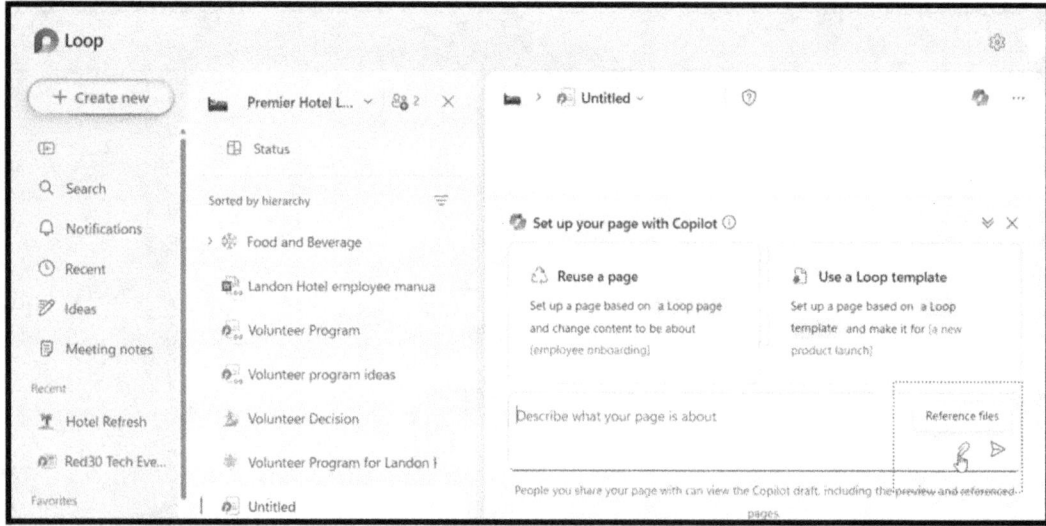

Figure 4-8. *Reference files used by Copilot for content creation*

This advanced feature supports more customized results as you gain familiarity with the tool. In summary, these steps outline the process for generating content on blank pages using Copilot within Microsoft 365.

Rewriting Content with Copilot Assistance

Copilot provides comprehensive assistance within your workspace, including content rewriting capabilities. We would like to demonstrate how Copilot can support you in enhancing the content on this page.

In the upper-right corner of Loop, you will notice that Copilot is always accessible for prompt initiation, as shown in Figure 4-9. Once you click on Copilot icon, you will see default prompts and space for custom prompts to query the Loop page content, as shown in Figure 4-10.

CHAPTER 4   REAL-TIME COLLABORATION USING LOOP

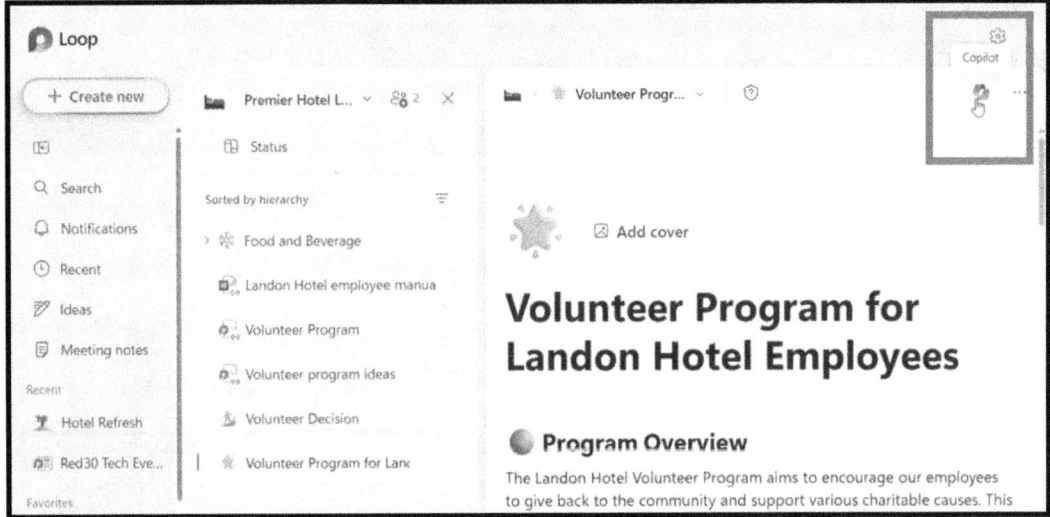

Figure 4-9. *Copilot part of Loop*

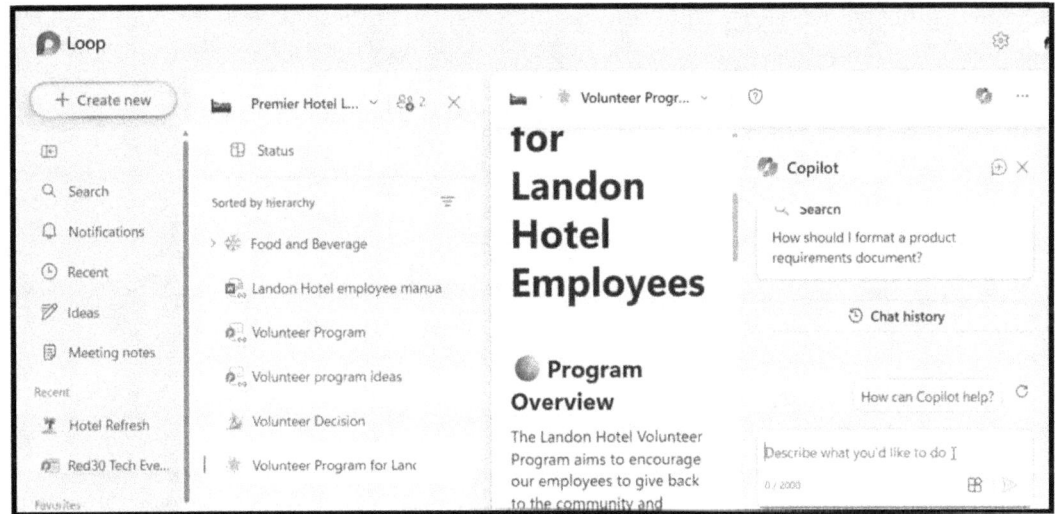

Figure 4-10. *Query Loop content using default and custom prompts*

Copilot is also available contextually, integrated directly with your workspace. For instance, when placing the mouse cursor within a paragraph or paragraph title, Copilot becomes visible, as shown in Figure 4-11 and 4-11-1, and helps relevant to the selected content. By clicking on the Copilot icon, the entire paragraph is selected, as shown in Figure 4-12, and a suggested prompt, such as "rewrite with Copilot," appears, as shown in Figure 4-13.

105

CHAPTER 4 REAL-TIME COLLABORATION USING LOOP

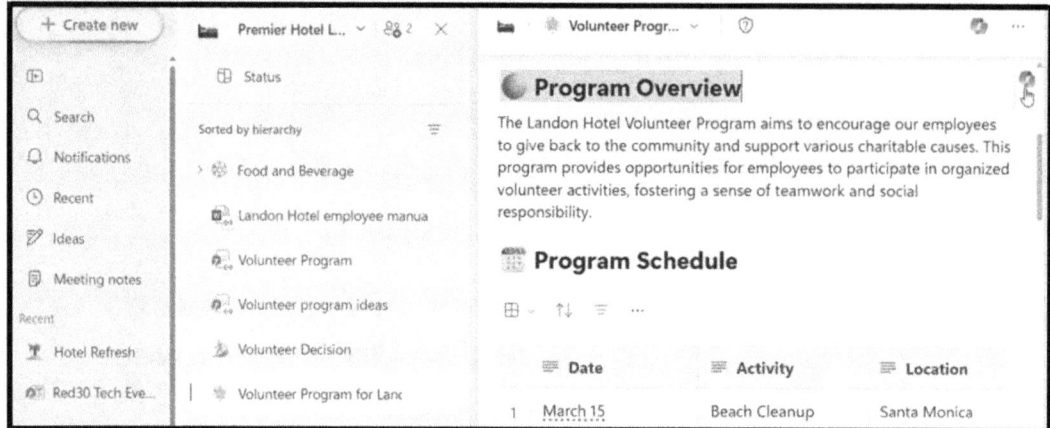

Figure 4-11. *Appearance of Copilot at the moment when paragraph Title is chosen*

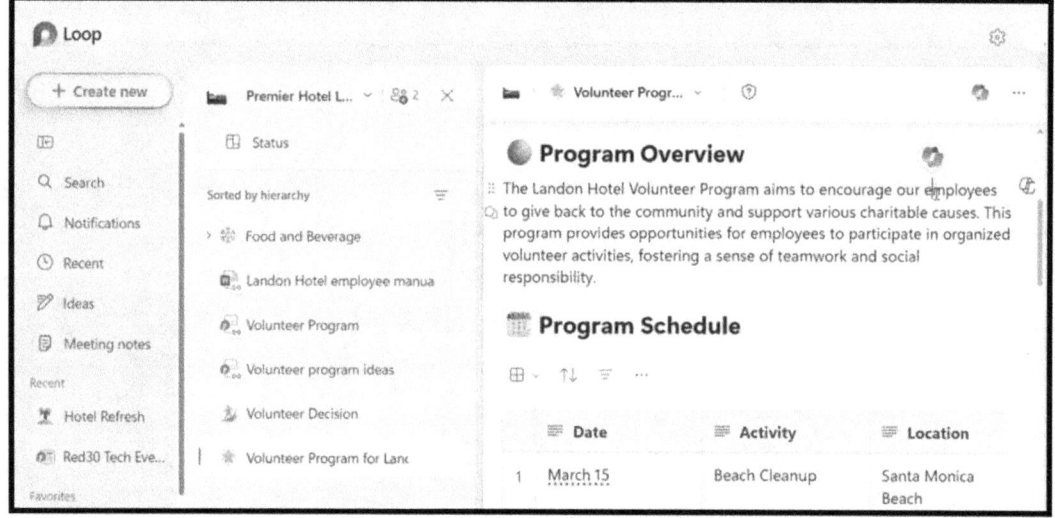

Figure 4-11-1. *Appearance of Copilot at the moment when paragraph is chosen*

CHAPTER 4   REAL-TIME COLLABORATION USING LOOP

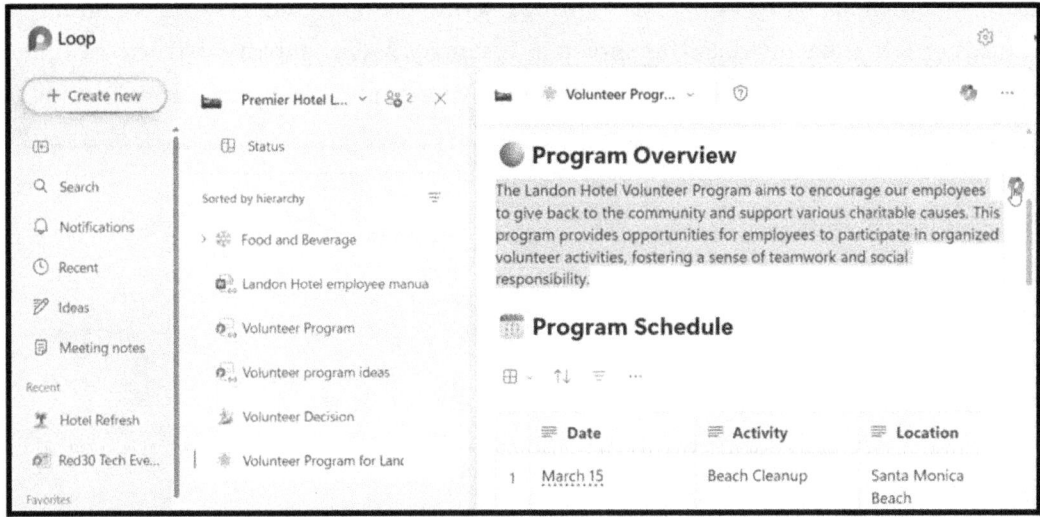

Figure 4-12. Selection of paragraph when Copilot icon is chosen

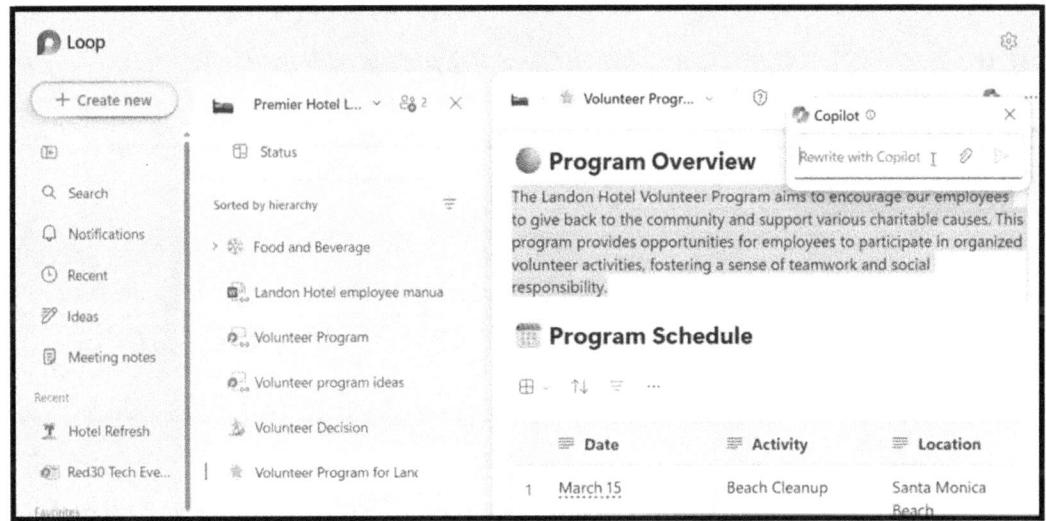

Figure 4-13. Prompt box with "Rewrite with Copilot"

At this stage, you can input specific instructions regarding the desired length, tone, or other parameters for rewriting the content, as shown in Figure 4-14. Additionally, it is possible to reference external files to inform the rewrite process, as shown in Figure 4-15. Upon submitting your instruction, Copilot notifies you while generating a

107

CHAPTER 4   REAL-TIME COLLABORATION USING LOOP

draft, as shown in Figure 4-16. The resulting rewritten content reflects your requested adjustments in tone and detail, as shown in Figure 4-17. This demonstrates how Copilot facilitates the process of refining and improving your content in a professional setting.

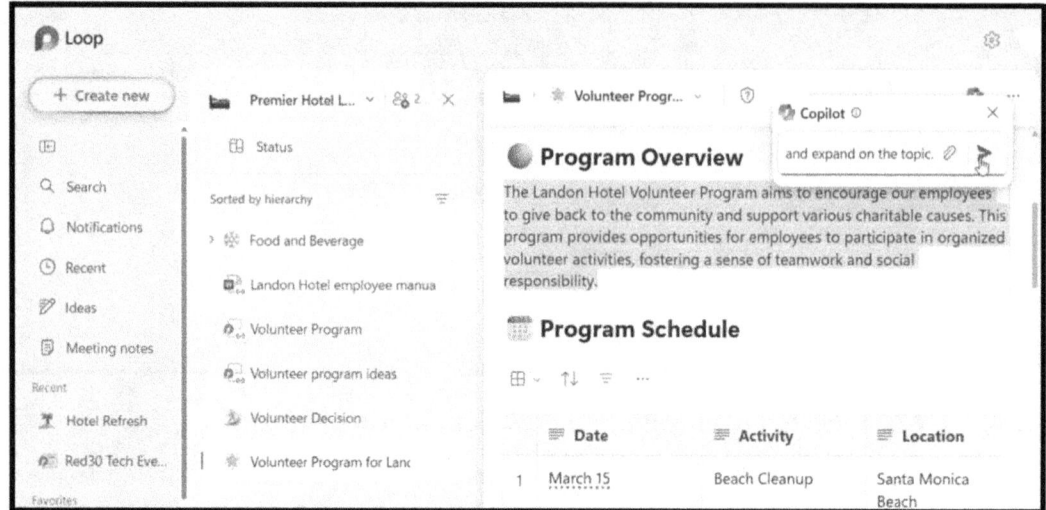

Figure 4-14.   Prompt to expand on the existing paragraph topic

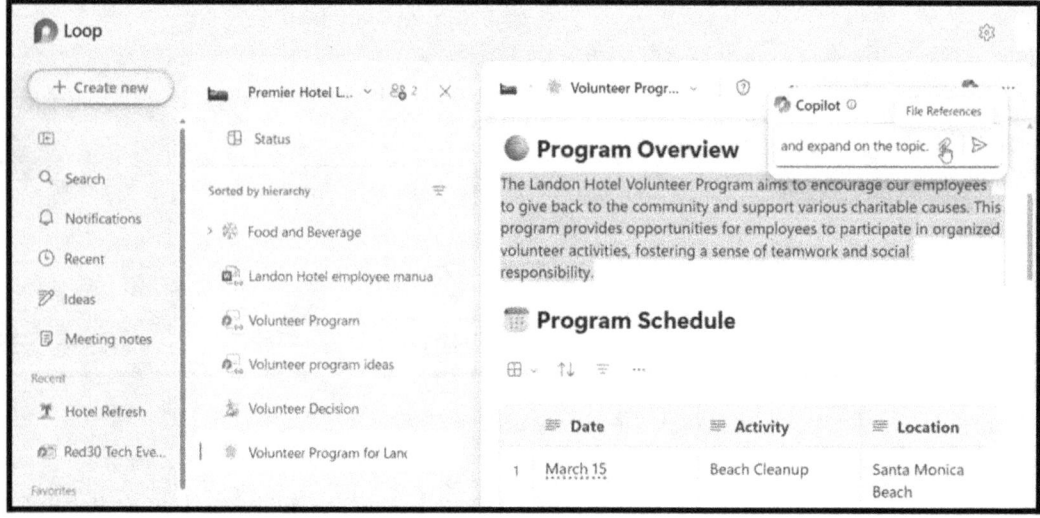

Figure 4-15.   File reference to rewrite paragraph

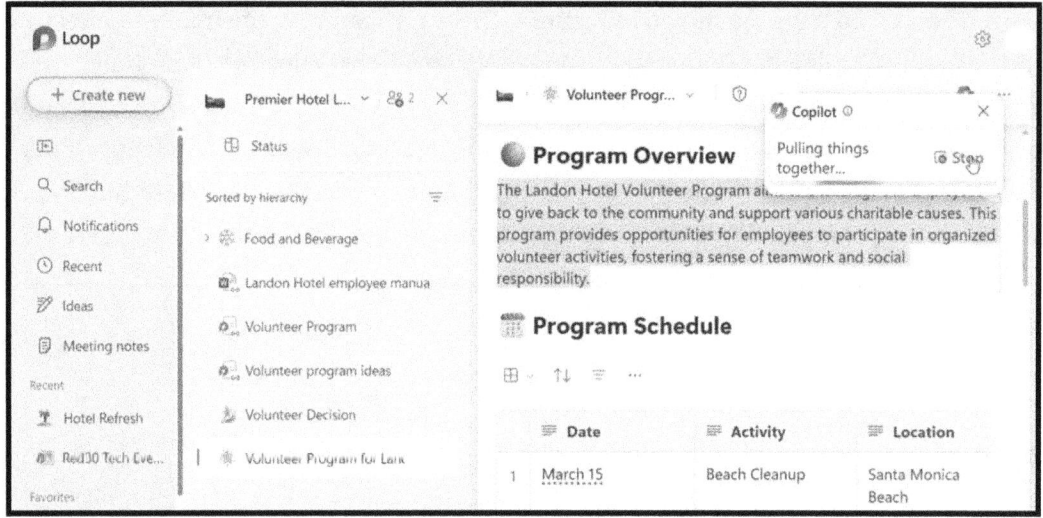

Figure 4-16. Copilot draft in progress

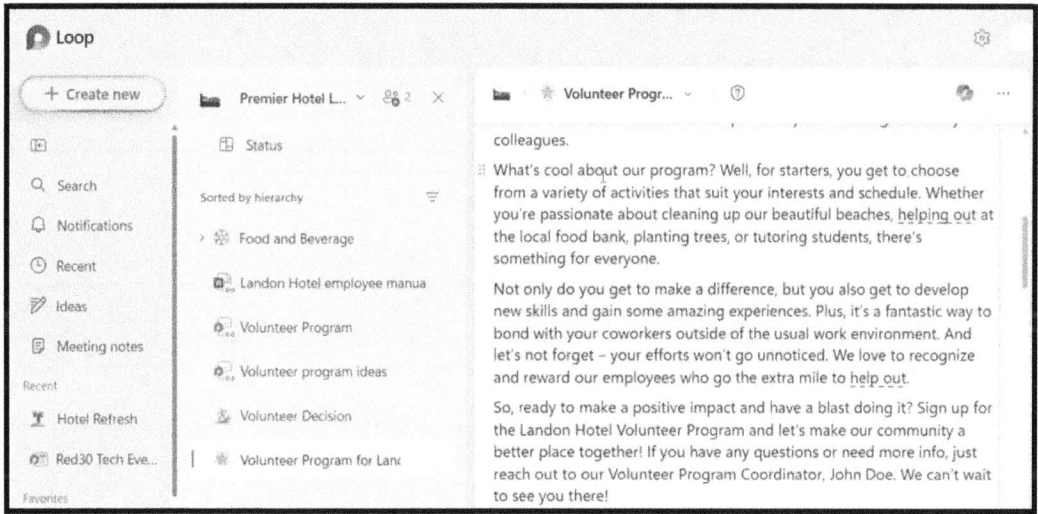

Figure 4-17. Resultant content from Copilot

Instructing Copilot to Summarize a Loop Workspace Page

Copilot offers robust support for a wide range of tasks within Loop workspace pages, including content creation, modification, and editing. An especially valuable feature is its ability to summarize large volumes of page content efficiently. To illustrate, consider

CHAPTER 4 REAL-TIME COLLABORATION USING LOOP

a recently created page. As shown in Figure 4-18, by navigating to the upper right corner and selecting Copilot, the Copilot pane appears, providing a selection of prebuilt prompts designed to facilitate prompt writing, as shown in Figure 4-19. Users may either select from these suggestions or compose their own prompts, as shown in Figure 4-20. For example, as shown in Figure 4-20, entering "Summarize this page in four bullet points" in the prompt area initiates the summarization process, as shown in Figure 4-21.

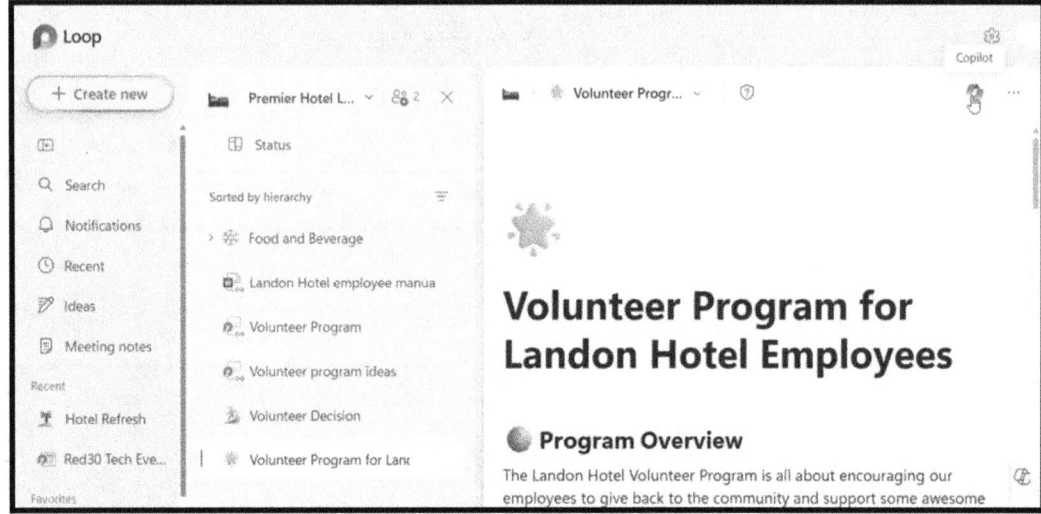

Figure 4-18. Access Copilot

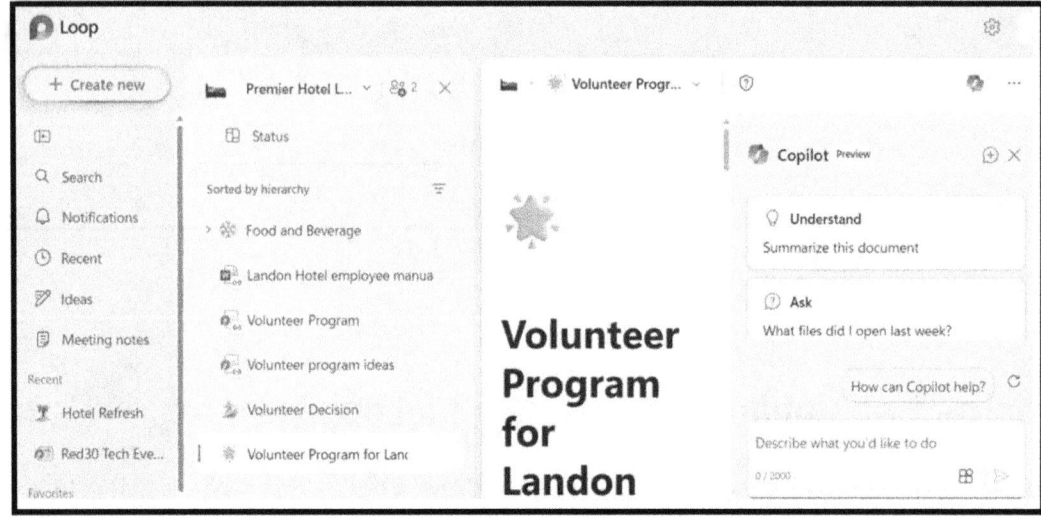

Figure 4-19. Prebuilt prompts designed to facilitate prompt writing

CHAPTER 4   REAL-TIME COLLABORATION USING LOOP

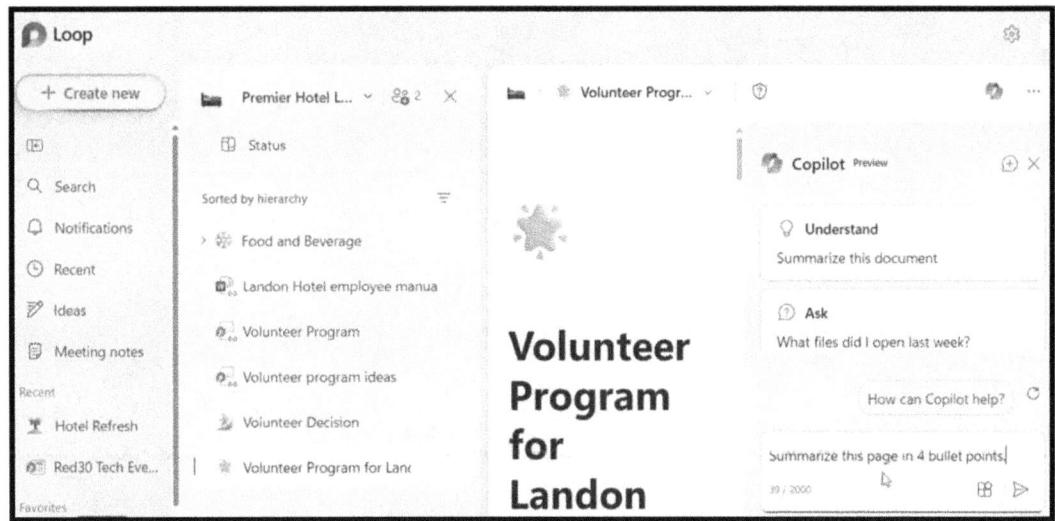

Figure 4-20. *Compose your own prompts*

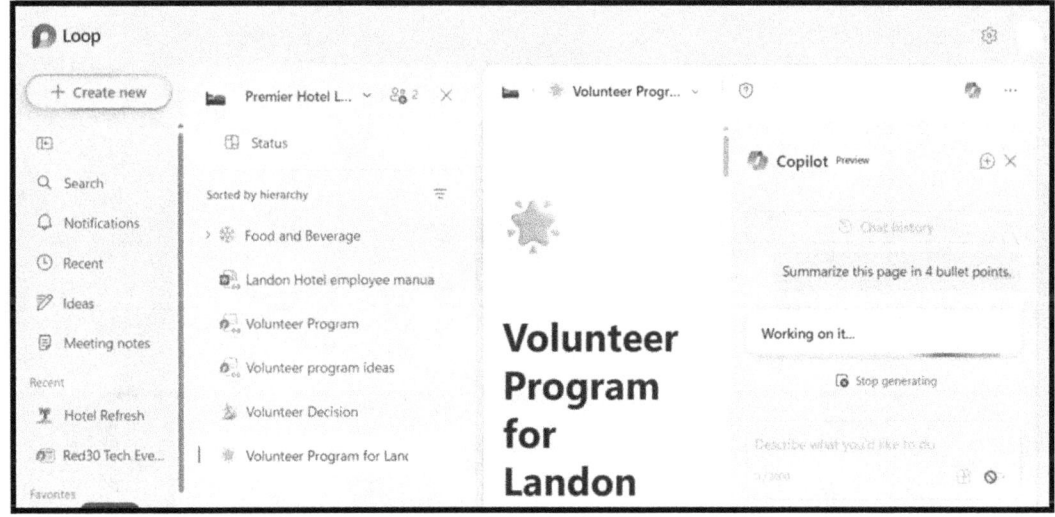

Figure 4-21. *Copilot result work-in-progress*

Once submitted, Copilot processes the information and displays a concise summary, as shown in Figure 4-22, which can then be easily copied, as shown in Figure 4-23, to the clipboard for use in other applications such as Microsoft Word, presentations, or email communications. This function effectively streamlines the inclusion of key ideas, decisions, or additional relevant content into various documents.

111

CHAPTER 4   REAL-TIME COLLABORATION USING LOOP

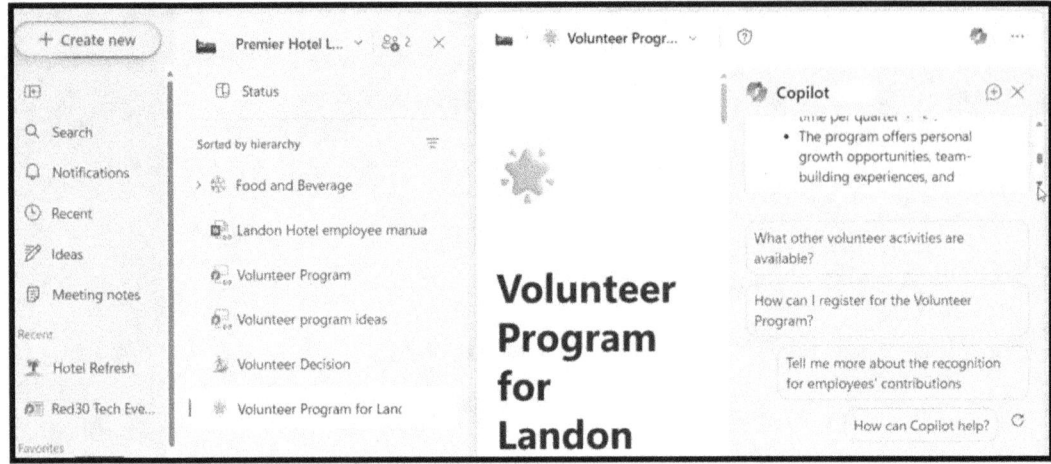

Figure 4-22. Summary Content generated by Copilot

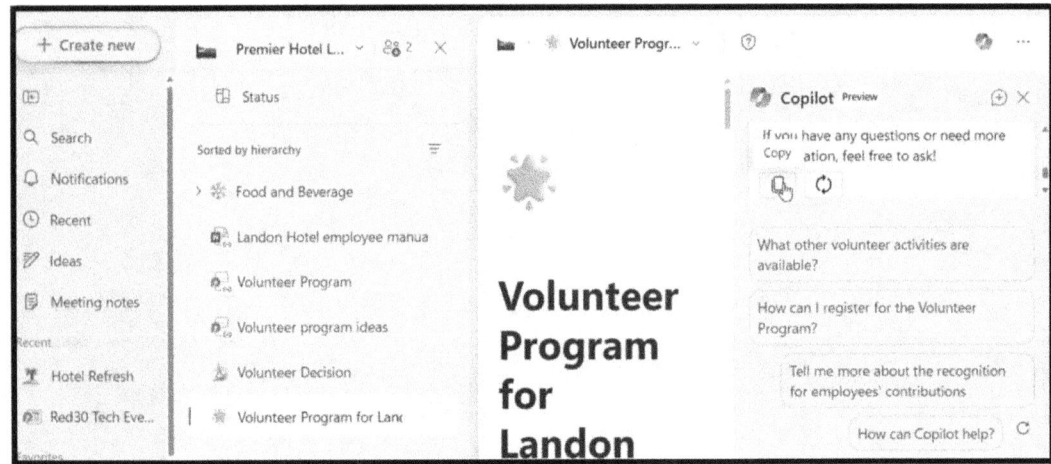

Figure 4-23. Summary content can be copied easily

As shown in Figure 4-24, beneath the generated response, Copilot suggests additional, contextually relevant prompts that may further assist users in extracting meaningful information from their workspace. Prompts such as "What other volunteer activities are available?" "How can I register for the volunteer program?" "Tell me more about the recognition for employees' contributions," and "How can Copilot help?" exemplify the breadth of possibilities Copilot provides.

CHAPTER 4 REAL-TIME COLLABORATION USING LOOP

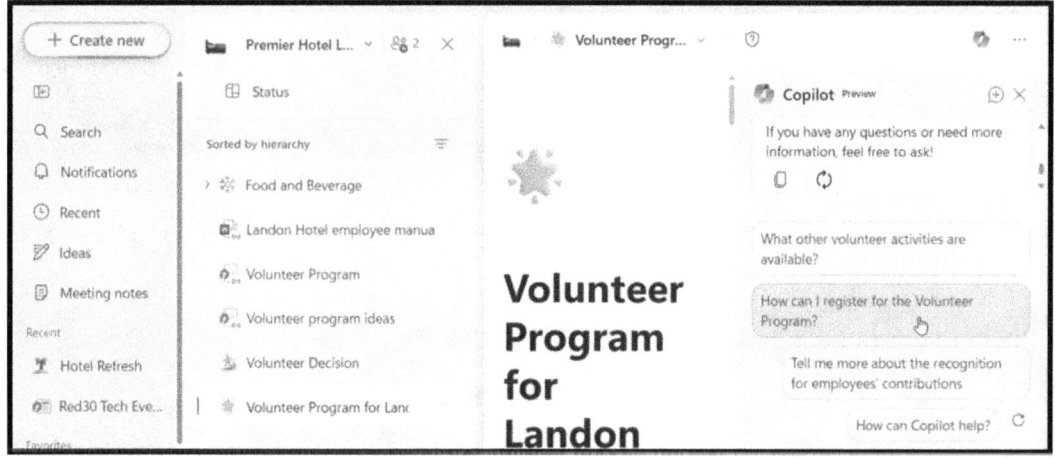

Figure 4-24. *Additional, contextually relevant prompts*

Selecting a suggestion, such as "What other volunteer activities are available?" as shown in Figure 4-25, prompts Copilot to aggregate information from accessible workspace files and communications within Microsoft 365, ensuring responses are grounded in available data, as shown in Figure 4-26. The chat interface allows users to initiate new conversations by selecting the plus sign, as shown in Figure 4-27, or to revisit previous interactions through the Chat history feature, as shown in Figure 4-28 and 4-28-1. These functionalities make it straightforward to summarize content and request further information from Copilot as needed.

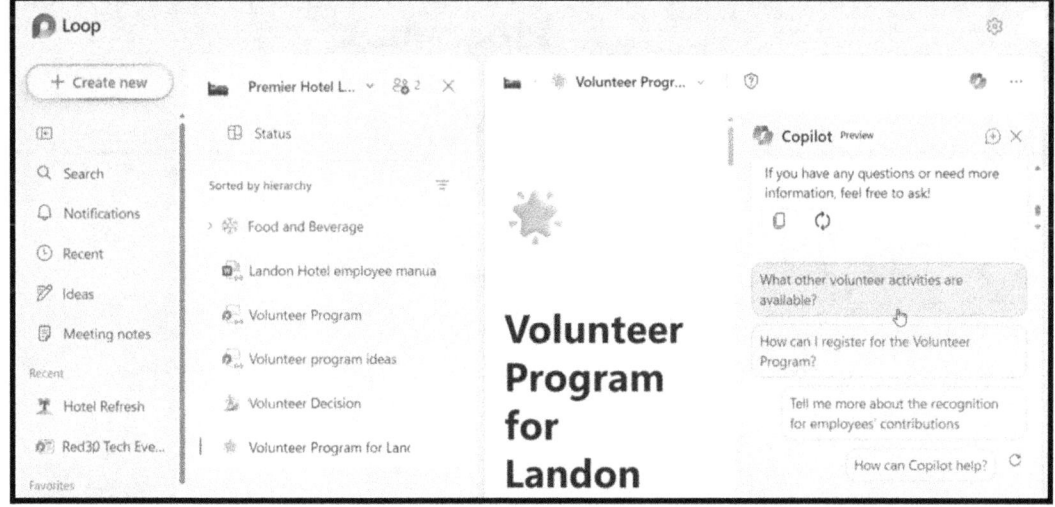

Figure 4-25. *Choosing a default prompt to find another set of information*

113

CHAPTER 4　REAL-TIME COLLABORATION USING LOOP

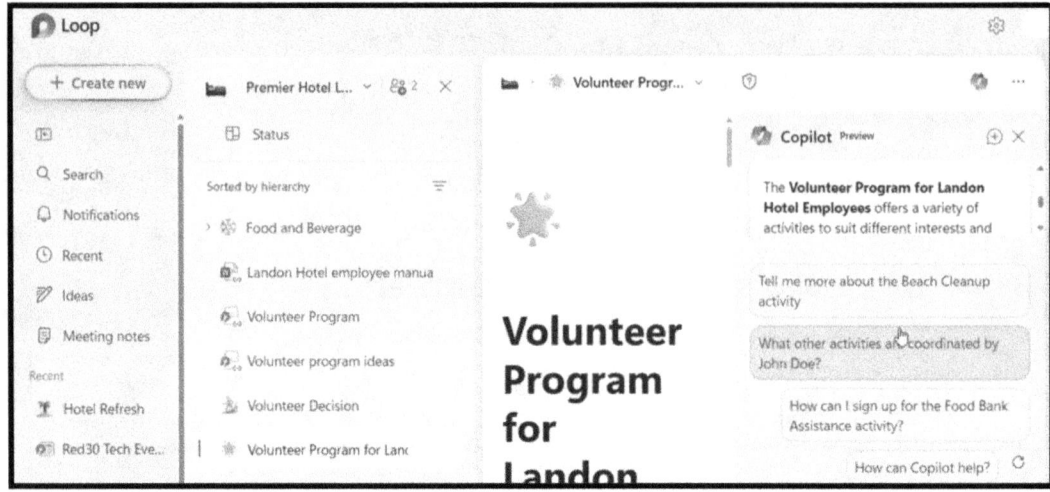

Figure 4-26. *Result from Copilot*

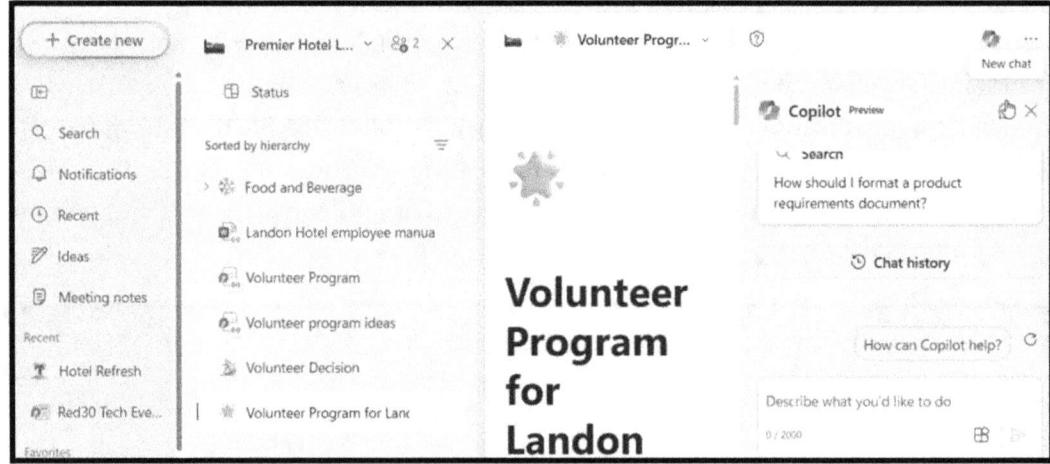

Figure 4-27. *Chat feature of Copilot*

CHAPTER 4   REAL-TIME COLLABORATION USING LOOP

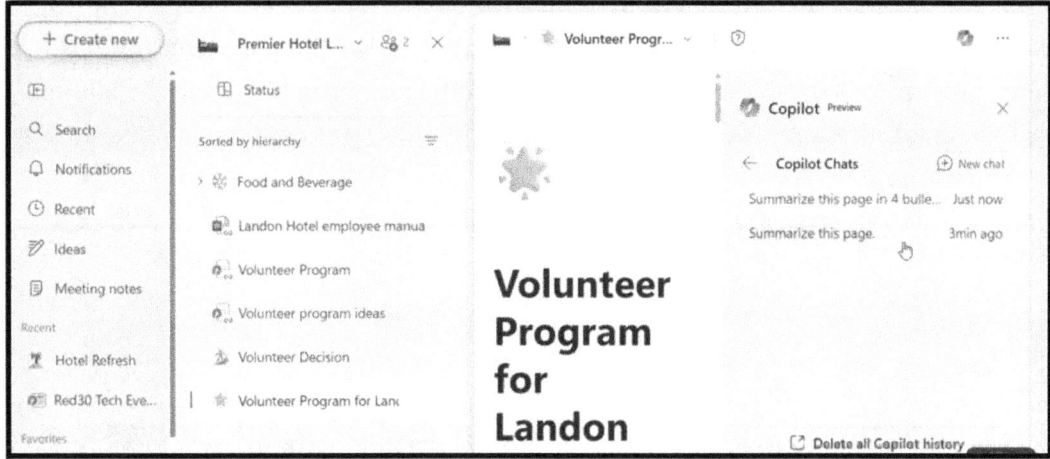

Figure 4-28. Copilot history

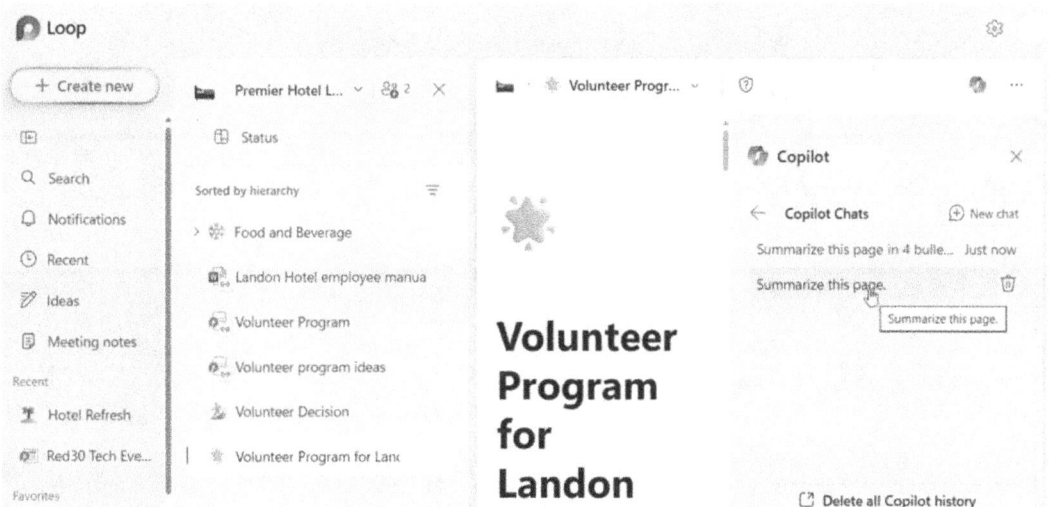

Figure 4-28-1. Access Copilot historical prompts

Asking Copilot to Brainstorm an Idea in a Loop Workspace Page

When you have an idea, Copilot can assist with brainstorming it further. For example, as shown in Figure 4-29, by selecting the volunteer program idea and then choosing Copilot on the right, users, as shown in Figure 4-30, can enter a prompt such as "Rewrite

115

CHAPTER 4 REAL-TIME COLLABORATION USING LOOP

with Copilot" and add instructions to brainstorm the idea with real-world examples before submitting, as shown in Figure 4-31. Notifications will indicate that a draft is being prepared, as shown in Figure 4-32. The resulting output expands on the idea and includes relevant examples, as shown in Figure 4-33. This process demonstrates how Copilot can support idea development.

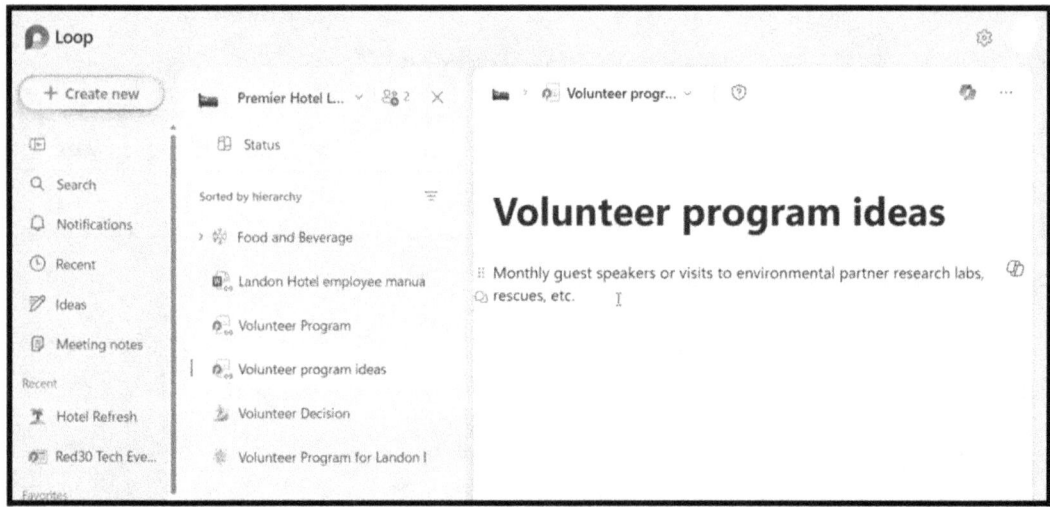

Figure 4-29. Raw idea

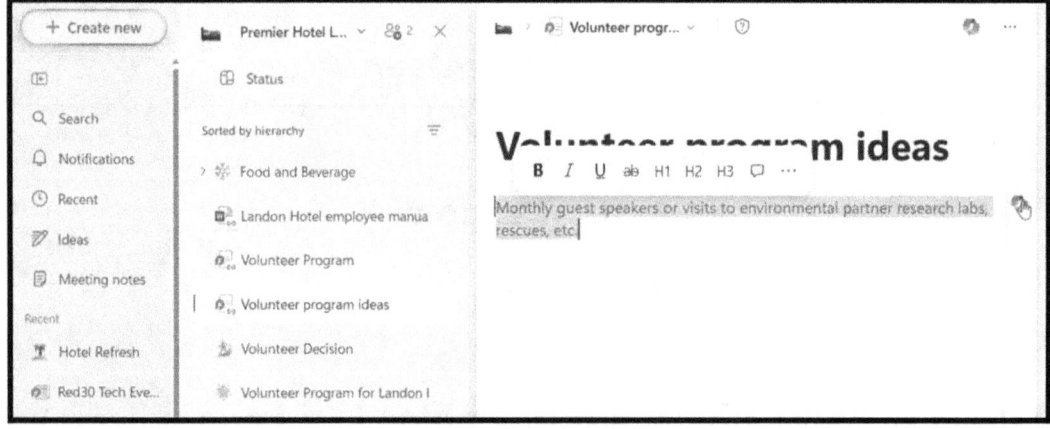

Figure 4-30. Choose Copilot to rewrite the idea

116

CHAPTER 4   REAL-TIME COLLABORATION USING LOOP

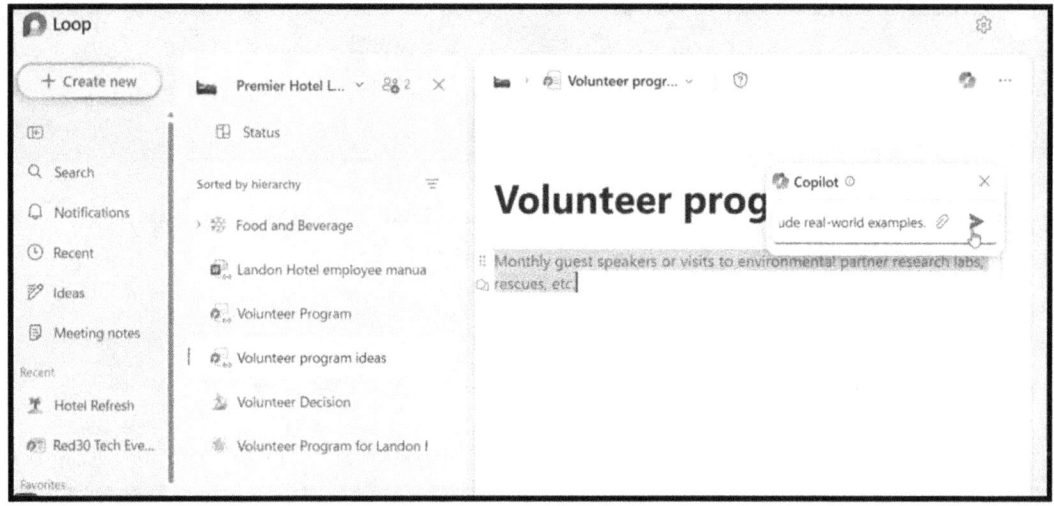

Figure 4-31. *Add instructions in the form of prompt*

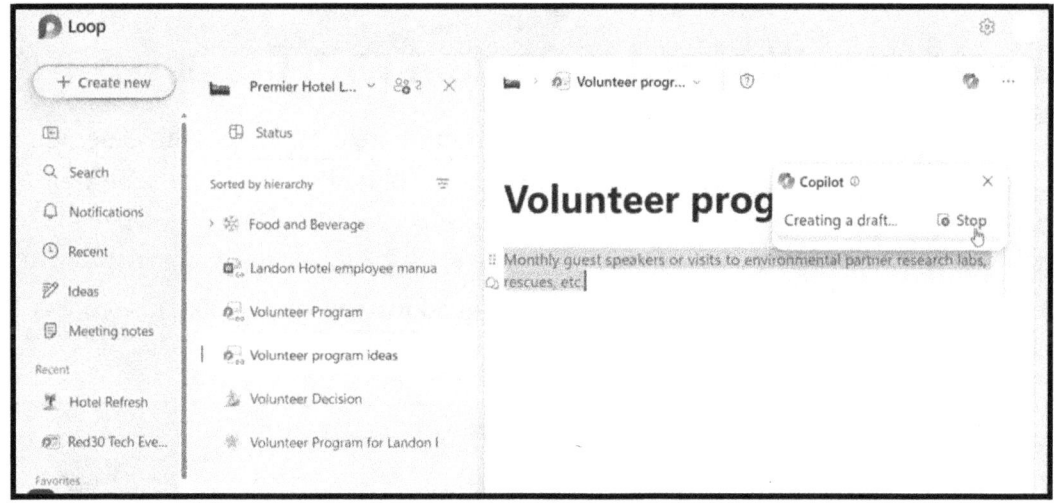

Figure 4-32. *Draft of new idea in progress*

117

CHAPTER 4   REAL-TIME COLLABORATION USING LOOP

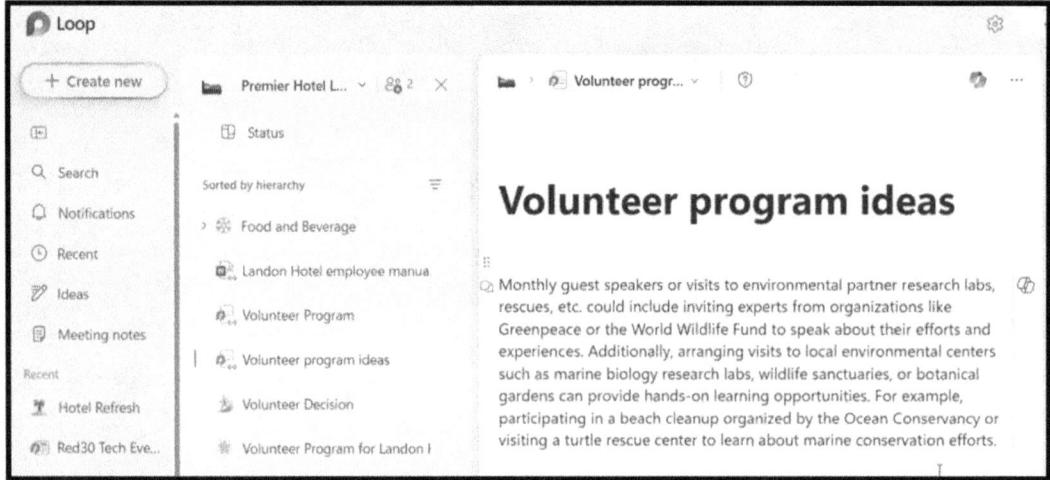

Figure 4-33. New idea created by Copilot

Create Loop Workspace Content with Copilot

If Copilot is included with your Microsoft 365 subscription, it can assist with generating content in a Loop workspace page. To use this feature, place the cursor at the desired location within the page, as shown in Figure 4-34, and select Copilot, as shown in Figure 4-35. Enter a prompt describing the desired content and select Send. The generated content will then appear on the page, as shown in Figure 4-36. This process allows users to create content within a Loop workspace page.

Figure 4-34. Place the cursor at the desired location within the page for Copilot prompt

CHAPTER 4 REAL-TIME COLLABORATION USING LOOP

Figure 4-35. *Draft idea using Copilot*

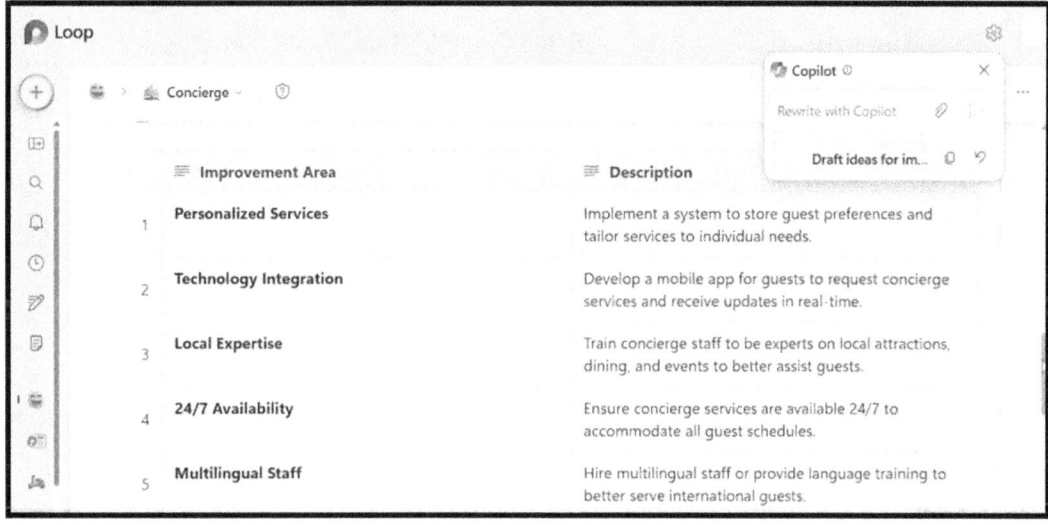

Figure 4-36. *Generated ideas by Copilot*

119

CHAPTER 4 REAL-TIME COLLABORATION USING LOOP

Understanding the Communication Process by Comparing Microsoft Loop with Microsoft Teams, Microsoft Outlook, and OneNote

Microsoft Loop vs. Microsoft Teams, Microsoft Outlook, and OneNote: A Deep-Dive Comparison

Overview

- Microsoft Teams is a unified communication and collaboration platform that integrates chat, video meetings, file sharing, and app integration. It's designed to centralize teamwork and streamline communication across organizations.

- Microsoft Loop, on the other hand, is a newer productivity tool focused on fluid collaboration through portable components that can be embedded across Microsoft 365 apps. It's built for dynamic, real-time co-creation and modular content sharing.

- Microsoft Outlook is a long-established email and calendar platform that serves as a central hub for communication, scheduling, and task management. It's widely used in enterprise environments for managing correspondence, appointments, and personal productivity.

- Microsoft OneNote is a digital notebook application designed for capturing, organizing, and sharing notes. It's widely used for personal productivity, academic work, and team documentation. OneNote allows users to create notebooks with sections and pages, supporting multimedia content and handwritten input.

Core Purpose and Philosophy

- Teams is built around structured communication—channels, teams, meetings, and threaded conversations. It's ideal for managing ongoing communication, organizing projects, and hosting virtual meetings.

- Loop is designed for flexible, component-based collaboration. It breaks down content into reusable blocks (Loop components) that can be edited in real time across apps like Teams, Outlook, Word, and OneNote. Loop emphasizes agility, decentralization, and real-time updates.

- Outlook is built around structured communication and scheduling. It's ideal for managing emails, organizing meetings, and tracking tasks. Its design supports asynchronous communication and personal productivity.

- OneNote is built around note-taking and information organization. It's ideal for capturing ideas, meeting notes, research, and personal reflections. Its structure mimics physical notebooks, making it intuitive for users familiar with traditional note-taking.

Collaboration Style

- Teams supports synchronous and asynchronous communication through chat, calls, and meetings. It's great for structured collaboration, especially when teams need to coordinate tasks, share files, and hold discussions.

- Loop supports fluid collaboration, where users can co-create content without being confined to a specific app or interface. A Loop component (e.g., a checklist or table) can live in a Teams chat, an Outlook email, or a Word document—and updates in one place reflect everywhere.

- Outlook supports asynchronous communication through email and calendar invites. It's excellent for formal communication, documentation, and time-based coordination.

- OneNote supports collaboration by allowing multiple users to edit shared notebooks. However, changes are not always reflected instantly, and simultaneous editing can sometimes lead to sync issues.

User Interface and Experience

- Teams has a dashboard-style interface with tabs for Chat, Teams, Calendar, Calls, and Files. It's designed for multitasking and managing multiple conversations and projects.

- Loop offers a minimalist, canvas-like interface. Users can create Loop pages and workspaces to organize components. The experience is more focused on content creation and less on communication threads.

- Outlook has a traditional interface with folders, inboxes, calendars, and task panes. It's optimized for managing large volumes of communication and scheduling.

- OneNote has a notebook-style interface with tabs for sections and pages. It supports rich formatting, drawing tools, and multimedia embedding. The experience is focused on personal organization and structured note-taking.

Integration with Microsoft 365

- Teams is deeply integrated with Microsoft 365. It connects with SharePoint, OneDrive, Planner, Power BI, and more. Users can access files, schedule meetings, and collaborate on documents directly within Teams.

- Loop is also integrated across Microsoft 365, but in a different way. Its components are portable and live, meaning they can be embedded in Outlook, Word, Teams, and OneNote, and remain editable and synchronized across all platforms.

- Outlook integrates deeply with Microsoft 365, including Teams, OneDrive, SharePoint, and To Do. Users can schedule meetings, share files, and manage tasks from within Outlook.

- OneNote integrates with Microsoft 365 apps like Outlook, Teams, and Word. Users can link notes to calendar events, share notebooks in Teams, and embed content from other apps.

Communication Features

- Teams excels in communication. It offers:
  - Persistent chat
  - Video and audio calls
  - Meeting scheduling and recording
  - Channel-based discussions
  - @mentions and notifications
- Loop does not offer direct communication features like chat or calls. Instead, it enhances communication by embedding collaborative content into communication tools. For example, a Loop component in a Teams chat allows users to collaborate on a table or checklist directly within the conversation.
- Outlook supports collaboration through shared calendars, meeting invites, and email threads. It also integrates with Microsoft To Do for task management and with Teams for meeting links and chat.

Content Collaboration

- Teams allows collaboration on files via SharePoint and OneDrive. Users can coauthor documents, share links, and comment on files.
- Loop takes content collaboration further by enabling real-time editing of modular components. These components are not tied to a single document—they can be reused and updated across multiple contexts.

- Outlook manages content through emails, attachments, and calendar entries. It's effective for storing and referencing communication history.

OneNote supports a wide range of content types as given below:

- Typed text
- Handwritten notes
- Images and audio
- Web clippings
- Tags and to-do lists
- Loop focuses on modular content:
- Tables
- Lists
- Checklists
- Paragraphs
- Voting components

Loop components are designed to be interactive and collaborative, while OneNote content is more static and personal.

Use Cases

Teams is ideal for

- Daily team communication
- Project coordination
- Virtual meetings
- Departmental collaboration
- Company-wide announcements

Loop is ideal for

- Brainstorming sessions
- Agile project planning
- Real-time feedback collection
- Meeting notes and action tracking
- Cross-functional collaboration

Outlook is ideal for

- Formal communication
- Scheduling meetings
- Managing tasks and reminders
- Tracking correspondence
- Organizing personal productivity

OneNote is ideal for

- Personal notetaking
- Meeting documentation
- Research organization
- Academic study
- Journaling and planning

Strengths

Teams:

- Robust communication tools
- Centralized workspace
- Strong integration with Microsoft 365
- Scalable for large organizations

CHAPTER 4   REAL-TIME COLLABORATION USING LOOP

Loop:

- Real-time, fluid collaboration
- Portable components
- Context-rich content sharing
- Enhances productivity across apps

Outlook:

- Mature and widely adopted
- Robust email and calendar features
- Strong integration with enterprise tools
- Effective for structured communication

OneNote:

- Rich formatting and multimedia support
- Intuitive notebook structure
- Great for personal productivity
- Offline access and syncing

Limitations

Teams:

- Can become cluttered with too many channels and chats
- Less flexible for modular content creation
- Real-time collaboration is limited to documents and files

Loop:

- Still evolving; not all features are fully mature
- Lacks built-in communication tools
- May require a mindset shift for traditional teams

Outlook:

- Less suited for real-time collaboration
- Can become cluttered with high email volume
- Static content (emails don't update once sent)

OneNote:

- Limited real-time editing capabilities
- Can become cluttered with large notebooks
- Not optimized for agile collaboration

Security and Compliance

Both Teams, Loop, and Outlook benefit from Microsoft's enterprise-grade security, including

- Data encryption
- Compliance with GDPR, HIPAA, and other standards
- Role-based access control
- Integration with Microsoft Purview for data governance

However, Teams has more mature administrative controls due to its longer presence in the enterprise ecosystem. Outlook has more mature administrative controls due to its long-standing role in enterprise environments. OneNote has more mature offline capabilities, while Loop relies more on cloud-based collaboration.

Workflow Integration

- Teams supports workflows via Power Automate, Planner, and third-party apps. It's a hub for task management, approvals, and notifications.
- Loop is beginning to support workflow integration, especially with Microsoft Copilot and AI-driven suggestions. It's more focused on content workflows than task automation (for now).

- Outlook supports workflows via Power Automate, To Do, and calendar-based triggers. It's a hub for task reminders, meeting scheduling, and email-based automation.

- OneNote supports workflows via Outlook and Teams. Users can link notes to meetings, share pages in chats, and use tags for task tracking.

AI and Copilot Integration

- Teams uses Copilot to summarize meetings, generate action items, and assist with communication.

- Loop uses Copilot to suggest content, summarize pages, and help with brainstorming. The AI integration in Loop is more focused on content generation and refinement, while in Teams it's focused on communication and productivity.

- Outlook uses Copilot to summarize emails, draft responses, and manage scheduling.

- OneNote uses Copilot to summarize notes, extract action items, and assist with organization.

Accessibility and Mobility

- Teams is available on desktop, mobile, and web. It's optimized for communication on the go.

- Loop is also available across devices, but its mobile experience is still being refined. It's best used on desktop for full functionality.

- Outlook is available on desktop, mobile, and web. It's optimized for communication and scheduling on the go.

- OneNote is available on desktop, mobile, and web. It supports offline access and is optimized for mobile notetaking.

Future Outlook

- Teams will continue to evolve as the central hub for enterprise communication, with deeper AI integration and an expanded app ecosystem.

- Loop is positioned to become the next-generation collaboration tool, especially for hybrid and agile teams. Its modular approach aligns with the future of work—flexible, decentralized, and AI-enhanced.

- Outlook will continue to evolve as the central hub for enterprise communication and scheduling, with deeper AI integration and smarter inbox management.

- OneNote will continue to serve as a robust personal and team note-taking tool, with deeper AI integration and improved syncing.

Conclusion

Microsoft Teams and Microsoft Loop serve complementary but distinct roles in the modern workplace. Teams is the backbone of communication, offering structured channels for chat, meetings, and collaboration. Loop is the future-forward tool for fluid, real-time content creation and sharing. While Teams centralizes communication, Loop decentralizes collaboration—allowing content to live and evolve across multiple contexts. Together, they form a powerful ecosystem that supports both structured and dynamic workflows. Choosing between them—or using them together—depends on your team's needs, work style, and goals.

Microsoft Outlook and Microsoft Loop serve distinct but complementary roles in the Microsoft 365 ecosystem. Outlook is the backbone of structured communication and scheduling, offering robust tools for managing emails, calendars, and tasks. Loop is the future-forward tool for fluid, real-time collaboration, enabling users to co-create content across apps. While Outlook centralizes communication, Loop decentralizes collaboration—allowing content to live and evolve wherever it's needed. Together, they empower teams to communicate effectively and collaborate dynamically, bridging the gap between traditional productivity and modern agility

CHAPTER 4   REAL-TIME COLLABORATION USING LOOP

Microsoft OneNote and Microsoft Loop serve distinct but complementary roles in the Microsoft 365 ecosystem. OneNote is the go-to tool for structured notetaking, personal organization, and documentation. Loop is the modern solution for real-time, modular collaboration across teams and platforms. While OneNote excels in capturing and organizing information, Loop shines in co-creating and evolving content dynamically. Together, they empower users to manage both personal productivity and team collaboration, bridging the gap between traditional note-taking and modern agile workflows.

Following our coverage of topics, including real-time collaboration via Loop, content rewriting with Copilot, summarizing Loop workspace pages, ideation support within Loop workspaces, creating content using Copilot, and examining the communication process by comparing Microsoft Loop to Teams, Outlook, and OneNote, this chapter will end. In the subsequent chapter, we will provide a comprehensive analysis of Microsoft Loop's integration with applications such as Outlook and OneNote, emphasizing how these integrations facilitate improved workforce collaboration, connectivity, and business operations. In particular, we will present examples of seamless email integration using Loop's Table Component in Outlook and demonstrate the efficient incorporation of a OneNote page with Loop's Retrospective Component.

CHAPTER 5

Integrating Loop with Microsoft 365 Apps

In the previous chapter, we explored real-time collaborative features of Microsoft Loop that helps any team achieving its project goals and objectives despite the team being spread across different time zones and multiple continents. In this chapter, we will take a deep dive into integration of Microsoft Loop with Microsoft Apps such as Outlook, OneNote, and experience with such integration how efficiently the workforce can collaborate, connect, and share business-related activities using Microsoft Loop.

Introduction

Microsoft Loop is an advanced collaboration platform engineered to redefine how teams conceptualize, co-develop, and manage tasks within the Microsoft 365 environment. At its core, Loop introduces a modular, real-time collaborative framework that transcends traditional document limitations, facilitating dynamic teamwork across applications such as Teams, Outlook, Word, OneNote, and Whiteboard. The system is structured around three primary components—**Loop components**, **Loop pages**, and **Loop workspaces**—each contributing distinct value to productivity and seamless collaboration.

Loop components comprise discrete units of productivity, including task lists, voting tables, progress trackers, and checklists, which can be embedded directly into Microsoft 365 applications. These live components synchronize instantaneously across all instances; for example, updates made in a Teams chat are immediately reflected in Outlook or Word wherever the same component appears. This real-time functionality is enabled by Microsoft's Fluid Framework, ensuring low-latency collaboration and data consistency. Components are initiated via the slash (/) command and are stored as ".fluid" files in OneDrive, enhancing discoverability and recoverability.

Loop pages function as flexible canvases, allowing users to organize components, links, files, and notes into adaptable documents suitable for brainstorming, project planning, and meeting documentation. Pages can be generated from Office.com or the Copilot app within Teams and accessed through the "Pages" tab on Microsoft365.com. They support collaborative editing, inline commenting, and integration with Copilot for content drafting and summarization. It is currently recommended, per enterprise guidelines, to avoid using Loop pages on mobile devices or sharing them externally due to existing limitations in eDiscovery and sensitivity labeling.

Loop workspaces act as collective hubs, aggregating related pages and components to enable team-based progress tracking, task assignment, and project management. Presently, only workspace creators possess editing rights, and ownership transfer is not yet supported—a limitation under active review. Workspaces are stored within SharePoint-Embedded containers and governed by retention and disposal protocols via Microsoft Syntex Repository Services.

From a deployment standpoint, Microsoft Loop is included in Microsoft 365 E3 and E5 enterprise subscriptions at no additional cost. The platform's development roadmap features integrations with external data sources such as Jira, Trello, and GitHub, enabling direct import, viewing, and editing of third-party items within Loop components. These integrations are controlled through Cloud Policy settings, providing tenant administrators with detailed management over external data synchronization. Such capabilities significantly enhance Loop's utility for software development, project oversight, and interdisciplinary collaboration.

User experience in Loop prioritizes simplicity and accessibility. Both components and pages are easily located via Office.com and OneDrive, with clear naming conventions recommended for efficient retrieval. Notably, users are advised not to move Loop files from OneDrive to SharePoint, as this action disrupts live component functionality in Teams. While sensitivity labels are available, enforcement remains pending, and external sharing is discouraged to preserve compliance and data integrity.

Compared to established platforms like Atlassian Confluence, Loop distinguishes itself with superior real-time collaboration, robust Microsoft 365 integration, and a contemporary, adaptable interface. Its bundled pricing within Microsoft 365 enhances accessibility for organizations already utilizing the ecosystem.

For information and data management professionals, Microsoft Loop provides an effective tool for optimizing workflows, knowledge sharing, and cross-functional alignment. The platform's modular architecture minimizes redundant effort, and its real-time features help maintain team cohesion and adaptability. As organizations increasingly adopt hybrid work environments, Loop's ability to centralize content and collaboration across diverse devices and platforms becomes ever more valuable.

In summary, Microsoft Loop represents a significant progression in collaborative technology. With deep integration into Microsoft 365, real-time coauthoring, and support for both structured and flexible content creation, Loop equips teams to operate with greater efficiency and transparency. While certain areas—such as mobile support, external sharing, and ownership flexibility—require further enhancement, the platform's ongoing development and strong enterprise foundation indicate a promising trajectory. As adoption expands and capabilities mature, Loop is positioned to become integral to modern digital collaboration.

Integration of Microsoft Loop with Microsoft 365 Apps

In this section, we will take a deep dive into how Microsoft Loop components are tightly and seamlessly integrated with Outlook and OneNote. In the case of Outlook, we will demonstrate how an email is seamlessly integrated with Loop component such as Table Component and in the case of OneNote, we will demonstrate how a OneNote page is seamlessly integrated with Retrospective component of Loop

Sharing a Collaborative Table Loop Component in an Outlook Message

Loop components offer portable content that can be integrated across various Microsoft 365 platforms, including email. Emails frequently contain substantial information on specific topics, and arranging this data in a tabular format enhances clarity and organization, enabling recipients to access key details efficiently. When updates to a table are required in multiple locations where it has been shared, loop table components provide an effective solution for collaborative editing and consistent content management.

First this section describes how to set up a loop table in a drafted email message. Other components such as insert Bullet List, Task List, Voting Table, Number List, Q&A Session, Progressive Tracker, Code, Kanban, and Team retrospective will follow similar lines. Loop components are available in both the Outlook web app and the Outlook desktop app and can be found in similar locations within the ribbons of each application. To insert a loop component, place the cursor at the desired location in the message, then navigate to the message ribbon, as shown in Figure 5-1. The loop components may appear either directly on the main ribbon or within a dropdown menu accessible via the ellipses. Additionally, the loop icon can be found on the insert ribbon; selecting this area will display a list of available loop components, as shown in Figure 5-2.

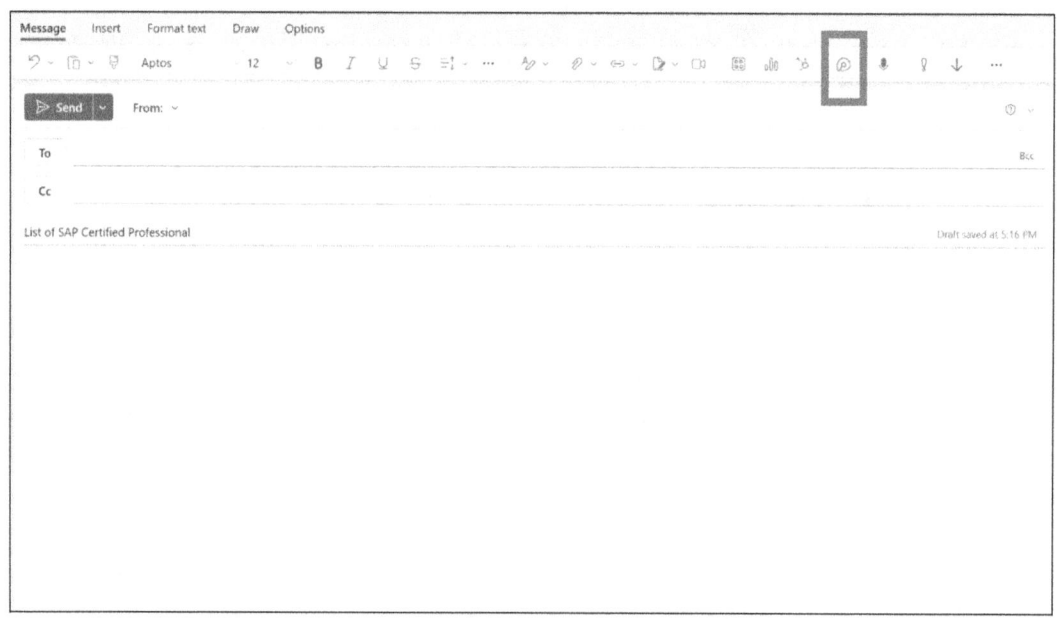

Figure 5-1. *Access Microsoft in the Outlook Email*

CHAPTER 5　INTEGRATING LOOP WITH MICROSOFT 365 APPS

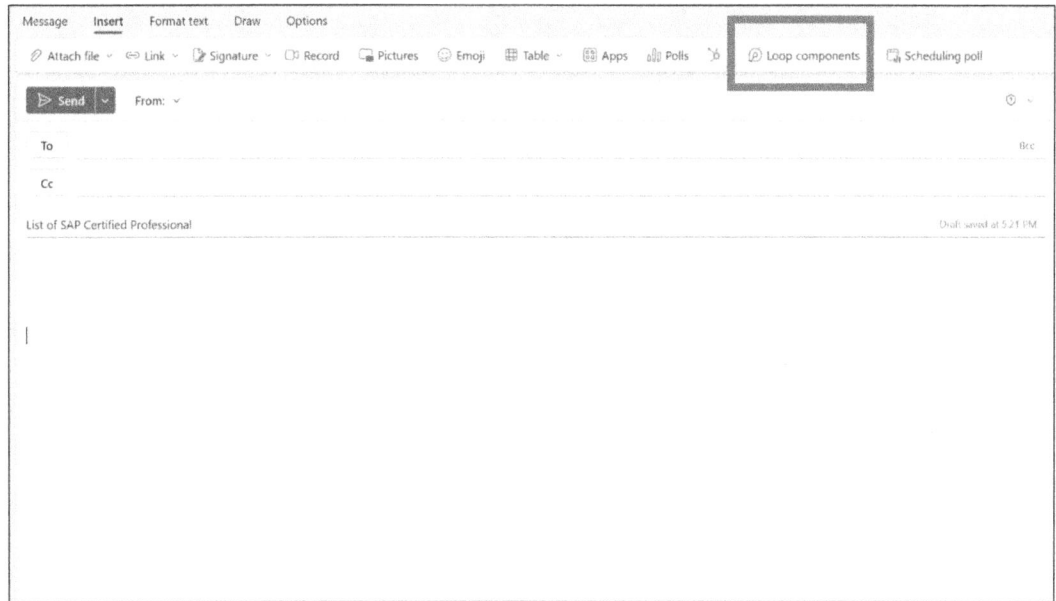

Figure 5-2. *Access Loop via Insert Menu*

Let's insert a Table Component first. All the components are supported within your Outlook email messages. To construct a table, select Menu and Click on Loop Components option, as shown in Figure 5-2. From the available list, Select Table component, as shown in Figure 5-3. The setup process will indicate "getting this ready," which then updates to reflect the subject of your email, as shown in Figure 5-4. If your subject line is pre-populated, as shown in this example, that information will also be assigned to the component, as shown in Figure 5-5. Next, proceed to build out the table; Click on Table component, as shown in Figure 5-6, and you will notice that several columns such as Column 1 and Column 2 are already provided as a starting point, as shown in Figure 5-7.

135

CHAPTER 5 INTEGRATING LOOP WITH MICROSOFT 365 APPS

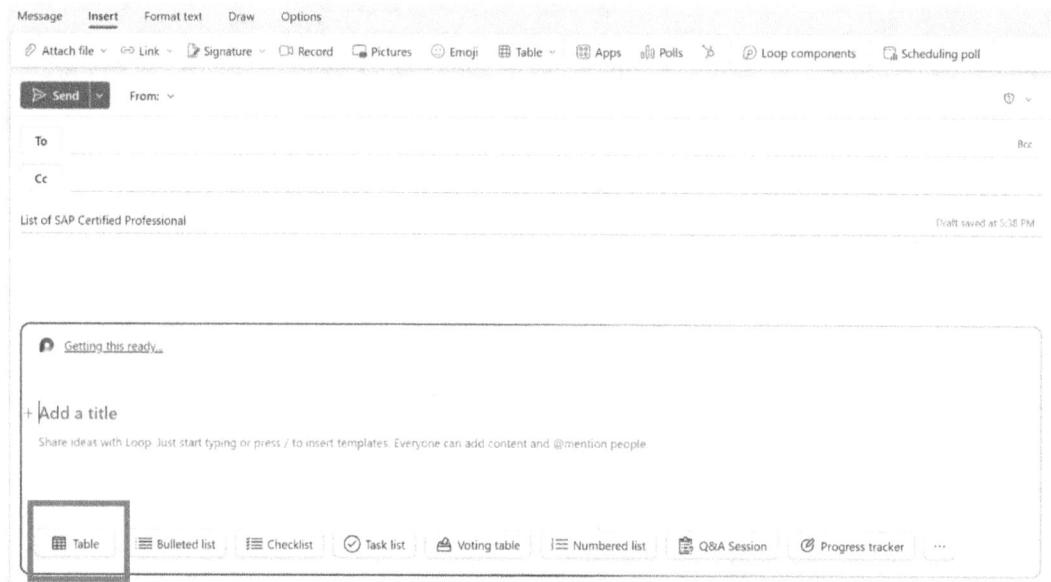

Figure 5-3. *Select Table Component after inserting Loop Components*

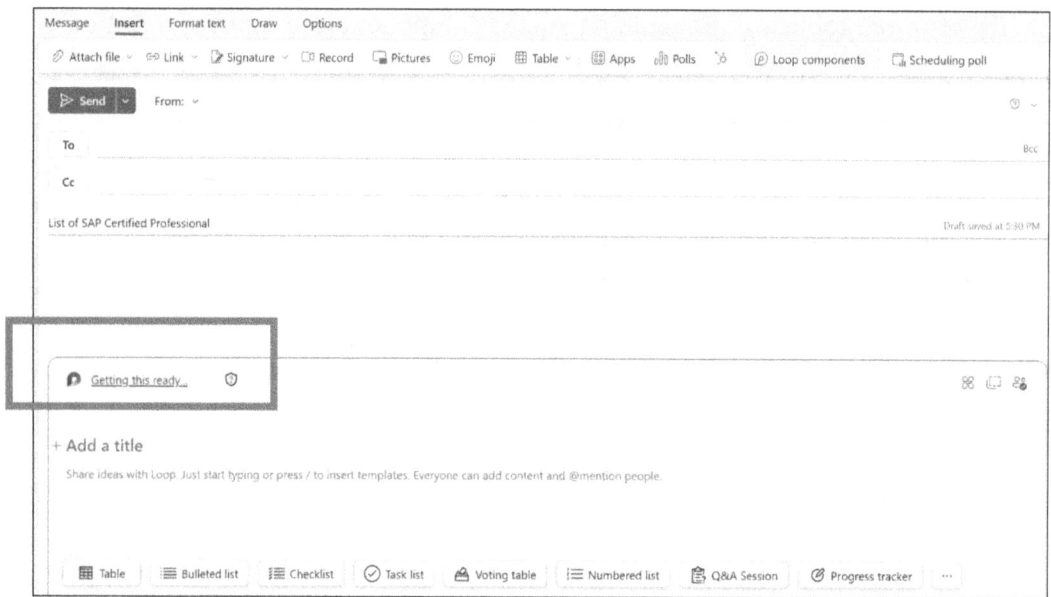

Figure 5-4. *Setup in process with "Getting this ready" message*

CHAPTER 5 INTEGRATING LOOP WITH MICROSOFT 365 APPS

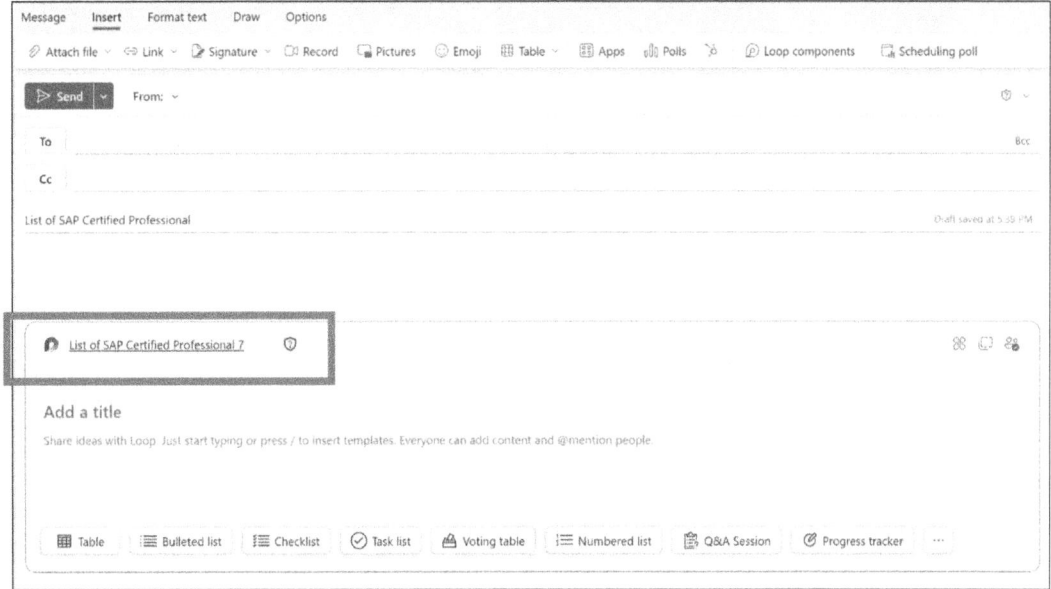

Figure 5-5. *Email subject line is prepopulated*

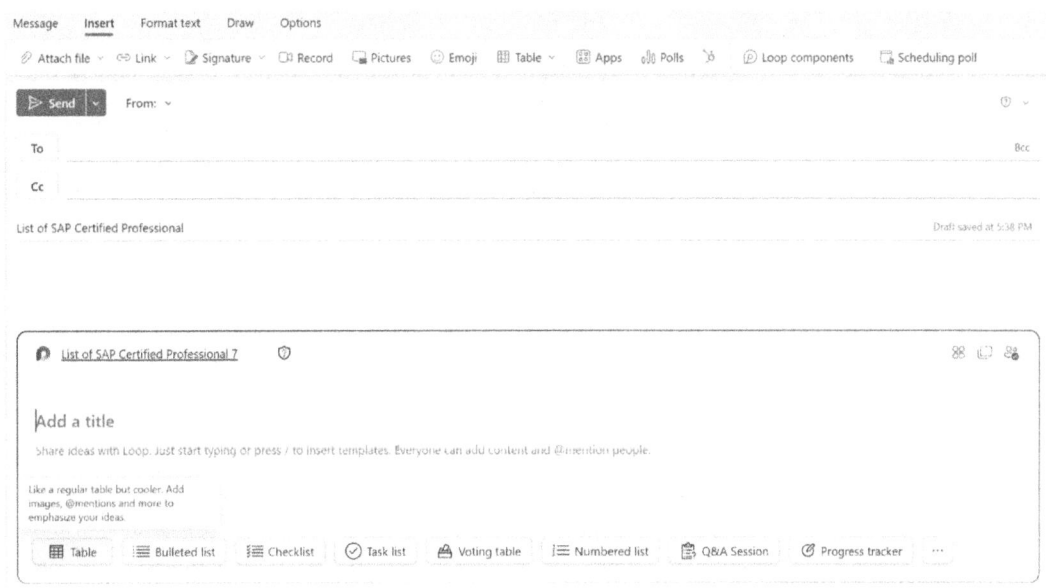

Figure 5-6. *Click on Component Table*

137

CHAPTER 5   INTEGRATING LOOP WITH MICROSOFT 365 APPS

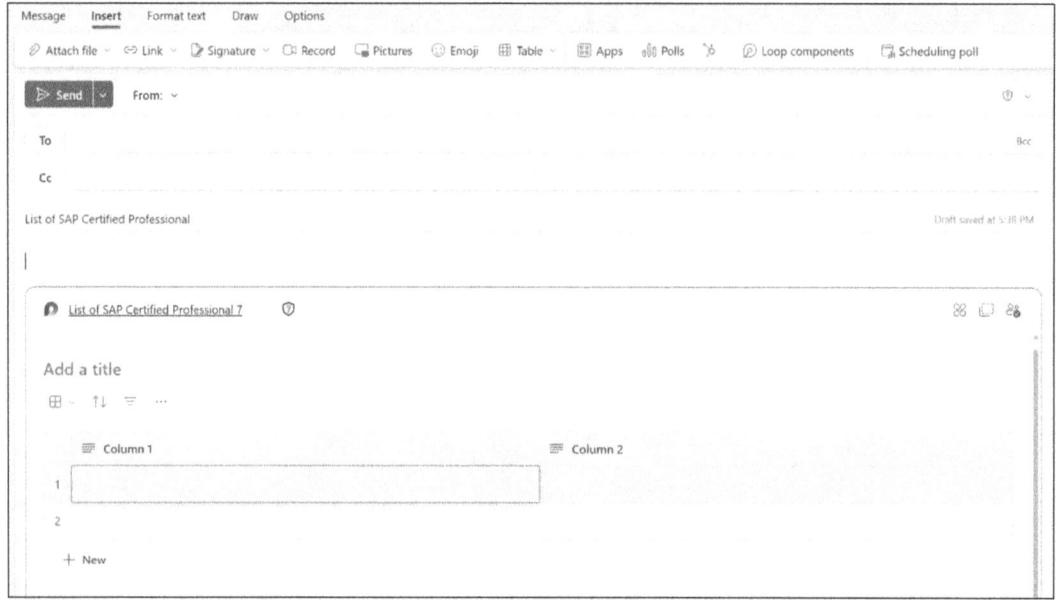

Figure 5-7. Table component with prepopulated columns Column 1 and Column 2

Now we will begin by updating the titles of the columns: rename the first column from "Column 1" to "Employee Name" and the second column from "Column 2" to "Certification Name", as shown in Figure 5-8. Next, add an additional column by selecting the plus sign located at the upper right corner, as shown in Figure 5-9; this option may only appear when you hover your mouse over the area. Name the third column "Certification Name" and finally, create one more column and designate it as "Certification Status," as shown in Figure 5-10.

CHAPTER 5 INTEGRATING LOOP WITH MICROSOFT 365 APPS

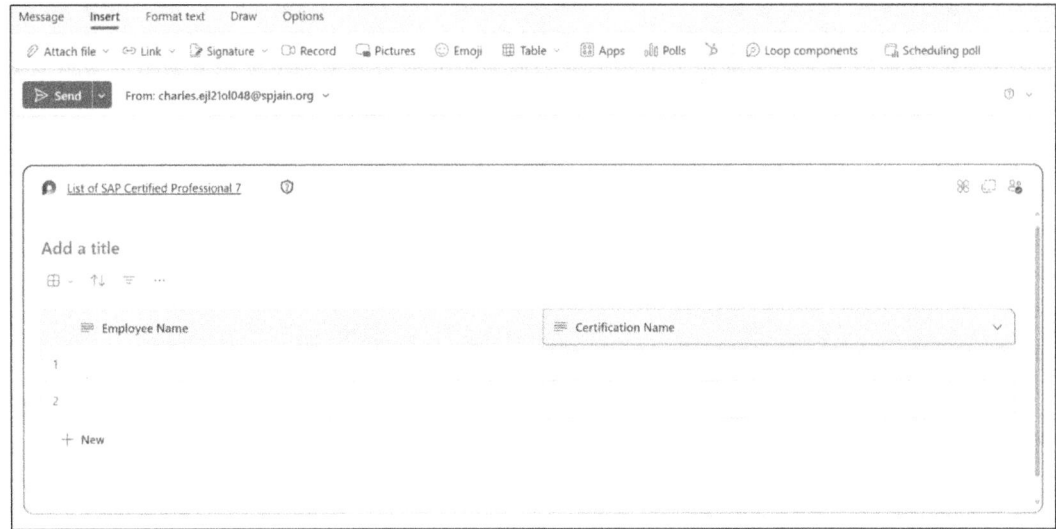

Figure 5-8. *Renaming of the Columns*

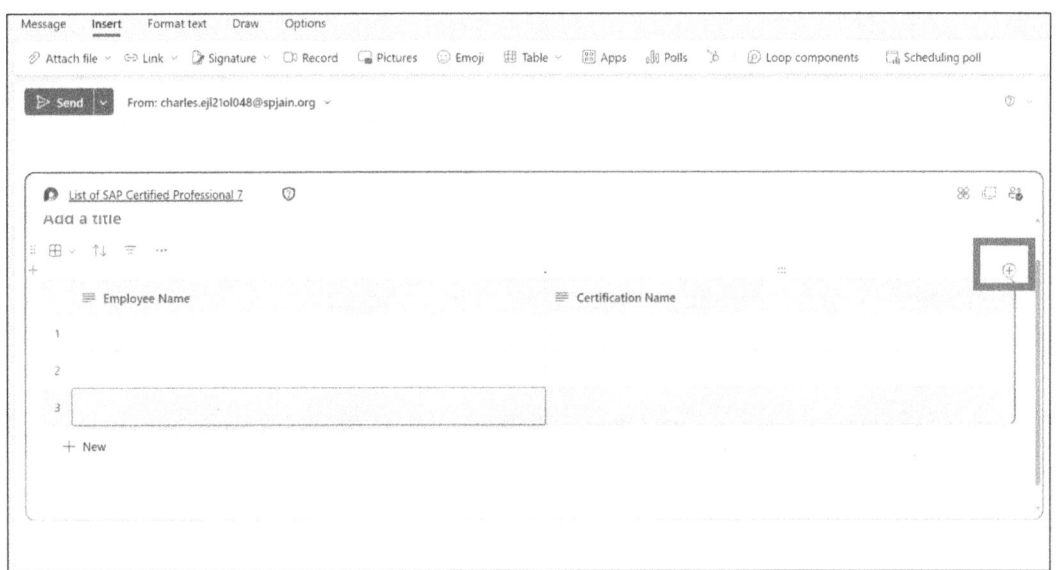

Figure 5-9. *"+" sign to add a new Column*

139

CHAPTER 5   INTEGRATING LOOP WITH MICROSOFT 365 APPS

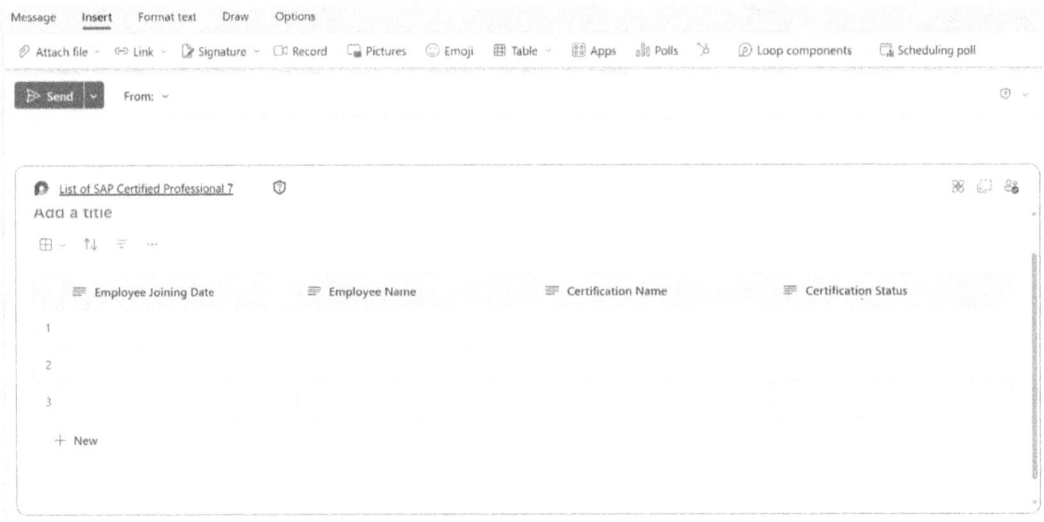

Figure 5-10. *Added two new columns "Certification Name" and "Certification Status"*

This email outlines a list of people who has passed SAP Certified. Begin by navigating the "Employee Joining Date" column. The input and display method for each column can be selected individually. For the Employee Joining Date column, which is a date field, select the dropdown arrow, as shown in Figure 5-11, and change the column type to "date," as shown in Figure 5-12. Table kind of icon appears next to ""Employee Joining Date" column indicating column type changes have been successfully changed, as shown in Figure 5-13. Other Column types are Text, Number, Person, Vote, and Label and default column type is the Text, as shown in Figure 5-14. The "Employee Name" column will remain as alphanumeric text to allow freeform entry, as shown in Figures 5-15 and 5-16, respectively.

CHAPTER 5 INTEGRATING LOOP WITH MICROSOFT 365 APPS

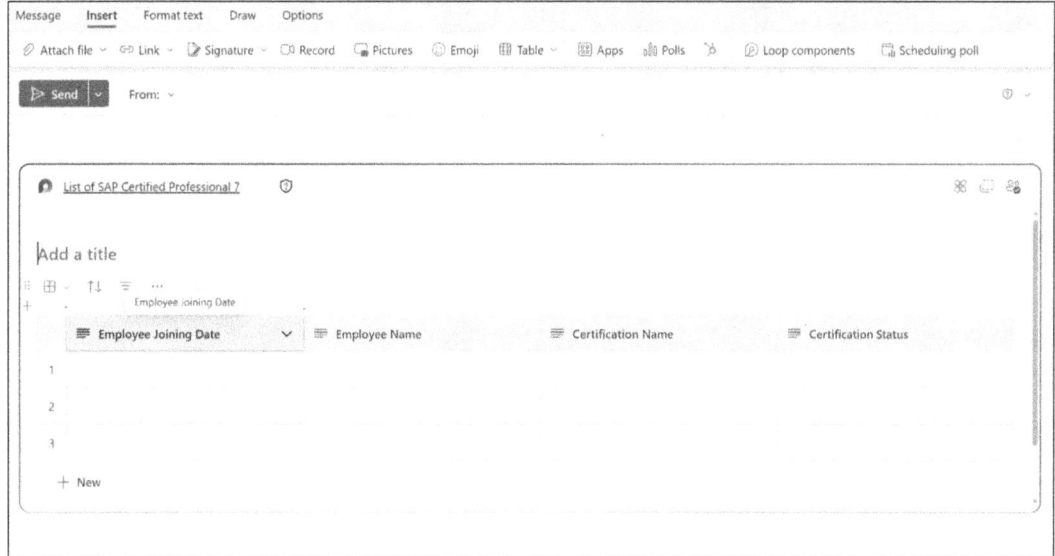

Figure 5-11. *Select Dropdown menu of "Employee Joining Date"*

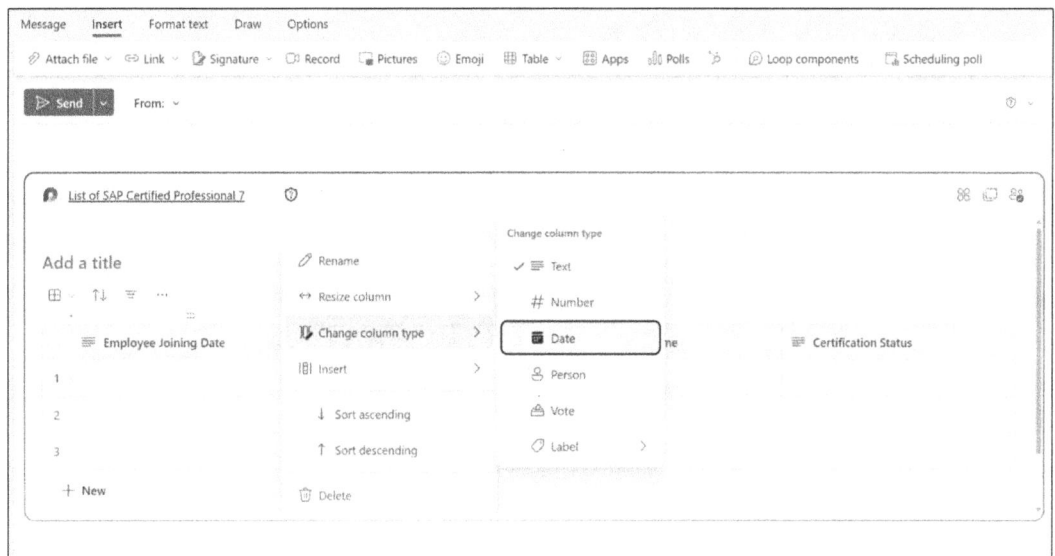

Figure 5-12. *Select Column Type*

141

CHAPTER 5   INTEGRATING LOOP WITH MICROSOFT 365 APPS

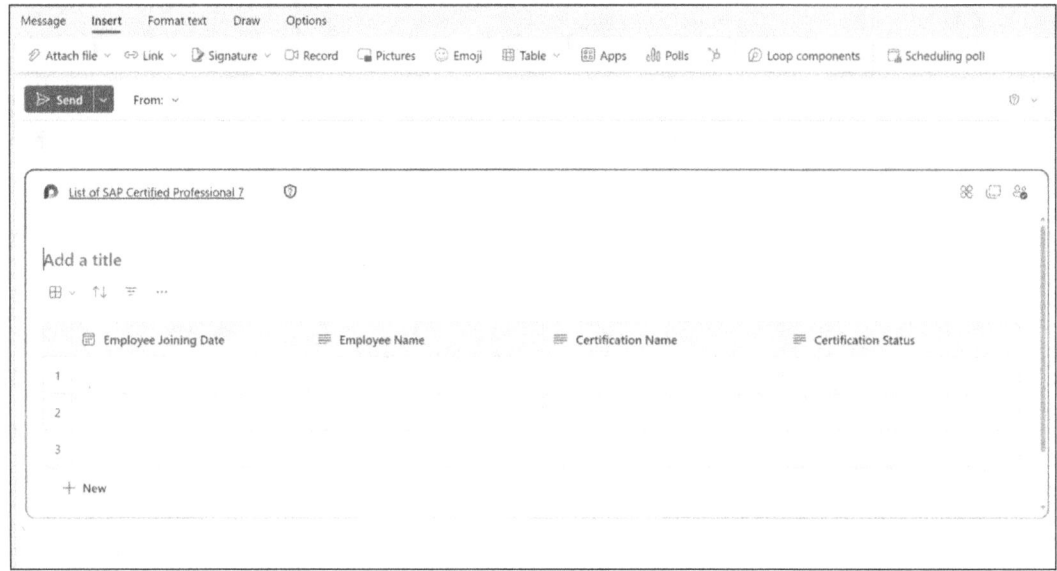

Figure 5-13. *Column type of "Employee Joining Date" changes successfully*

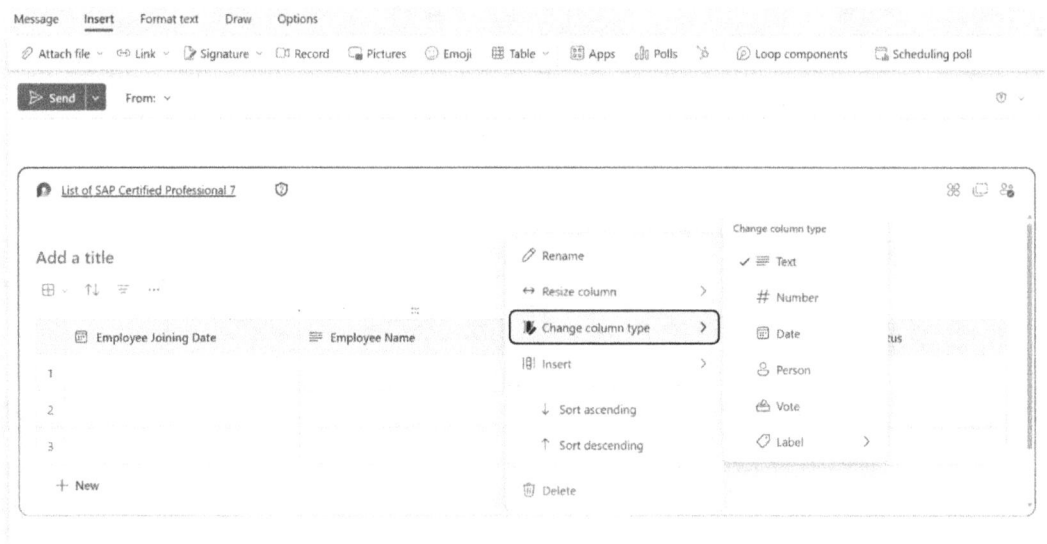

Figure 5-14. *Default Column type is Text*

142

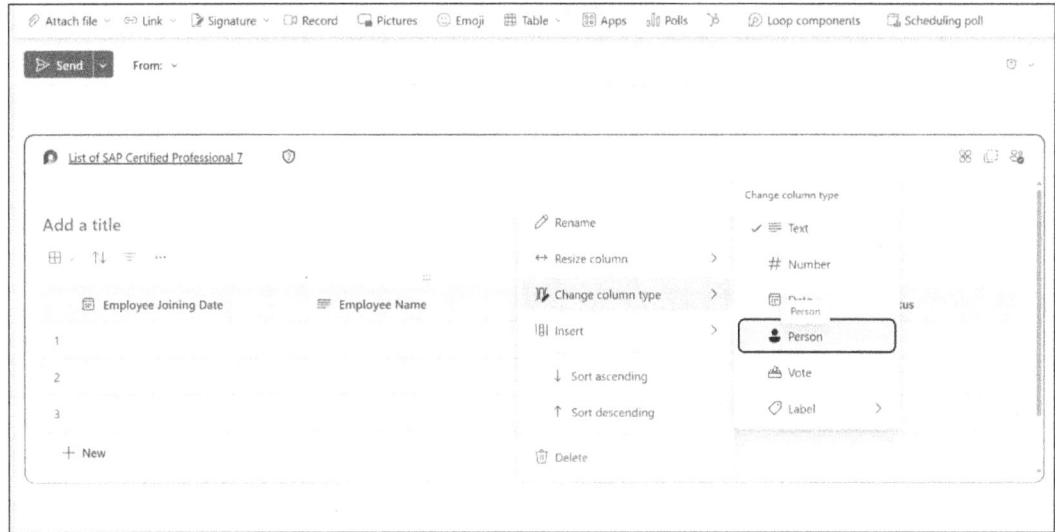

Figure 5-15. *Choose Person as Column Type*

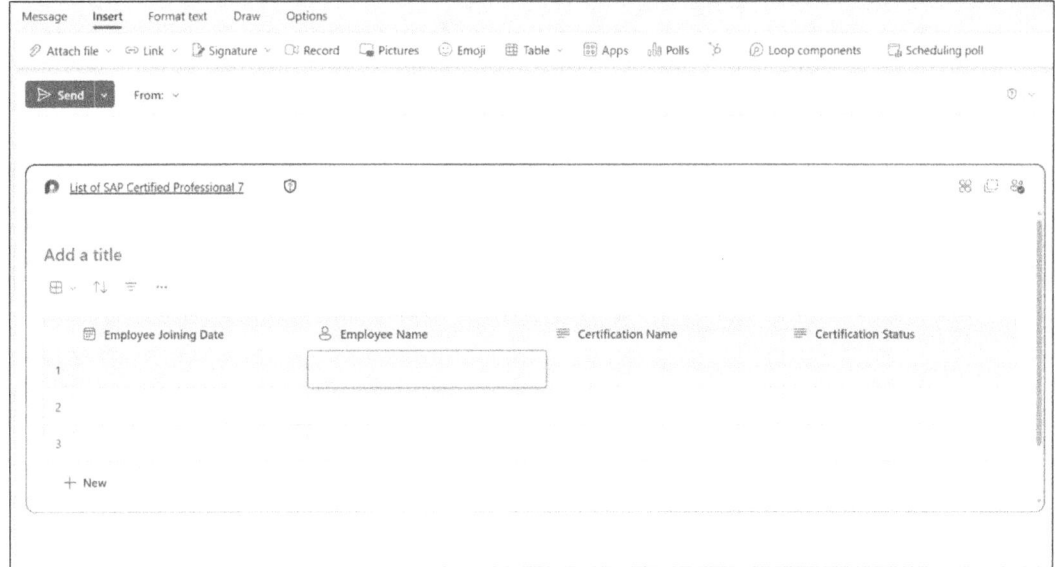

Figure 5-16. *Employee Name Column type changed to Person*

Proceed to the "Certification Name," open the dropdown menu, and set the column type to "Text," as shown in the Figures 5-17 and 5-18. For the "Certification Status" Column, use the dropdown arrow to access the column type options and select "label," as shown in Figure 5-19. There are prebuilt label groups such as priority levels, but in this case, create a new label group called Status, as shown in Figure 5-20. Enter the desired options: Completed, Incomplete, Work-in-Progress, as shown in Figure 5-21. Save these settings to enable custom label selection within the "Certification Status" column and when you hover over any cell of this column, label values become visible, as shown in Figure 5-22.

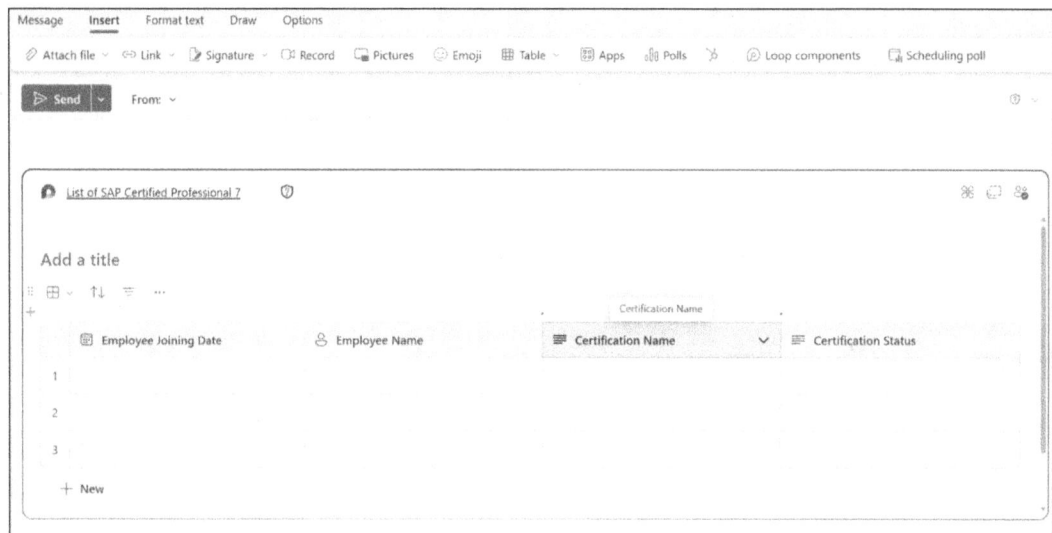

Figure 5-17. Access dropdown menu of "Certification Name" column

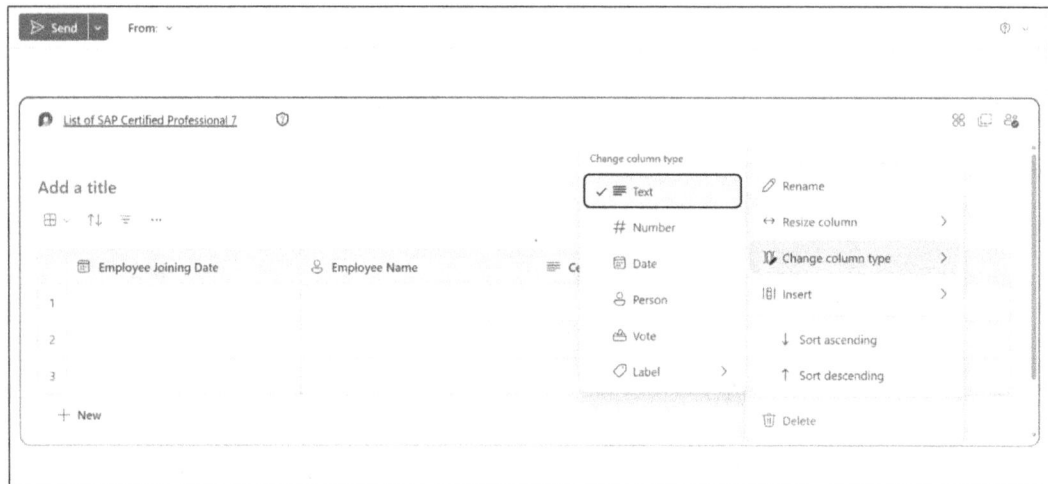

Figure 5-18. Column Type changed to Text

CHAPTER 5   INTEGRATING LOOP WITH MICROSOFT 365 APPS

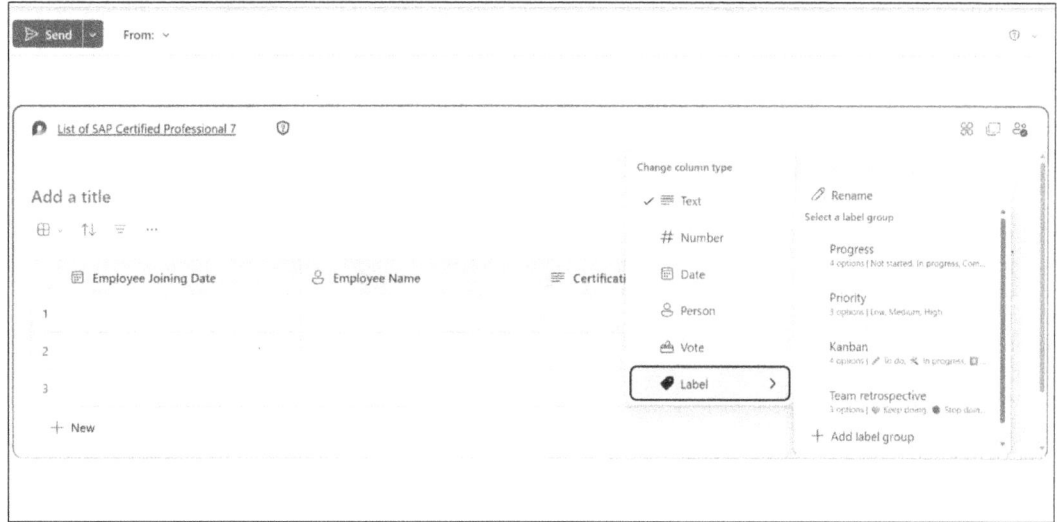

Figure 5-19. *Change Column of Certification Status column to Label*

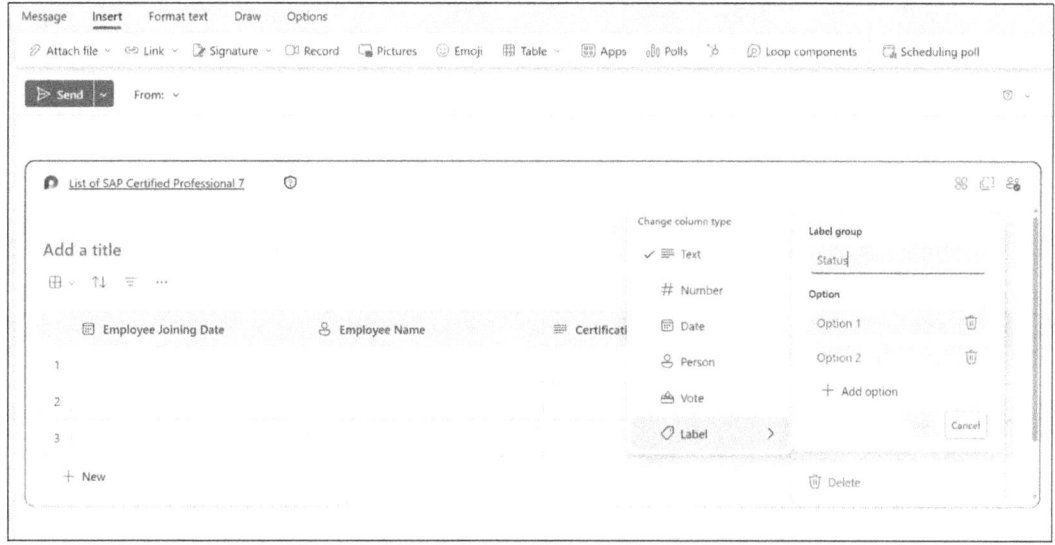

Figure 5-20. *Create Label called "Status"*

CHAPTER 5 INTEGRATING LOOP WITH MICROSOFT 365 APPS

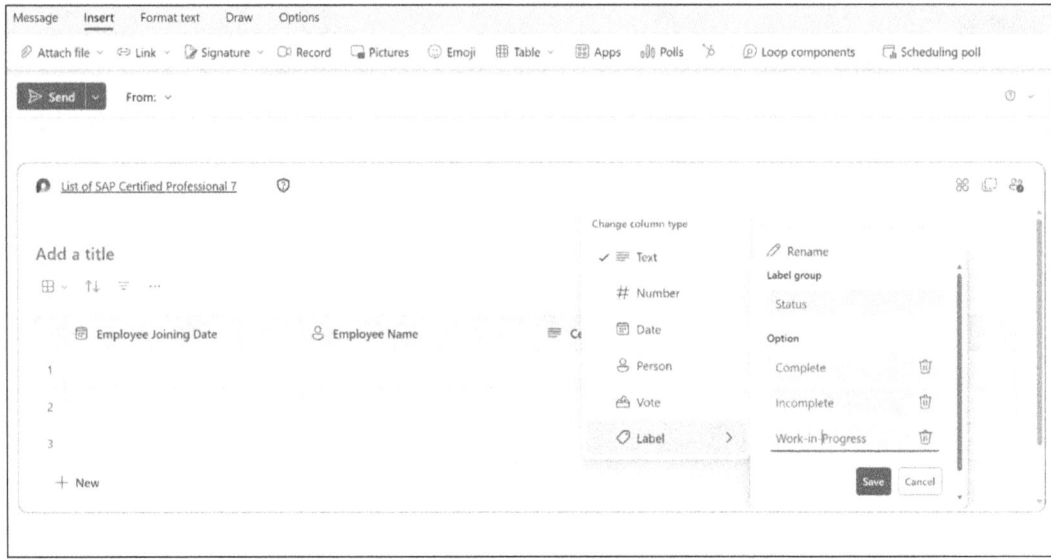

Figure 5-21. Update Label values

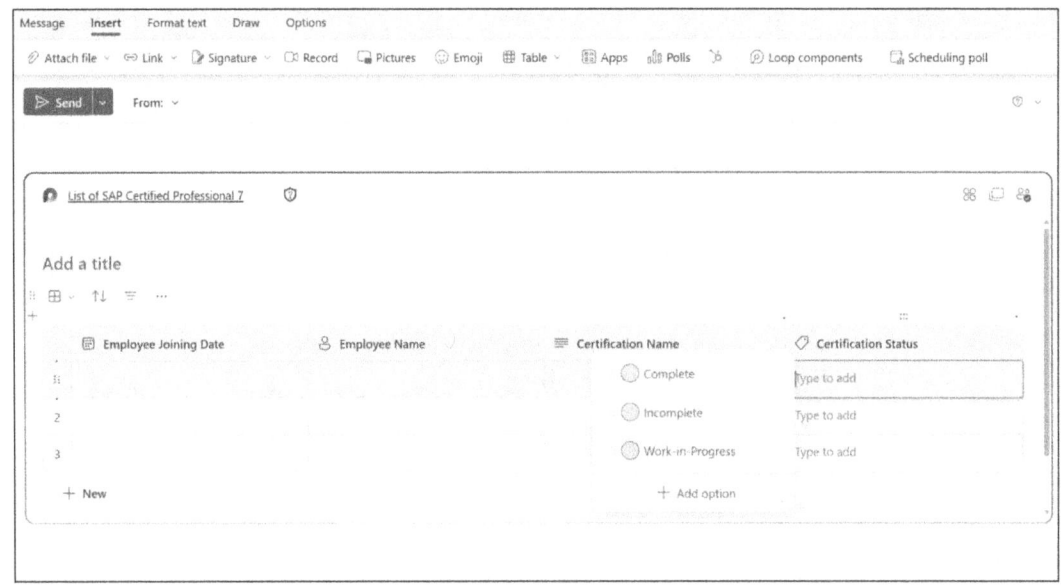

Figure 5-22. Label values visible after saving changes

CHAPTER 5 INTEGRATING LOOP WITH MICROSOFT 365 APPS

Next, enter the data into the table. For instance, select a month—such as September 9th of the next year—2024, as shown in Figure 5-23. Add employee names, as "Charles Waghmare," Certification Name as "SAP Finance" and Choose Certification Status as Completed, as shown in Figure 5-24, respectively.

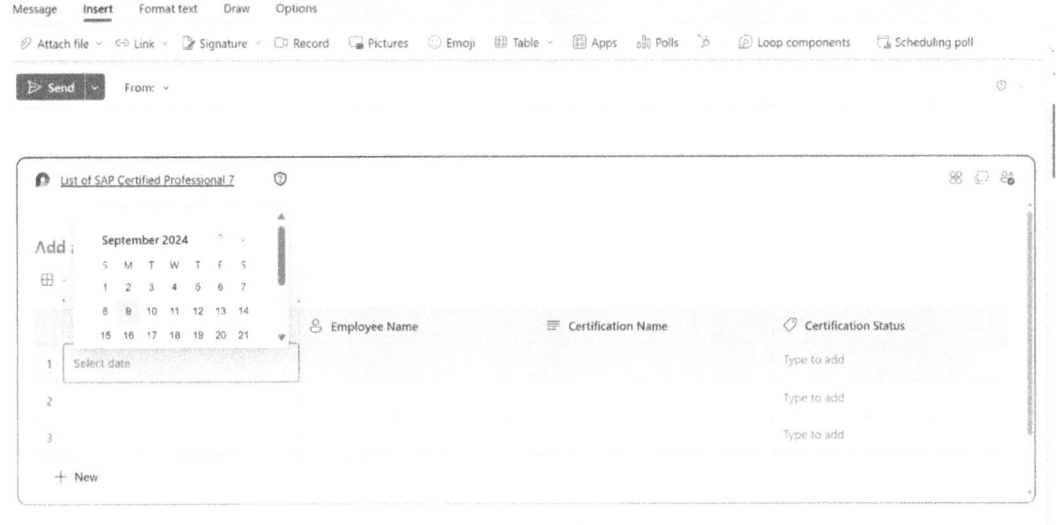

Figure 5-23. Choose September 9, 2024, as Employee Joining Date

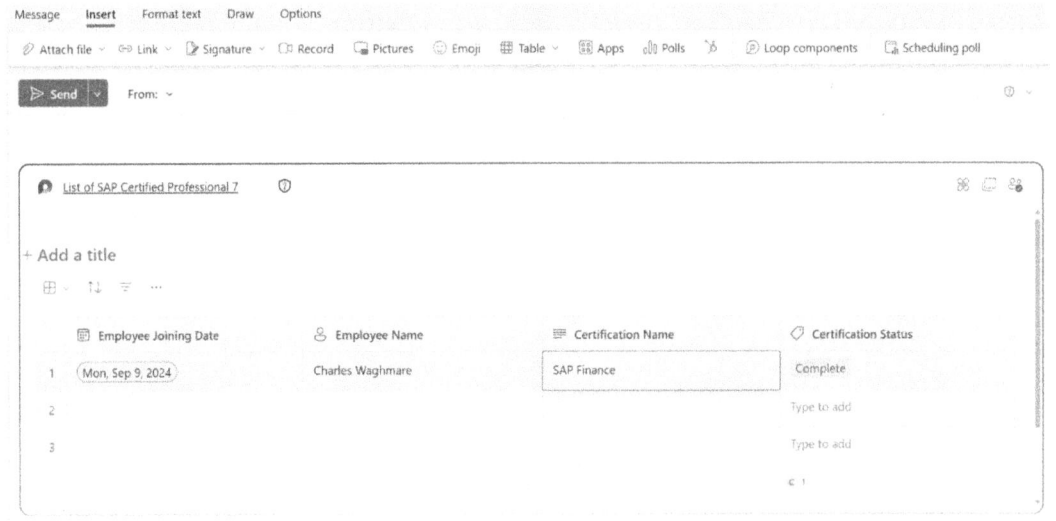

Figure 5-24. Data entry for all columns

147

Once distributed, recipients of the email can update the table collaboratively by adding their information. The table will always display the most current version, whether viewed in email, OneDrive, or another platform. This component can be shared in different Microsoft applications—such as Teams chat messages, channel conversations, Word documents, or OneNote notebooks.

For missing Title "Add a Title" is default message, as shown in Figure 5-25. The Title for the Table Component can be given with free text or @mention to some person or link file, as shown in Figure 5-26.

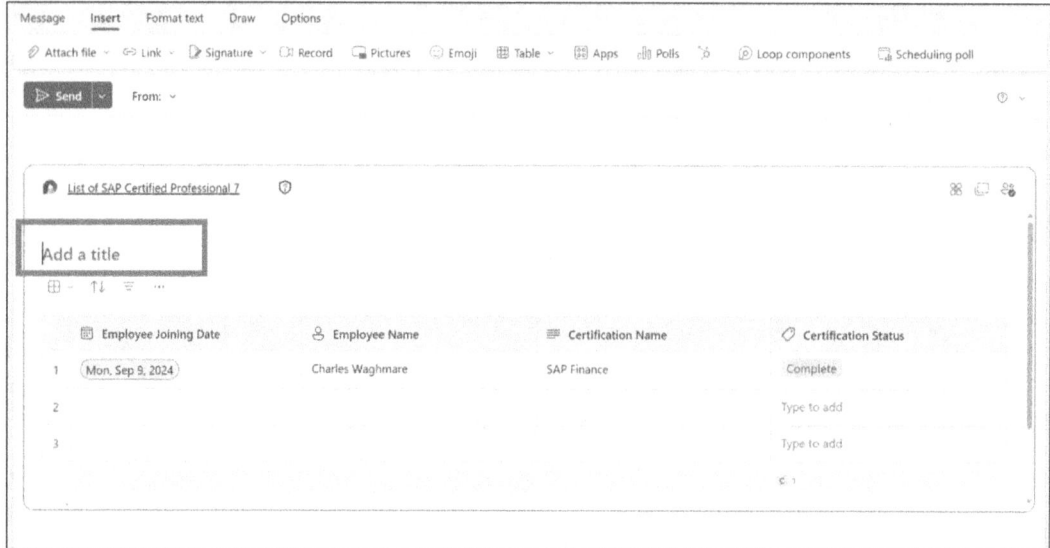

Figure 5-25. *Default missing Title Message*

CHAPTER 5   INTEGRATING LOOP WITH MICROSOFT 365 APPS

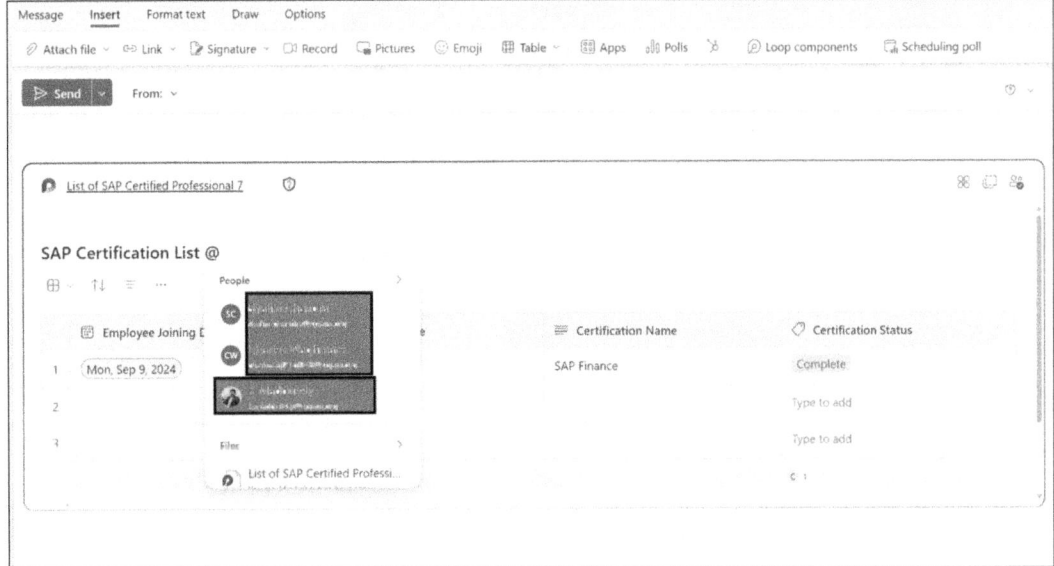

Figure 5-26. *SAP certification List as Title and @mention to tag to person or file in Title*

Besides, component has features display Table content in the form of Table, Board, and Calendar views depending upon user requirements, as shown in Figure 5-27. Figure 5-27-1 displays board view of the content and Figure 5-27-2 displays calender view of the content.

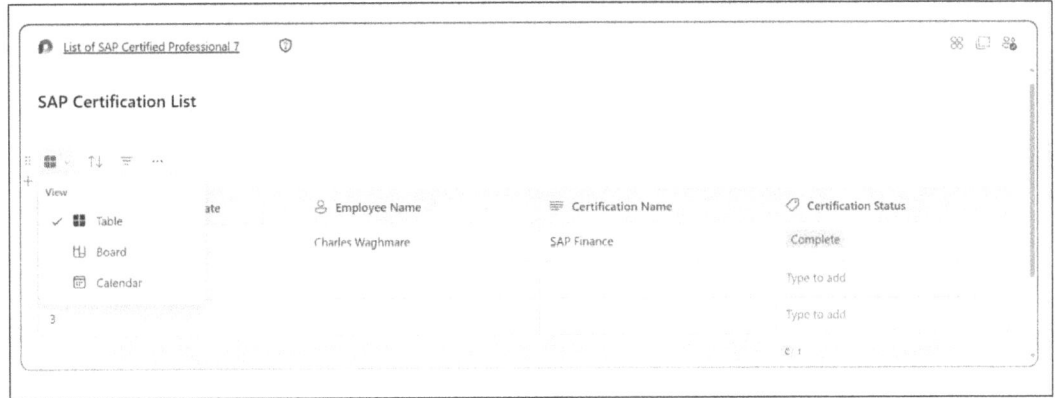

Figure 5-27. *Different Content views*

149

CHAPTER 5   INTEGRATING LOOP WITH MICROSOFT 365 APPS

Figure 5-27-1. Board view of content

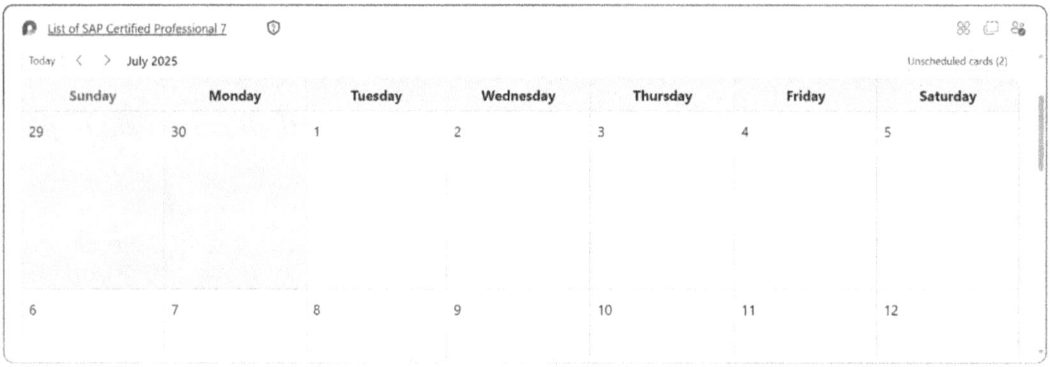

Figure 5-27-2. Calander view of content

In addition to different views of the content, a user can sort content in ascending or descending format based upon the column defined in the component, as shown in the Figures 5-28 and 5-29.

CHAPTER 5 INTEGRATING LOOP WITH MICROSOFT 365 APPS

Figure 5-20. Access "Sort" option

Figure 5-29. Sort content based on a chosen field

Further, user can filter Table content bases on conditions shown in the Figure 5-30. Conditional statement are very similar to one that we use in Excel.

CHAPTER 5   INTEGRATING LOOP WITH MICROSOFT 365 APPS

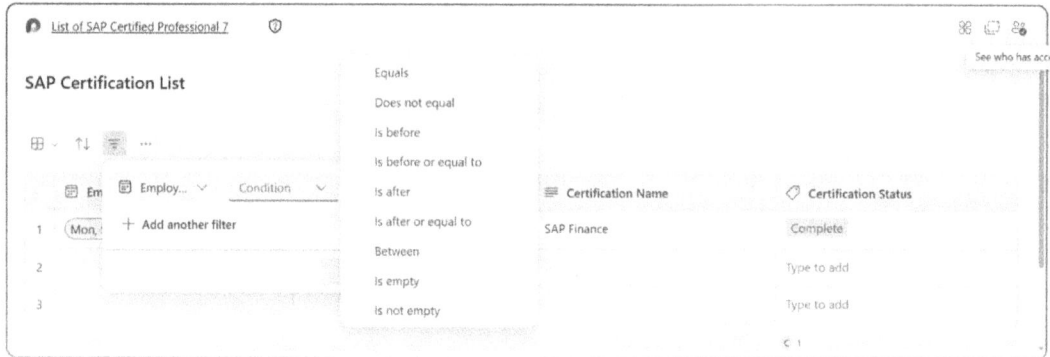

Figure 5-30. *Explore conditions for data filter*

Finally, there are option management Row as "Tall" or Short, as shown in Figure 5-31. Option to Hide existing columns also exists, as shown in Figure 5-32, and at the last Table, content can be exported to excel or ".csv," as shown in Figure 5-33.

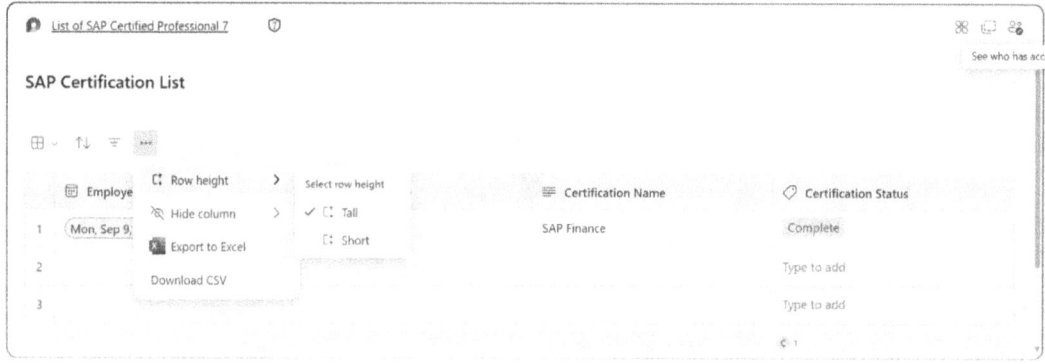

Figure 5-31. *Adjust row height*

152

CHAPTER 5   INTEGRATING LOOP WITH MICROSOFT 365 APPS

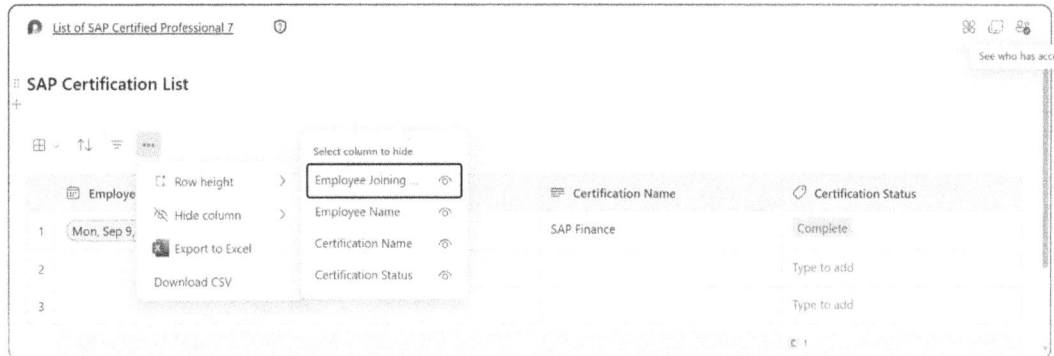

Figure 5-32. Hide existing Columns

Figure 5-33. Export data to excel and ".CSV"

Table component can be shared across different Loop workspaces using Shared Location options, as shown in Figure 5-34, and copied using copy component, as shown in Figure 5-35. Finally, user can view list of people who have access to the component, as shown in Figure 5-36, to read and edit content.

153

CHAPTER 5   INTEGRATING LOOP WITH MICROSOFT 365 APPS

Figure 5-34. *Shared Location to copy across other Loop workspaces*

Figure 5-35. *Copy Table component*

Figure 5-36. *List of users having access to Table component to read and edit content*

CHAPTER 5 INTEGRATING LOOP WITH MICROSOFT 365 APPS

Developing a Team Retrospective Loop Component Within a OneNote Notebook Page

When a team reviews a project's performance, this process typically includes identifying areas for improvement, which is referred to as a team retrospective. Microsoft Loop offers a Loop component specifically for this activity. If project notes are being taken within a OneNote Notebook, the following steps outline how to set up this Loop component on a Notebook page.

Begin by positioning the cursor where the component should be inserted on the page. Then select the Insert tab, locate the Collaborate group in the middle of the ribbon, and choose Loop Components, as shown in Figure 5-37. All available components for use with Notebook pages will be displayed. Select Team Retrospective from the options, as shown in Figures 5-38 and 5-38-1.

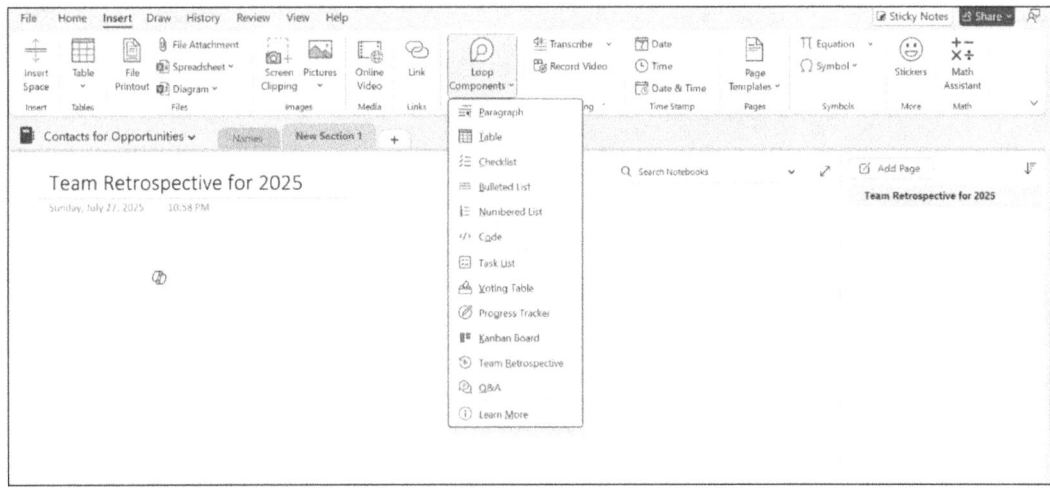

Figure 5-37. Select Loop Component from Insert Menu

155

CHAPTER 5   INTEGRATING LOOP WITH MICROSOFT 365 APPS

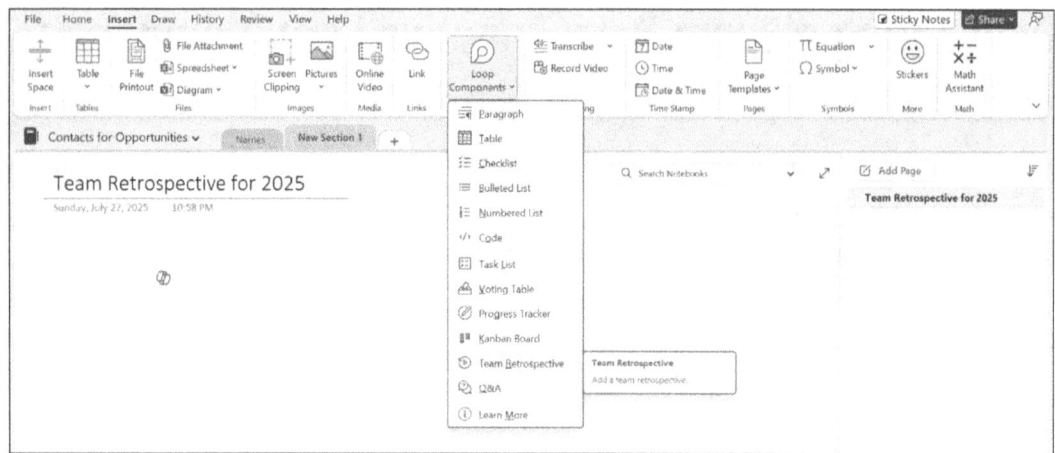

Figure 5-38. *Choose Team Retrospective*

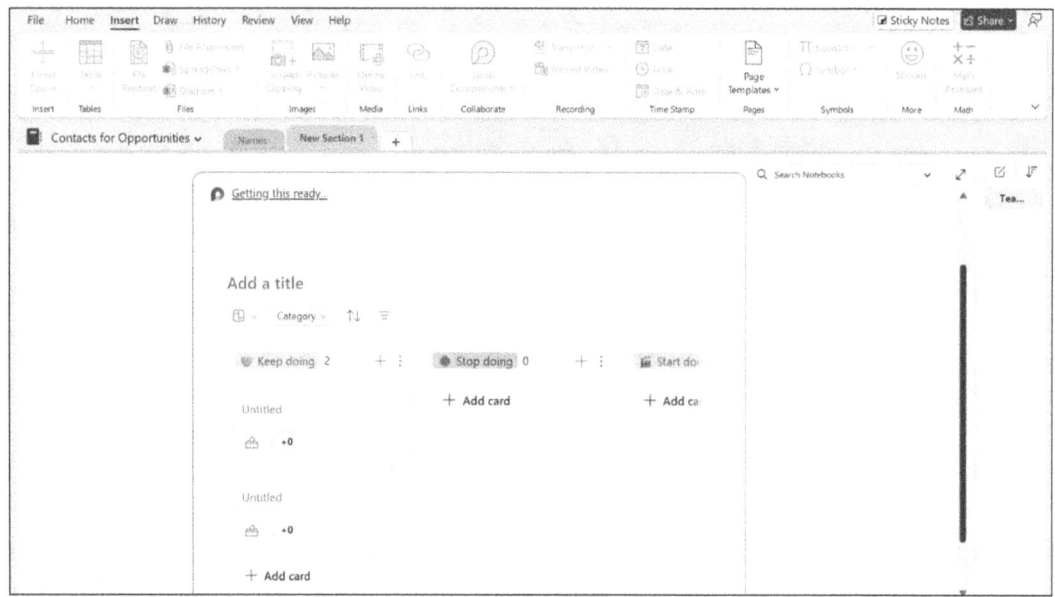

Figure 5-38-1. *Post selecting Team retrospective component*

The component will be inserted, initially displaying "Getting this ready" in the upper left corner before updating to reflect the page's name, as shown in Figure 5-39. For example, if the page is named Team Retrospective 2025, this title will also appear in the newly inserted component.

CHAPTER 5   INTEGRATING LOOP WITH MICROSOFT 365 APPS

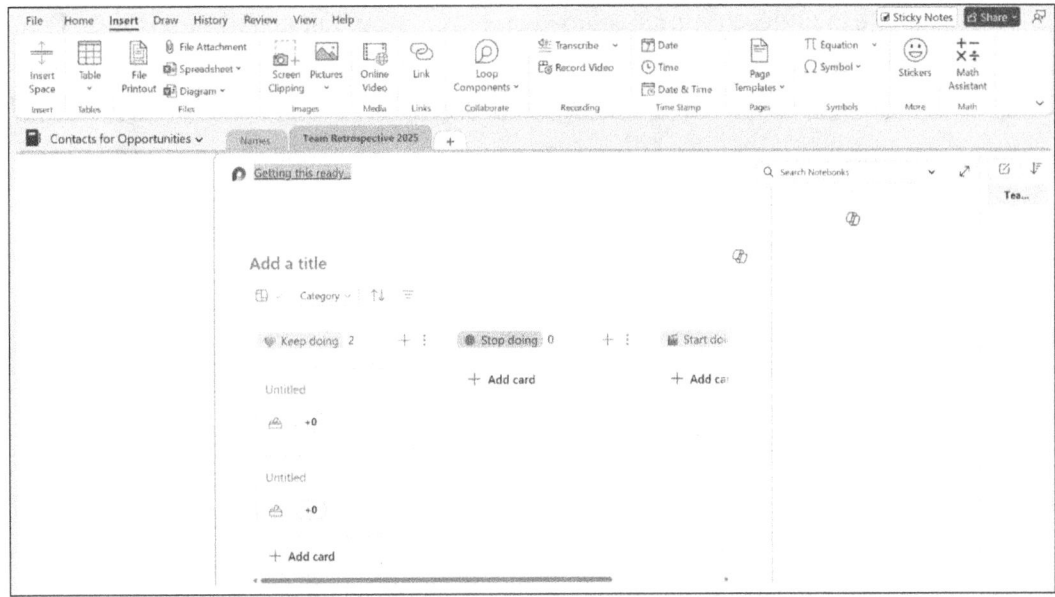

Figure 5-39. *Retrospective component with "Getting this ready" Title*

At this point, a cursor appears at Add a Title, where a title can be entered as "Team Retrospective 2025," as shown in Figure 5-40. This step is useful if the component is used or shared elsewhere within the Microsoft 365 tenant.

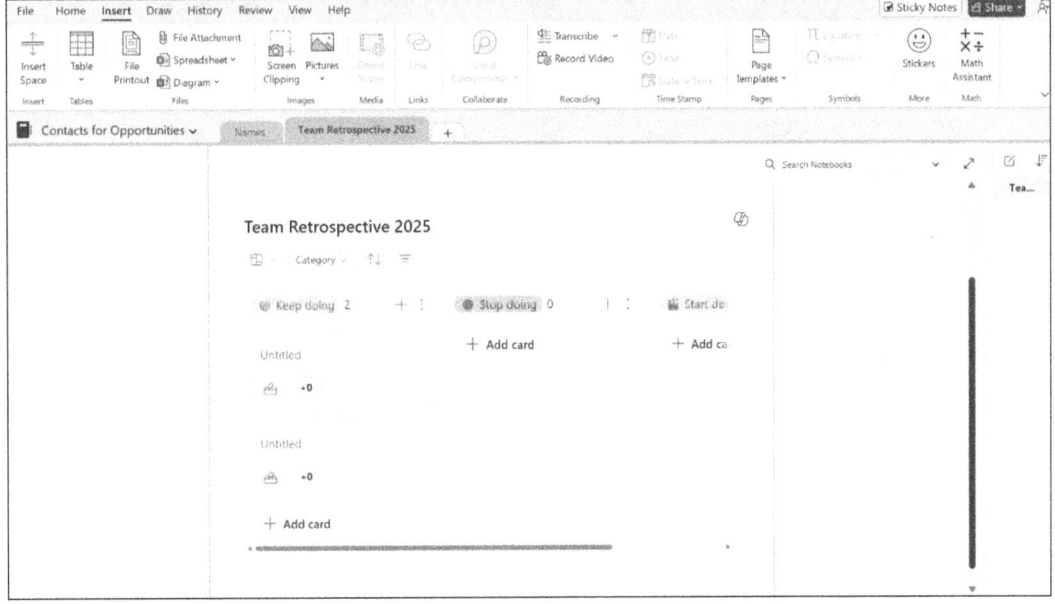

Figure 5-40. *Add Title to component*

157

CHAPTER 5   INTEGRATING LOOP WITH MICROSOFT 365 APPS

The template includes groups labeled keep doing, stop doing, and start doing. The note container and component width can be adjusted by dragging the right edge using the double-headed arrow, as shown in Figure 5-41.

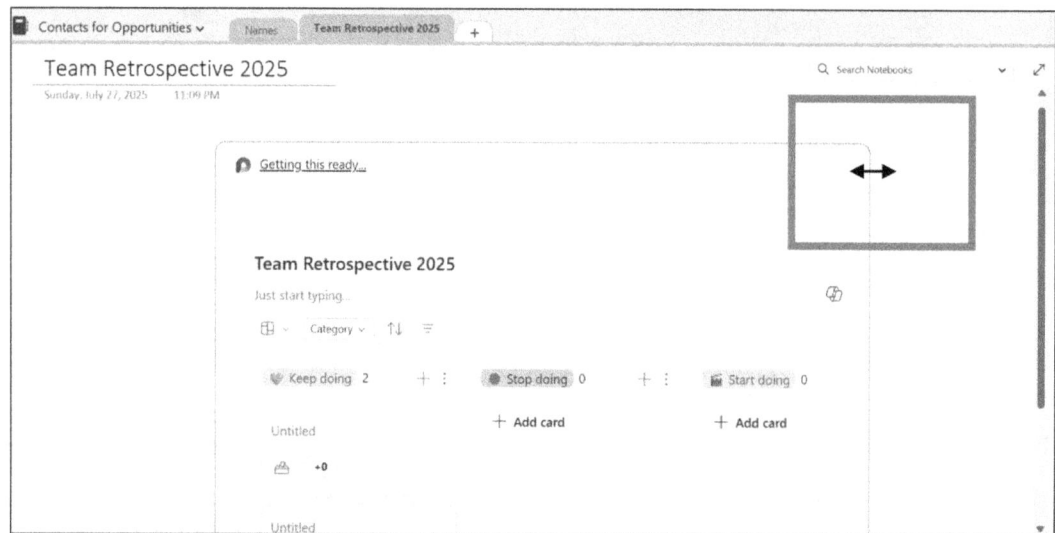

Figure 5-41. *Adjut size of component using double-headed arrow*

Under "keep doing" group, there are two untitled cards provided for initiating the activity. To add similar cards to the other groups, navigate to "stop doing" group and select Add Card as needed, as shown in Figures 5-42 and 5-42-1, repeating the process for "start doing" group, as shown in Figure 5-43.

CHAPTER 5 INTEGRATING LOOP WITH MICROSOFT 365 APPS

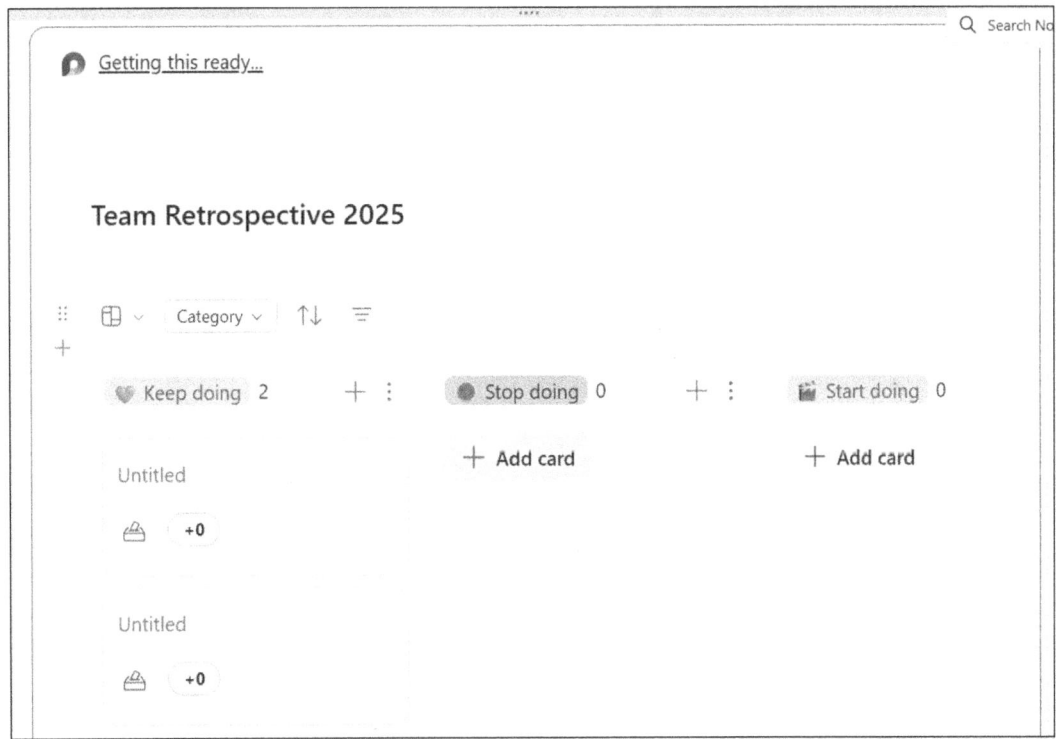

Figure 5-42. *Select "Add Card" option*

CHAPTER 5   INTEGRATING LOOP WITH MICROSOFT 365 APPS

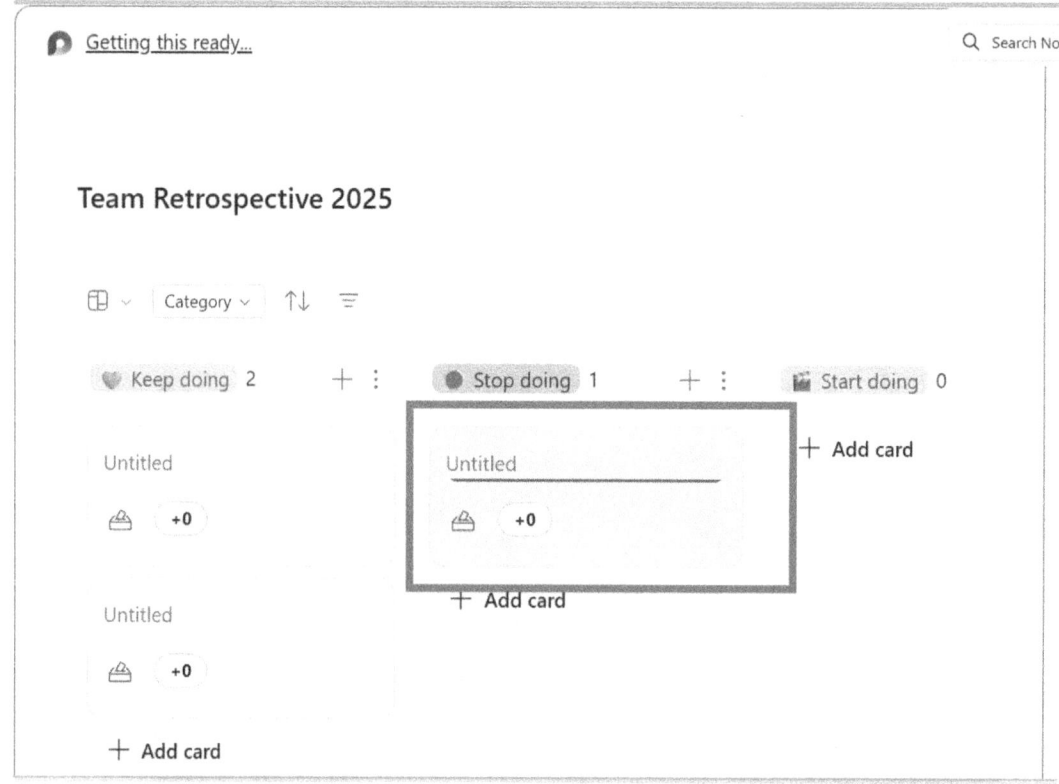

Figure 5-42-1. *Post selecting "Add Card" option*

CHAPTER 5   INTEGRATING LOOP WITH MICROSOFT 365 APPS

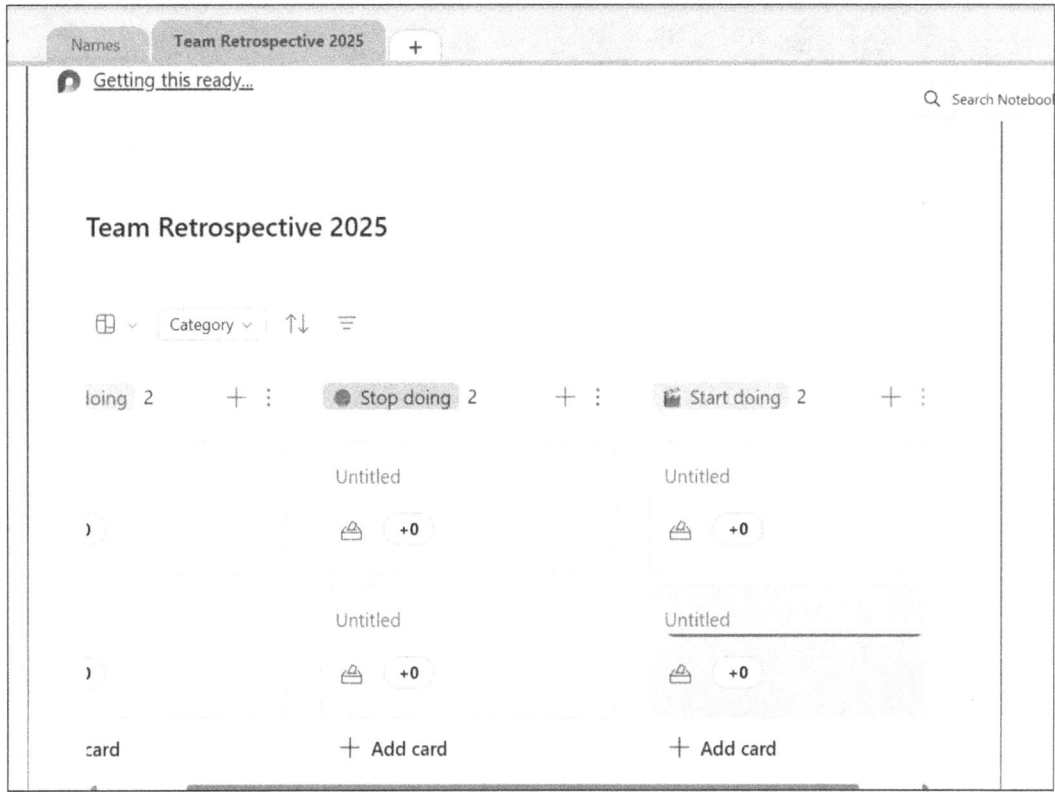

Figure 5-43. *Chosen "Add Card" option for "Start doing" group*

Additional groups can be added by selecting Group Options via the three ellipses next to the group, as shown in Figure 5-44. Here, it is possible to rename the group, change its order, or insert new groups to the left or right of the selected one, as shown in Figures 5-45, 5-45-1, and 5-45-2.

CHAPTER 5   INTEGRATING LOOP WITH MICROSOFT 365 APPS

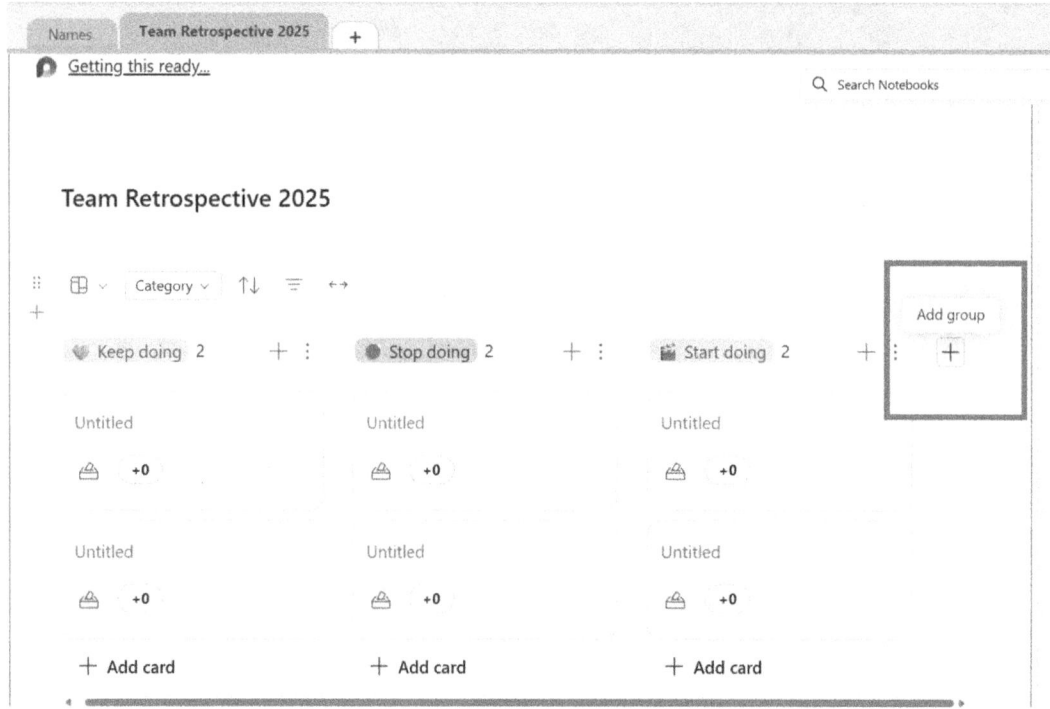

Figure 5-44. *Option to add additional group*

CHAPTER 5 INTEGRATING LOOP WITH MICROSOFT 365 APPS

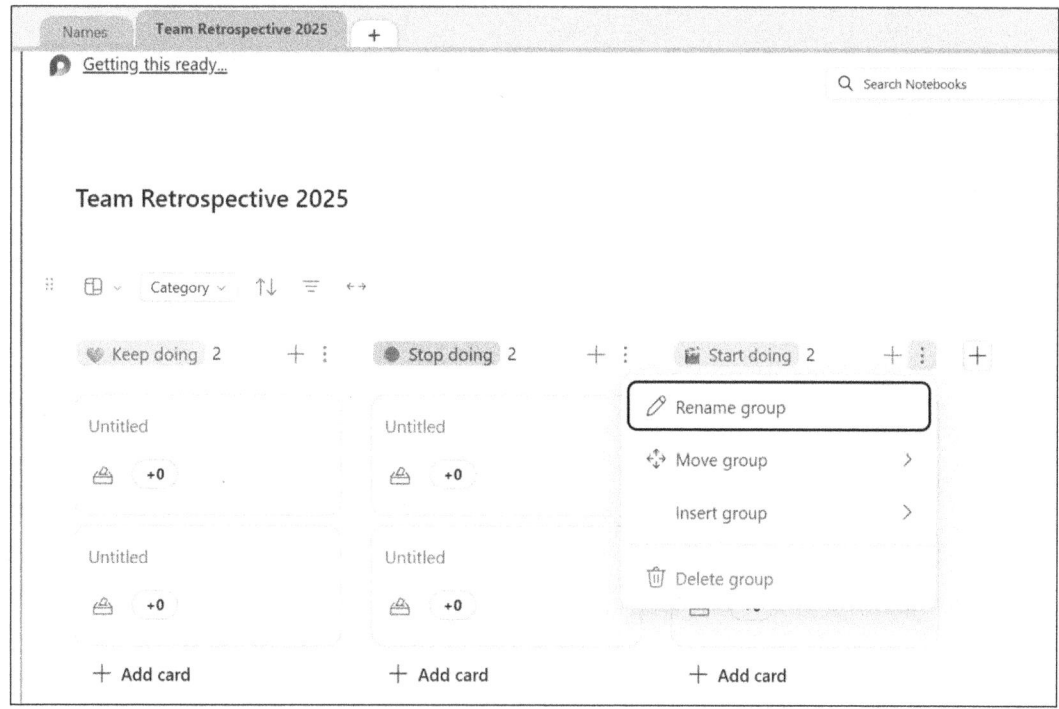

Figure 5-45. *Rename existing group*

CHAPTER 5   INTEGRATING LOOP WITH MICROSOFT 365 APPS

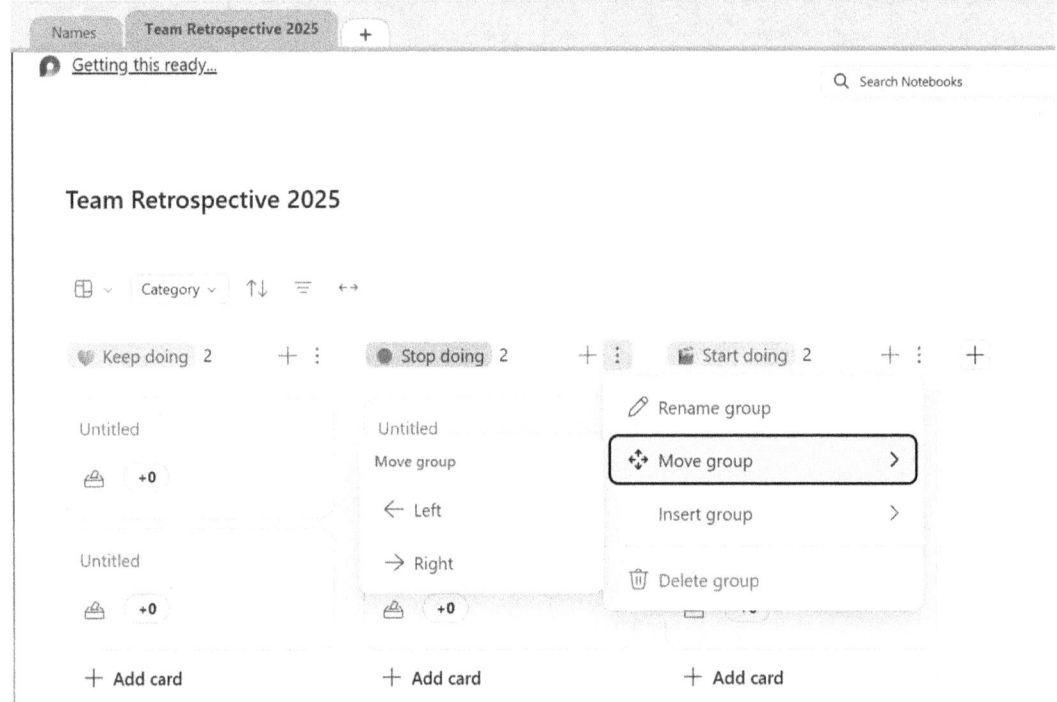

Figure 5-45-1. *Move Group left or right*

CHAPTER 5   INTEGRATING LOOP WITH MICROSOFT 365 APPS

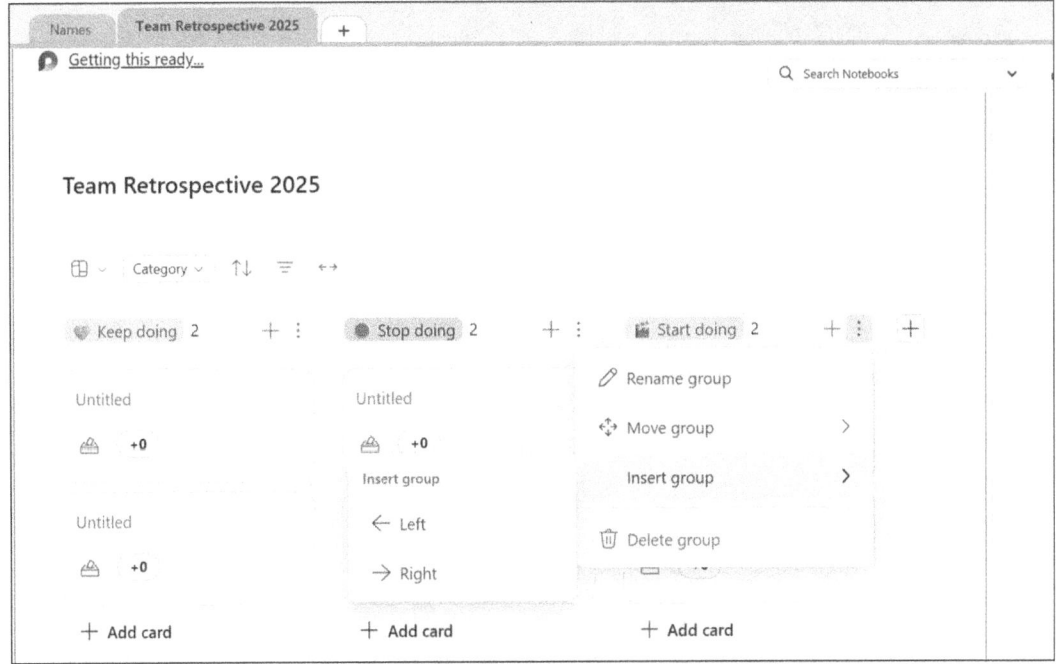

Figure 5-45-2. *Insert group left or right*

In the upper left corner, there are options for changing the view of the component. It can be viewed as a board or switched to a table format, as shown in Figures 5-46 and 5-46-1, and back again if desired. The team retrospective component is then prepared for project team members to assess achievements, recognize areas for improvement, and develop an action plan.

165

CHAPTER 5   INTEGRATING LOOP WITH MICROSOFT 365 APPS

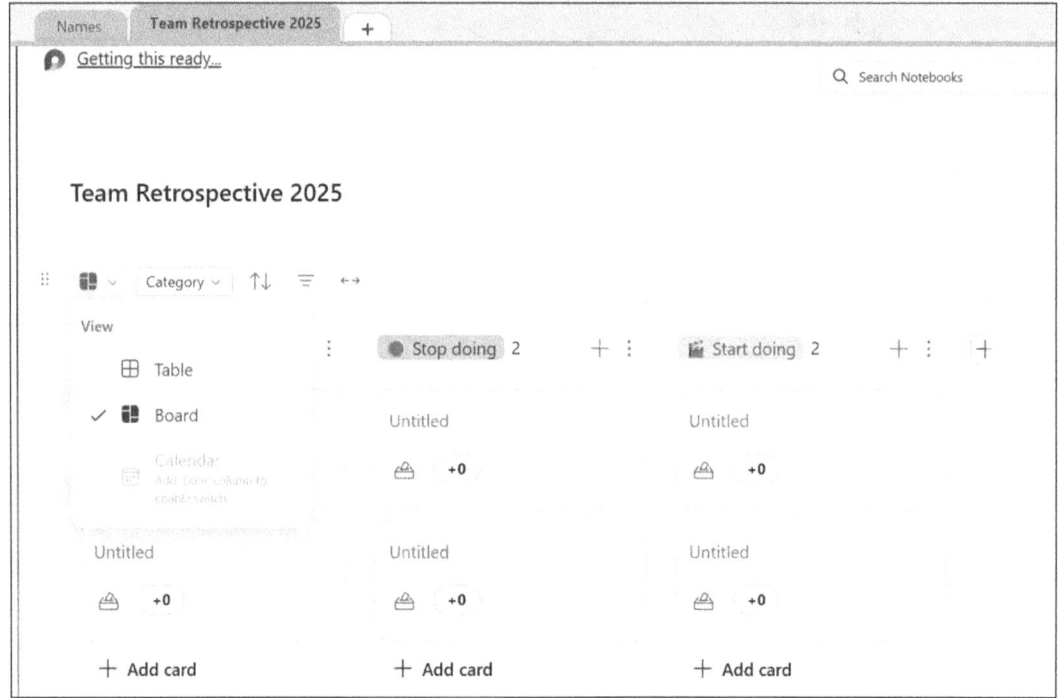

Figure 5-46. *Board view of restrospective*

CHAPTER 5   INTEGRATING LOOP WITH MICROSOFT 365 APPS

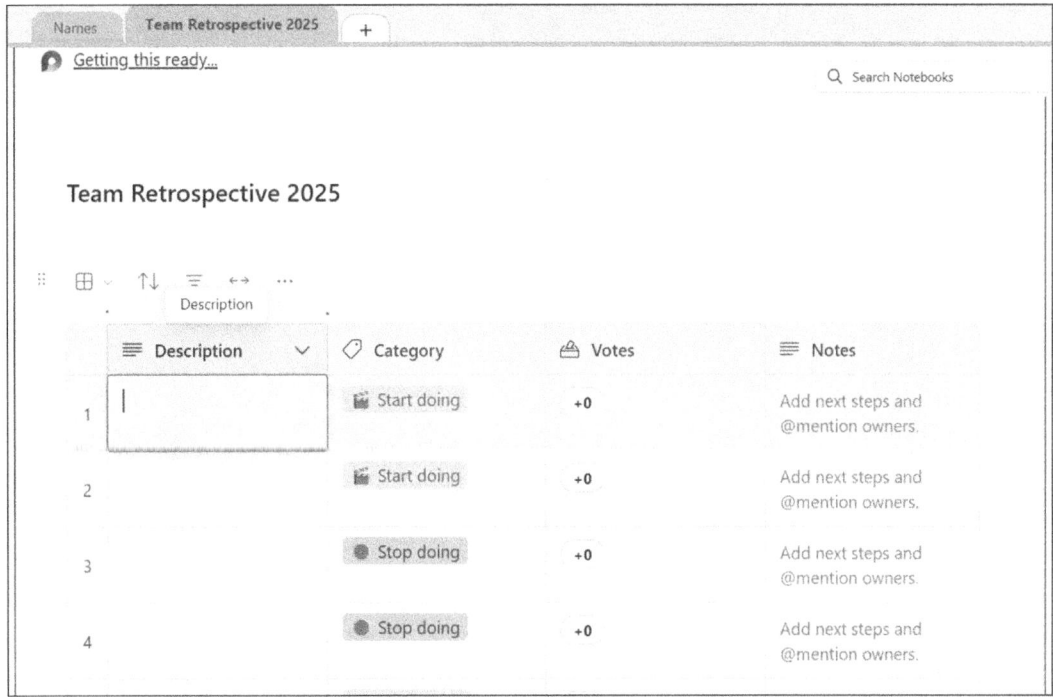

Figure 5-46-1. *Table view of restrospective*

As we have seen in the Table component of Outlook, similary restrospective component has options to sort, filter, adjust row height, and hide columns.

This concludes the chapter. In this section, we conducted an in-depth exploration of Microsoft Loop's integration with Microsoft applications such as Outlook and OneNote, highlighting how these integrations can enhance workforce collaboration, connectivity, and business-related activities. Specifically, we demonstrated seamless email integration with Loop's Table Component in Outlook and illustrated how a OneNote page can be efficiently incorporated with Loop's Retrospective Component. In the next chapter, we will explore features such as Kanban Boards, Ideas Tab, Page Linking, Templates, and customization to fit real-time needs and others to continue our journey of collaborative content co-creation.

CHAPTER 6

Exploring Advanced Features and Customizations

In the preceding chapter, we provided a comprehensive analysis of Microsoft Loop's integration with Microsoft applications, including Outlook and OneNote. Our discussion emphasized how these integrations facilitate improved collaboration, connectivity, and efficiency within business environments. We examined the smooth integration of email communications via Loop's Table Component in Outlook and demonstrated the effective incorporation of Loop's Retrospective Component within OneNote pages. In the following chapter, we will review features such as Kanban Boards, the Ideas Tab, page linking, templates, and customization options designed to address real-time operational needs, further advancing collaborative content creation. In short, we will explore all possible Loop components in this chapter.

Task List

The Task List component within Microsoft Loop serves as an effective and versatile solution for collaborative task management. This interactive checklist enables users to create, assign, and monitor tasks, set deadlines, and oversee progress, all within a unified workspace that synchronizes seamlessly across Microsoft 365 applications. In contrast to conventional task management systems limited to specific platforms, Loop's Task List is both portable and dynamic; it can be integrated into Microsoft Teams chats, Outlook emails, Word documents, and Loop pages, with real-time updates reflected universally. Such instant synchronization distinguishes Loop, making its Task List component particularly valuable for environments where collaboration and rapid workflow are essential.

CHAPTER 6   EXPLORING ADVANCED FEATURES AND CUSTOMIZATIONS

To access Task List component, go to any Loop page, and look for "+" option, as shown in the Figure 6-1. Then from the list of components, look for Task list, as shown in Figure 6-2, and Task list appears, as shown in Figure 6-3.

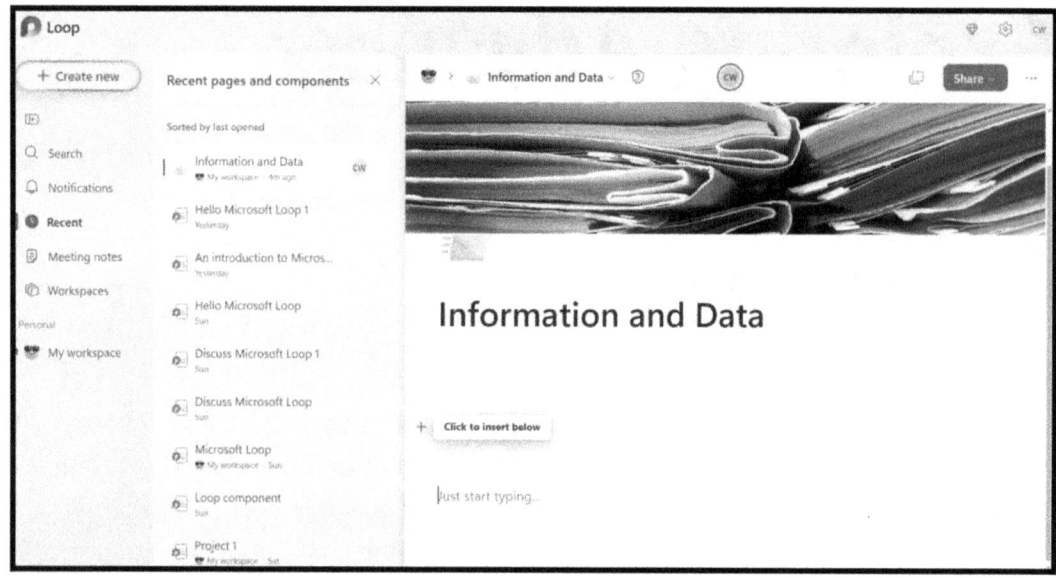

Figure 6-1. *"+" option visible*

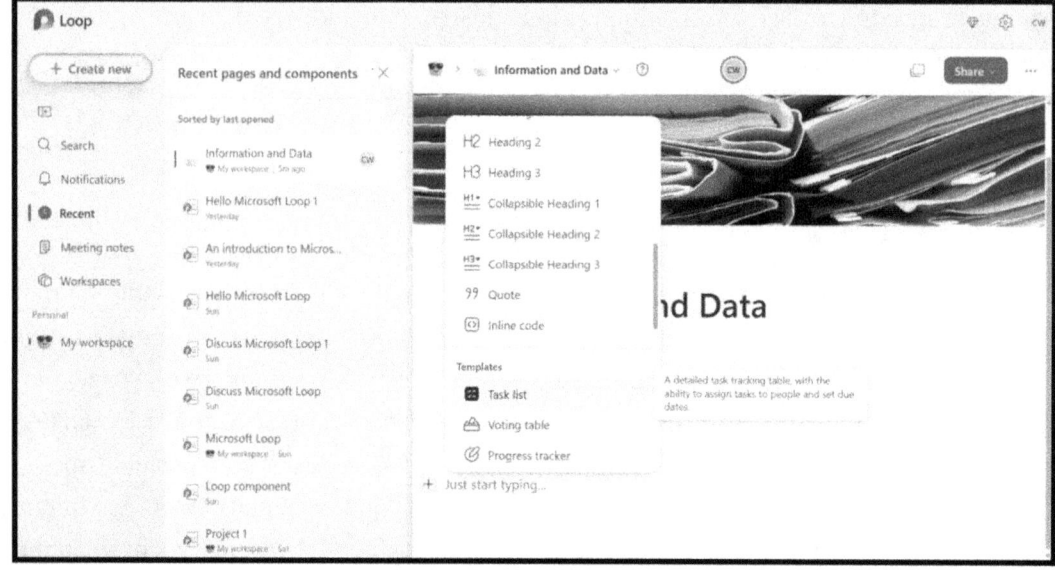

Figure 6-2. *Choose Task List as component*

170

CHAPTER 6   EXPLORING ADVANCED FEATURES AND CUSTOMIZATIONS

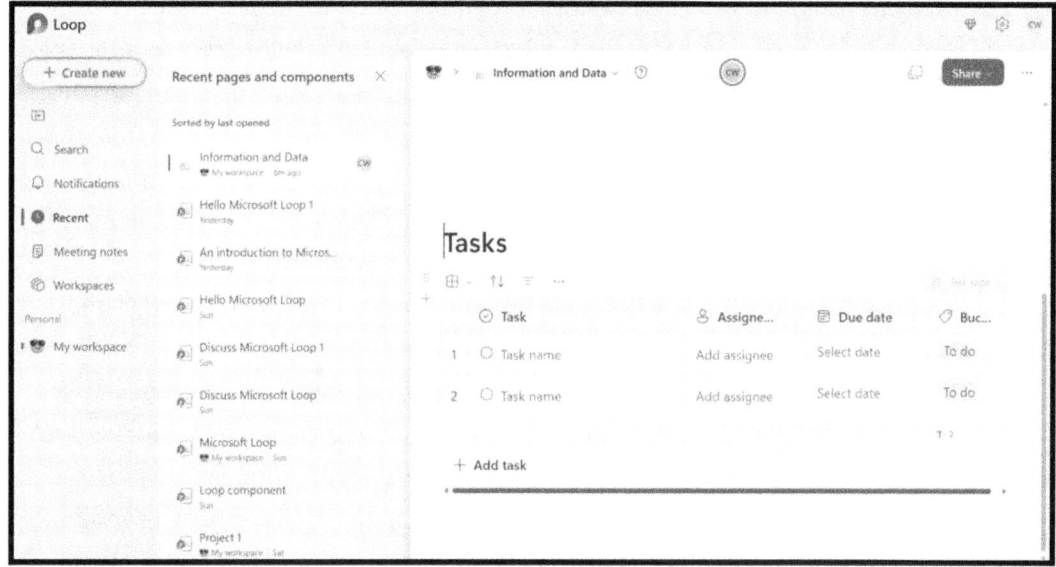

Figure 6-3. *Appearance of Task List*

The Task List component features several configurable fields for each task, permitting users to specify a task name or description, assign responsibility through the Microsoft 365 identity system, and establish deadlines via an integrated date picker. Each task offers a completion checkbox that serves as a visual progress indicator. Designed for clarity and ease of use, these fields enable teams to efficiently record and organize work without transitioning between applications or tools. Additionally, the component supports inline editing, allowing users to modify task details within ongoing conversations or documents, thereby eliminating the need to access a separate task management platform.

A primary benefit of the Task List component is its capability to support real-time collaboration. Multiple users are able to view and edit the task list concurrently, with changes instantly reflected for all participants. This feature eliminates the necessity for version control or manual updates, thereby ensuring that all team members access the most up-to-date information. For instance, within a Microsoft Teams meeting, a Task List can be seamlessly integrated into chat or meeting notes. As action items are discussed, tasks may be added, responsibilities assigned, and deadlines established in real time. These updates are immediately visible to all attendees and remain accessible within the same context following the meeting.

The Task List component is designed to integrate efficiently with other Microsoft Loop features, including Loop Pages and Workspaces. A Loop Page serves as a flexible canvas that enables the combination of various components—such as Task Lists, tables, and paragraphs—to facilitate the creation of comprehensive project dashboards or collaborative workspaces. Within a Loop Workspace, related pages and components are systematically grouped, allowing teams to structure their activities by project, department, or initiative. This organizational framework supports both detailed task tracking and overarching project management, positioning the Task List component as an effective solution for diverse professional scenarios.

The Task List component offers significant versatility across a broad range of use cases. It is suitable for daily task management, agile sprint planning, tracking meeting action items, onboarding procedures, event coordination, and more. For instance, marketing teams may utilize a Task List to monitor campaign deliverables by assigning responsibilities such as "Design banner ad," "Write blog post," and "Schedule social media posts" to individual team members with defined deadlines. Product teams can leverage the component to oversee feature development, with tasks like "Finalize UI mock-ups," "Conduct user testing," and "Prepare release notes." As the component integrates seamlessly with platforms such as Outlook and Teams, it aligns with existing workflows, minimizing the need for additional systems.

An additional significant advantage of the Task List component is its seamless integration with Microsoft Copilot, the AI-powered assistant embedded within Microsoft 365. Copilot assists users in generating task lists by analyzing meeting transcripts, emails, or project briefs. For example, following a meeting, Copilot may automatically propose tasks derived from the discussion, such as "Follow up with client," "Send proposal draft," or "Schedule next review." Furthermore, it can summarize task lists, highlight overdue items, and recommend prioritization strategies. This AI-driven integration enhances productivity by minimizing manual input and enabling teams to concentrate on their most critical objectives.

The Task List component is designed to be responsive and straightforward to navigate. Tasks are arranged vertically, with indicators showing assignees and due dates. Completed tasks are marked visually, often by being grayed out or checked, which assists users in tracking progress. The component offers drag-and-drop functionality for reordering tasks, as well as options to filter and sort tasks according to status, assignee, or deadline.

The Task List component fosters a culture of collaboration by promoting transparency and accountability within teams. With tasks made visible and clearly assigned to team members, responsibility and deadlines are easily identifiable. This level of visibility minimizes misunderstandings, supports consistent alignment, and encourages collective ownership. Additionally, the component facilitates proactive communication as team members are able to comment, update statuses, and identify issues directly within the system.

Security and compliance are integral to the Task List component, leveraging Microsoft 365's enterprise-grade protection. Strict access controls ensure that only authorized personnel can view or modify tasks, with data encryption implemented both in transit and at rest. Organizations have the capability to manage permissions at either the workspace or page level, thereby protecting sensitive information while enabling effective collaboration.

In conclusion, the Microsoft Loop Task List component serves as a comprehensive, adaptable, and intelligent solution for task management in collaborative settings. With its real-time editing functionality, seamless integration across Microsoft 365 applications, and support for AI-powered features, it distinguishes itself as a key element of the Loop platform. Suitable for both simple task lists and complex project management needs, the Task List component enhances team organization, alignment, and productivity. It redefines task management, transforming it from an isolated process to a dynamic, shared workflow that adapts to evolving team requirements and operational pace.

Voting Table

The Voting Table component within Microsoft Loop offers an advanced collaborative decision-making solution, enabling teams to evaluate options, articulate preferences, and achieve consensus efficiently. As part of the broader Loop platform, it facilitates modular and dynamic content creation throughout Microsoft 365 applications such as Teams, Outlook, Word, and OneNote. The Voting Table distinguishes itself as an interactive tool permitting users to vote on proposals or items directly within shared documents, chats, or emails—proving particularly effective for brainstorming, prioritization, or planning sessions. Using "+" option, a voting table can be accessed and published inside a loop page, as shown in Figures 6-4 and 6-5, respectively.

CHAPTER 6　EXPLORING ADVANCED FEATURES AND CUSTOMIZATIONS

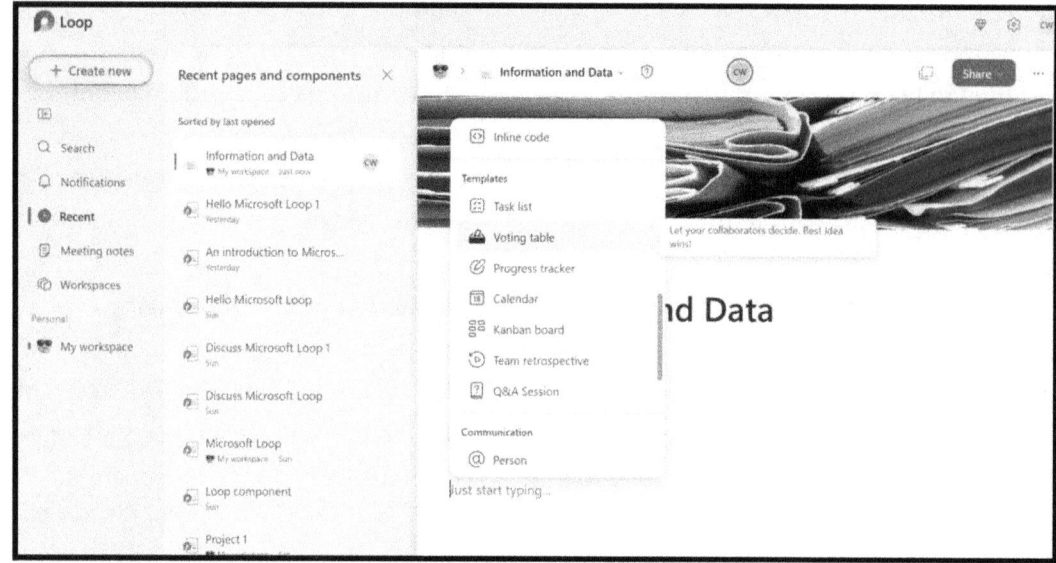

Figure 6-4. *Access Voting table using "+" option*

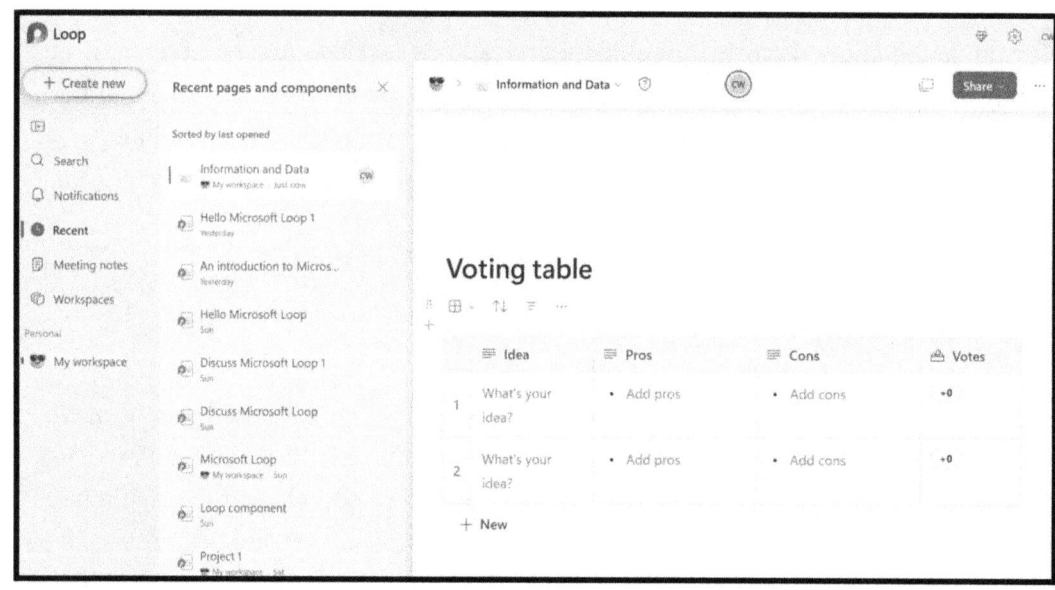

Figure 6-5. *Appearance of Voting table*

Fundamentally, the Voting Table is structured similarly to a spreadsheet or matrix: each row represents an item under consideration, while columns allow participants to cast votes or submit input. Its voting mechanisms are adaptable, featuring thumbs-up/thumbs-down icons, numerical ratings, emoji reactions, or custom labels according to specific use cases. This versatility ensures suitability for scenarios ranging from informal polls to formal evaluations.

A key feature of the Voting Table is its real-time collaboration capability. Any modifications made are instantly synchronized across all embedded instances, removing the need for manual tallying or version control. For instance, during a meeting in Microsoft Teams, participants may vote on ideas with immediate updates visible to all. The same synchronicity applies when the Voting Table appears in Outlook emails, guaranteeing unified and current data wherever accessed.

Additionally, the Voting Table supports rich contextual collaboration, allowing users to append comments or notes alongside each item. This fosters thoughtful participation and provides clarity regarding individual voting rationales and suggestions for improvement. Such annotations enhance the depth and quality of team discussions, promoting more informed decisions.

From a design and usability standpoint, the Voting Table is intuitive and visually organized. Items are presented in rows with voting options in columns, facilitating straightforward result comparison. It supports sorting and filtering to highlight popular or contentious topics, as well as visual enhancements like color-coding, progress bars, and vote counts for improved engagement and readability.

Regarding use cases, the Voting Table is highly adaptable. It can be employed for task prioritization in sprint backlogs, workshop topic selection, design mockup reviews, vendor proposal assessments, and team event planning. For example, marketing teams may use the component to determine preferred campaign initiatives, while human resources may gather feedback on employee programs through collaborative voting.

Integration with Microsoft Copilot further amplifies the Voting Table's utility. Copilot can summarize voting results, identify trends, and recommend next steps, expediting movement from discussion to action. Additionally, Copilot assists in generating Voting Tables by suggesting items based on meeting transcripts, emails, or project briefs.

The Voting Table encourages a democratic and inclusive culture in collaboration by providing every team member with an opportunity to participate in decision-making processes. It enhances transparency, inclusiveness, and brings forth diverse perspectives, particularly within hybrid or remote teams.

Robust security and compliance measures are integral, leveraging Microsoft 365's enterprise-grade protection. Access controls restrict viewing and editing to authorized personnel, and all data benefits from encryption both in transit and at rest. Permission management is available at workspace and page levels, ensuring sensitive information remains secure.

Furthermore, the Voting Table can be embedded within Loop Pages, which function as comprehensive workspaces incorporating multiple components such as Task Lists, summary paragraphs, or progress trackers. These pages can be grouped into Loop Workspaces for project, team, or initiative-based organization, supporting both detailed input and overarching strategies.

In conclusion, the Microsoft Loop Voting Table component serves as a sophisticated, versatile, and intelligent resource for collaborative decision-making. Its seamless integration, real-time capabilities, and AI support position it as an invaluable asset for fast, informed, and inclusive team actions, fundamentally transforming how groups engage in voting and consensus-building across Microsoft 365.

Progressive Tracker

The Progress Tracker component within Microsoft Loop is an advanced and user-friendly solution engineered to support teams in visualizing and overseeing the status of tasks, projects, or workflows in real time. Integrated into the broader Loop ecosystem, which prioritizes modularity, portability, and live collaboration across Microsoft 365 applications, the Progress Tracker significantly enhances transparency, accountability, and team alignment. It presents a systematic framework for delineating stages of work, simplifying comprehension of completed, ongoing, and pending items for all stakeholders. This component proves particularly beneficial in collaborative settings involving multiple contributors working on interdependent tasks where visibility is essential for effective coordination and decision-making. Using "+" option, a Progressive Tracker can be accessed and published inside a loop page, as shown in Figures 6-6 and 6-7, respectively.

CHAPTER 6 EXPLORING ADVANCED FEATURES AND CUSTOMIZATIONS

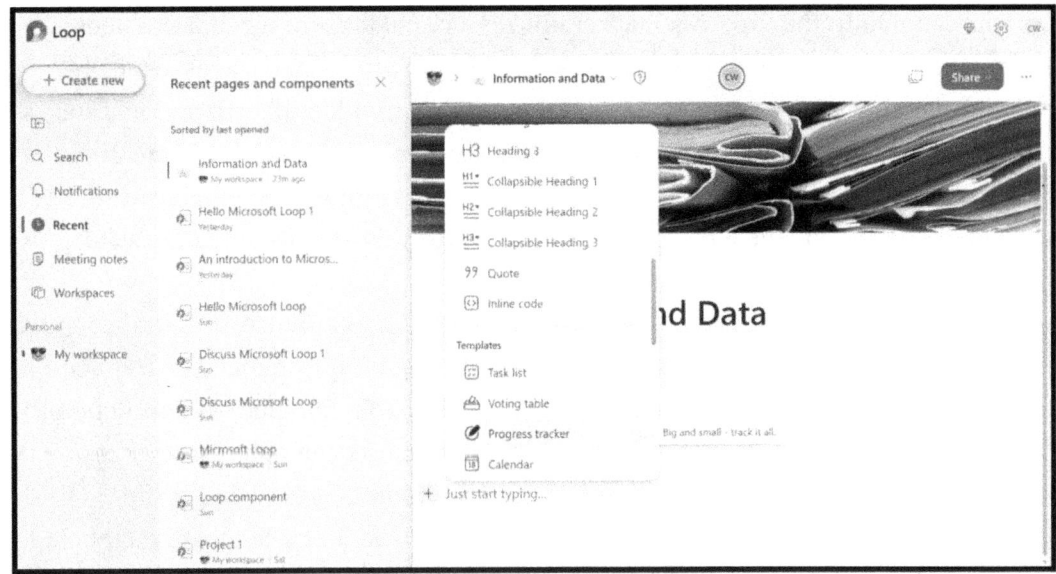

Figure 6-6. *Access Progressive Tracker*

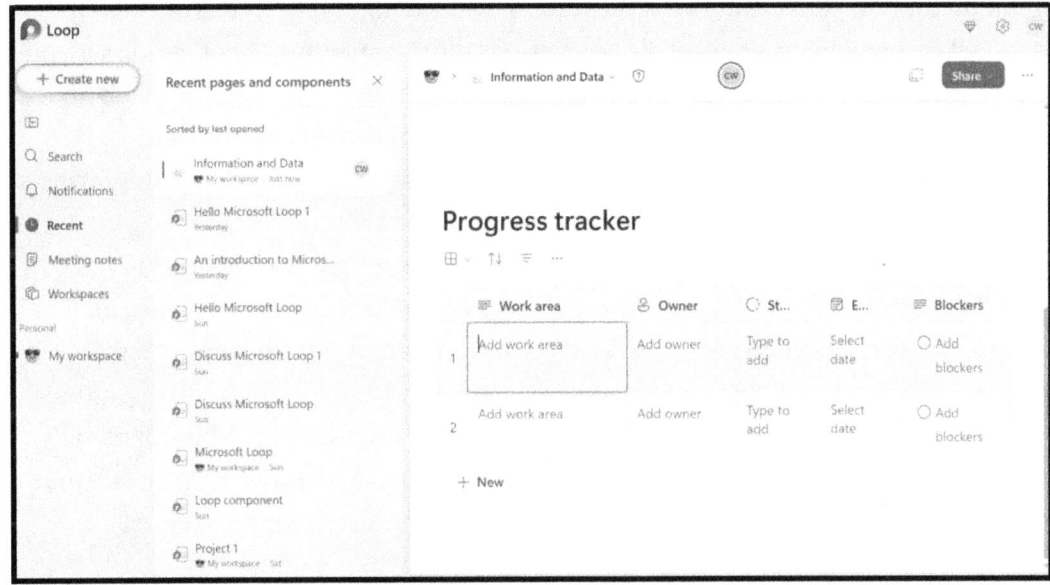

Figure 6-7. *Display of Progressive Tracker*

CHAPTER 6   EXPLORING ADVANCED FEATURES AND CUSTOMIZATIONS

Fundamentally, the Progress Tracker utilizes a visual table or list that classifies items—such as tasks, deliverables, or milestones—into predefined stages, typically including labels such as "Not Started," "In Progress," "Completed," with optional stages such as "Blocked" or "Deferred" tailored to specific workflows. Each entry receives a status, and the tracker updates instantaneously as users modify content, ensuring all participants access the most accurate information regardless of their platform, be it Microsoft Teams, Outlook, Word, or Loop itself.

The design of the component emphasizes clarity and ease of use, presenting items in rows and their statuses in corresponding columns, frequently enhanced by color coding for improved legibility. For instance, green may indicate "Completed," yellow denotes "In Progress," and grey marks "Not Started." These visual cues enable quick assessment of project health. The Progress Tracker also accommodates filtering and sorting functions, empowering users to concentrate on particular categories, team members, or deadlines—a versatility that suits both comprehensive overviews and detailed management requirements.

A notable feature is the real-time collaboration capability, allowing multiple users to simultaneously update and view the tracker, with changes reflected immediately across all embedded instances. This is invaluable during meetings or planning sessions, enabling live status updates and issue identification. Updates made during such interactions are instantly accessible, providing a continuous record of progress.

Seamless integration with other Loop components and Microsoft 365 tools further enhances utility. The Progress Tracker can be embedded alongside Task Lists, Voting Tables, Paragraphs, and additional elements within Loop Pages to construct holistic project dashboards. Within Loop Workspaces, related pages and components are organized for enhanced oversight and strategic planning, supporting both granular tracking and broader initiative management across diverse team sizes and disciplines.

Regarding use cases, the Progress Tracker demonstrates considerable adaptability. It is suitable for managing software development sprints, marketing campaigns, event planning, product launches, onboarding processes, among others. For example, a product team might monitor feature development with tasks such as "Design UI," "Implement backend," "Conduct QA," and "Deploy to production," updating each item's status as progress occurs. Similarly, human resources teams can oversee onboarding via tasks like "Complete paperwork," "Set up accounts," and "Schedule orientation."

An additional advantage is its integration with Microsoft Copilot, the AI-powered assistant within Microsoft 365. Copilot analyzes tracker data to generate summaries, identify trends, and recommend actions. For instance, it can highlight if a significant portion of tasks remain "Not Started" and suggest resource reallocation or timeline adjustments. It can also pinpoint bottlenecks, thereby enabling more proactive management.

The Progress Tracker fosters a culture of transparency and accountability by making statuses visible to all team members, clarifying responsibilities and progress. This encourages timely updates, shared ownership, and supports informed decision-making by managers and stakeholders without necessitating extra reporting or meetings.

Security and compliance are integral, with the Progress Tracker inheriting Microsoft 365's enterprise-grade protections. Access controls ensure only authorized personnel can view or edit the component, and data encryption protects information in transit and at rest. Organizations may manage permissions at various levels to safeguard sensitive data while facilitating appropriate collaboration.

From a usability perspective, the component is designed for efficiency and intuitiveness. Users can easily modify statuses, add context through comments or notes, and rearrange items as priorities evolve, thanks to drag-and-drop functionality. Integration with other Microsoft tools, such as Planner and To Do, enables task synchronization and consistency across platforms.

In summary, the Microsoft Loop Progress Tracker component represents a robust, adaptable, and intelligent instrument for visualizing and managing work progression in collaborative environments. Its real-time editing, seamless integration throughout Microsoft 365, and AI-driven insights distinguish it as an essential element of the Loop platform. Whether deployed for task tracking, workflow management, or milestone monitoring, the Progress Tracker enables teams to remain aligned, informed, and productive, transforming the nature of progress tracking into a dynamic, shared endeavor responsive to organizational needs and evolving work demands.

Kanban Board

The Kanban Board component in Microsoft Loop serves as a sophisticated, visual tool for effective task and workflow management. Drawing from traditional Kanban methodology, it organizes work into columns that represent various stages of progress. Microsoft Loop's implementation of the Kanban Board offers dynamic tracking of tasks from initiation to completion with customizable formatting to suit specific team processes. Integration with Microsoft 365 applications—including Teams, Outlook,

CHAPTER 6 EXPLORING ADVANCED FEATURES AND CUSTOMIZATIONS

Word, and OneNote—ensures accessibility and seamless collaboration. Using "+" option, a Kanban Board can be accessed and published inside a loop page, as shown in Figures 6-8 and 6-9, respectively.

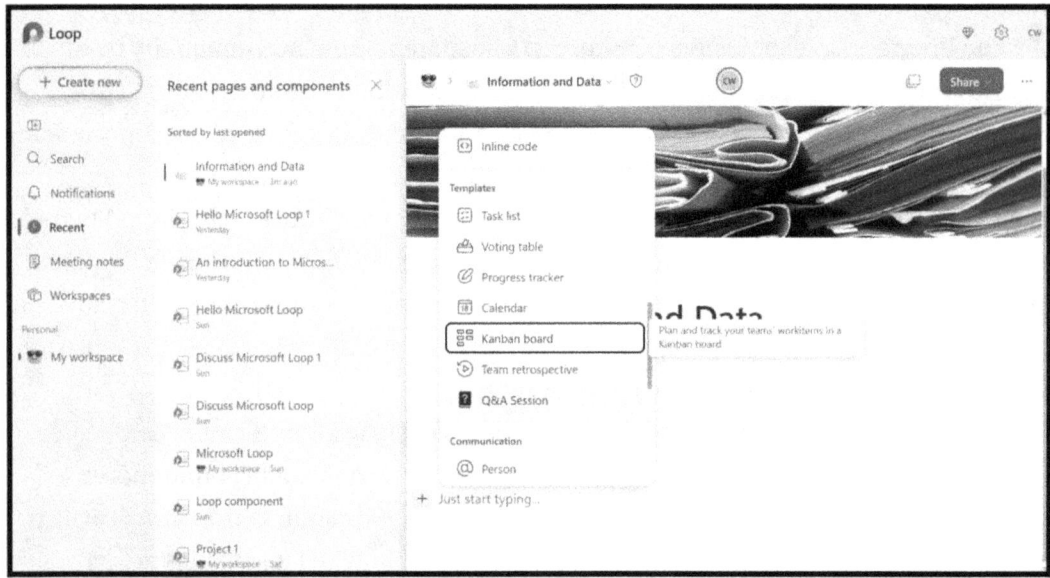

Figure 6-8. *Access Kanban Board*

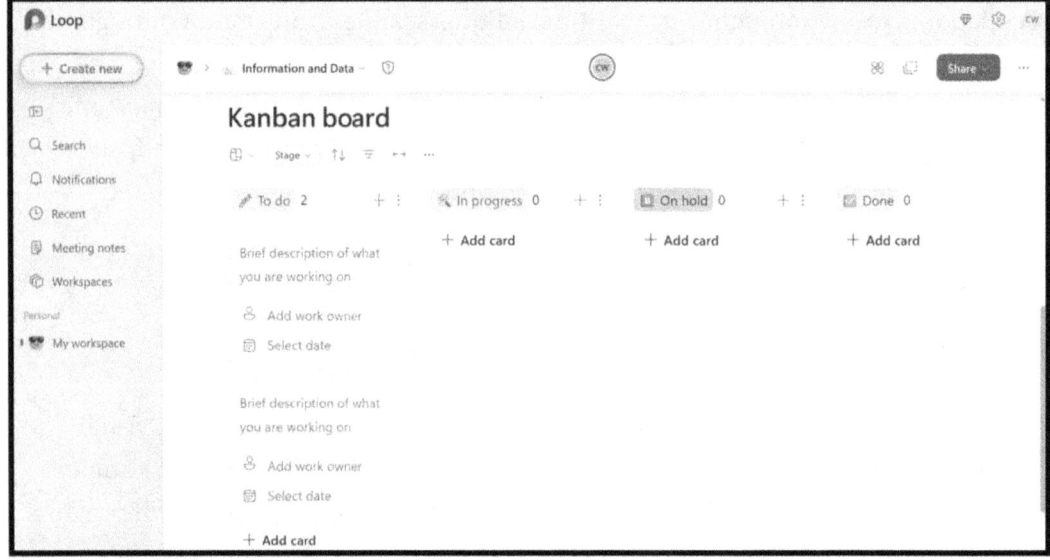

Figure 6-9. *Display Kanban Board*

To utilize the Kanban Board within Loop, users can insert the component by typing /Kanban board on a Loop page. The default configuration includes "To Do," "In Progress," and "Done" columns, which can be renamed for workflow customization. For instance, design teams may select "Draft," "Review," and "Publish," while development teams may opt for "Backlog," "In Development," and "QA." This adaptability ensures accurate reflection of operational stages.

Each board item is presented as a card, containing essential details such as titles, descriptions, labels, assignees, due dates, and embedded Loop components like checklists or notes. Cards are easily moved between columns via drag-and-drop, facilitating efficient status updates during meetings or collaborative sessions. Comments added directly to cards streamline communication, reducing reliance on separate channels and supporting contextual dialogue—beneficial for both remote and hybrid teams.

A key attribute of the Kanban Board is its real-time synchronization, ensuring immediate visibility of changes, such as moving cards, updating labels, or adding comments, for all collaborators. Regardless of the platform—Teams, Outlook, Word—the board remains interactive and current, eliminating issues arising from outdated information or version discrepancies.

The Ribbon Menu provides extensive customization options, including alternative views such as Table or Calendar format. Cards can be grouped by label to facilitate organization by criteria like priority, department, or theme. Users can add labels using /Label in the card description and create new groupings as needed. Sorting and filtering features further support targeted task management based on parameters such as due date, assignee, or status.

Another notable capability is the option to convert the Kanban Board into a Loop component, enabling portability and embedding across multiple Loop pages and workspaces. Centralized boards maintain consistency, reflecting updates wherever embedded and reducing redundant administration.

Integration extends to additional Microsoft tools, including Teams and Whiteboard. Teams can embed boards within channels to enhance stand-ups or sprint reviews; card titles may link to individual Loop pages for comprehensive task management without overburdening the main board. This layered structure accommodates both high-level planning and detailed execution.

The Kanban Board supports a wide range of professional use cases: agile sprint planning, marketing campaign management, product development, event coordination, and content creation. Product teams, for example, may track feature development across "Design," "Development," "Testing," and "Release," while marketing teams can manage assets through "Ideation," "Production," and "Scheduled" columns.

Moreover, the Kanban Board fosters transparency and accountability by making task assignments and progress visible to all team members. This clarity minimizes misunderstandings, aligns team efforts, and encourages shared ownership. Direct commenting, status updates, and issue flagging within the board promote proactive communication.

Security and compliance considerations are integral, as the Kanban Board leverages Microsoft 365's enterprise-grade protections. Access controls restrict view and edit permissions to authorized individuals, and all data is encrypted in transit and at rest. Organizations can further tailor permissions at workspace or page levels to safeguard sensitive information.

Finally, integration with Microsoft Copilot introduces AI-driven assistance for task management. Copilot can summarize activity, identify workflow bottlenecks, suggest prioritization strategies, and generate new cards based on meeting notes or project briefs. Following planning discussions, Copilot may recommend actions such as finalizing budgets, drafting timelines, and assigning roles—enhancing productivity and focus.

In conclusion, the Microsoft Loop Kanban Board component offers an advanced, flexible solution for visual task management. Its real-time editing, customizable layouts, comprehensive Microsoft 365 integration, and AI-enabled insights position it as a valuable asset for team organization and productivity. The board transforms static task lists into dynamic, collaborative workspaces responsive to evolving project needs.

Team Retrospective

The Team Retrospective component in Microsoft Loop is a collaborative tool designed to help teams reflect on their work, share feedback, and continuously improve their processes. Rooted in agile methodologies, retrospectives are a key practice for teams that value transparency, learning, and iterative development. Microsoft Loop brings this practice into the modern digital workspace by offering a dynamic, real-time retrospective board that can be embedded across Microsoft 365 apps such as Teams, Outlook, Word, and OneNote. This component enables teams to conduct structured

CHAPTER 6 EXPLORING ADVANCED FEATURES AND CUSTOMIZATIONS

retrospectives directly within their existing workflows, making it easier to capture insights, foster open communication, and drive actionable improvements. Using "+" option, a Team Retrospective can be accessed and published inside a loop page, as shown in Figures 6-10 and 6-11, respectively.

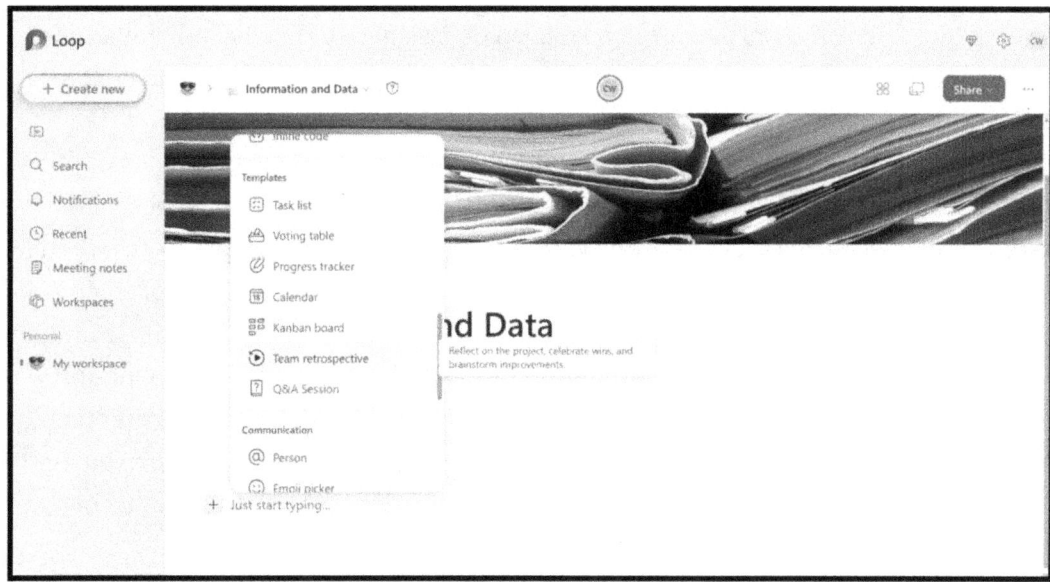

Figure 6-10. *Access Team Retrospective*

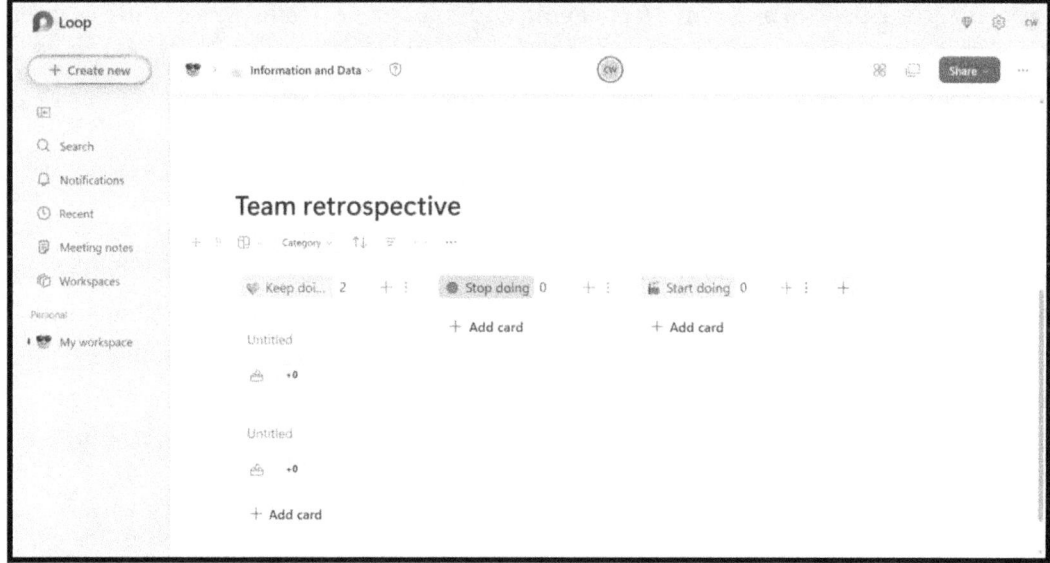

Figure 6-11. *Display Team retrospective*

CHAPTER 6   EXPLORING ADVANCED FEATURES AND CUSTOMIZATIONS

The Team Retrospective component is typically structured around three core categories: What went well, What didn't go well, and What can be improved. These categories provide a simple yet effective framework for organizing feedback and guiding discussion. When a retrospective board is created in Loop, team members can add their thoughts under each category in the form of editable cards. Each card can include a title, description, and comments, and can be tagged or assigned to specific individuals for follow-up. This format encourages participation from all team members and ensures that feedback is captured in a consistent and actionable way.

One of the most powerful aspects of the Team Retrospective component is its real-time collaboration capability. As with all Loop components, any changes made to the retrospective board are instantly visible to all collaborators, regardless of where they're accessing it. For example, during a retrospective meeting in Microsoft Teams, participants can add feedback to the board as the discussion unfolds, and those updates will be reflected live for everyone. Similarly, if the board is embedded in an Outlook email or a Word document, team members can contribute asynchronously, and their input will sync automatically. This real-time synchronization eliminates the need for manual consolidation and ensures that everyone is working with the most current information.

The component also supports rich contextual collaboration. Users can comment on individual cards, mention teammates to draw attention to specific items, and use emojis or reactions to express agreement or highlight important points. These features make the retrospective board more engaging and interactive, fostering a culture of open communication and psychological safety. For example, a team member might add a card under "What didn't go well," noting that sprint planning felt rushed, and others can comment with their perspectives or suggest solutions. This threaded discussion helps teams explore issues in depth and build consensus around improvements.

From a design and usability standpoint, the Team Retrospective component is clean, intuitive, and customizable. Teams can rename the default categories to better suit their needs—for instance, using "Start," "Stop," and "Continue" or "Highlights," "Challenges," and "Ideas." Cards can be color-coded, grouped, or sorted to enhance readability and organization. The board supports drag-and-drop functionality, allowing users to rearrange items as priorities shift or themes emerge. These features make it easy to adapt the retrospective format to different team cultures and workflows.

CHAPTER 6 EXPLORING ADVANCED FEATURES AND CUSTOMIZATIONS

In terms of use cases, the Team Retrospective component is highly versatile. It can be used by software development teams at the end of each sprint, by marketing teams after a campaign launch, by operations teams following a major incident, or by any group looking to reflect on a completed project or milestone. For example, a product team might use the board to review a recent release, capturing feedback on collaboration, timelines, and quality. A customer support team might use it to analyze a spike in support tickets, identifying what worked well in their response and what could be improved for future incidents.

Another major benefit of the Team Retrospective component is its integration with Microsoft Copilot, the AI-powered assistant built into Microsoft 365. Copilot can help summarize the feedback collected on the board, identify recurring themes, and suggest action items. For instance, after a retrospective session, Copilot might generate a summary like "Team noted strong collaboration and timely delivery as positives. Key challenges included unclear requirements and limited testing time. Suggested improvements include earlier stakeholder engagement and dedicated QA resources." This AI-generated insight helps teams move from reflection to action more efficiently and ensures that learning is documented and shared.

The Team Retrospective component also promotes a culture of continuous improvement. By regularly reflecting on their work and discussing what can be done better, teams build habits of learning and adaptation. The visibility of the board encourages accountability, as action items can be tracked and revisited in future retrospectives. It also helps teams celebrate successes, recognize contributions, and maintain morale. For example, highlighting "What went well" can reinforce positive behaviors and motivate team members.

Security and compliance are built into the Team Retrospective component, as it inherits Microsoft 365's enterprise-grade protections. Access controls ensure that only authorized users can view or edit the board, and all data is encrypted both in transit and at rest. Organizations can manage permissions at the workspace or page level, ensuring sensitive feedback is protected while enabling collaboration where appropriate.

The retrospective board can be embedded within Loop Pages, which serve as canvases for organizing multiple components into a cohesive workspace. A Loop Page might include the Team Retrospective board alongside a Task List for action items, a Paragraph summary of the meeting, and a Progress Tracker for follow-up. These pages can be grouped within Loop Workspaces, which organize related content by project, team, or initiative. This structure supports both reflection and execution, making the Team Retrospective component a valuable part of the broader collaboration ecosystem.

CHAPTER 6 EXPLORING ADVANCED FEATURES AND CUSTOMIZATIONS

In summary, the Microsoft Loop Team Retrospective component is a robust, flexible, and intelligent tool for facilitating team reflection and continuous improvement. Its real-time editing capabilities, customizable layout, seamless integration across Microsoft 365 apps, and support for AI-powered insights make it a standout feature of the Loop platform. Whether used for agile retrospectives, project reviews, or team health checks, the component empowers teams to share feedback, learn from experience, and grow together. It transforms retrospectives from a static reporting exercise into a dynamic, collaborative experience that evolves with the needs of the team and the pace of work.

Q&A Session

The **Q&A Session component** in Microsoft Loop is a collaborative tool intended to facilitate structured question-and-answer interactions within teams, projects, and shared documents. It is part of the Loop ecosystem, which supports modular, real-time, and portable collaboration across Microsoft 365 applications such as Teams, Outlook, Word, and OneNote. The Q&A component allows users to pose questions and provide answers in a format that can be easily read, updated, and shared. This structure is used for knowledge sharing, onboarding, brainstorming, and feedback collection. Using "+" option, a Q&A Session can be accessed and published inside a loop page, as shown in Figures 6-12 and 6-13, respectively.

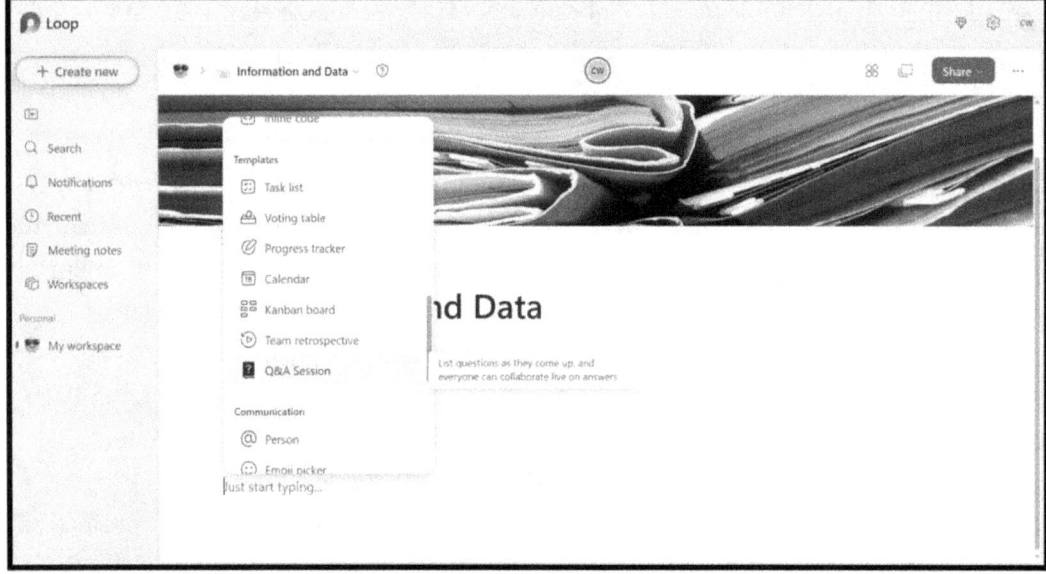

Figure 6-12. *Access Q&A Session*

CHAPTER 6   EXPLORING ADVANCED FEATURES AND CUSTOMIZATIONS

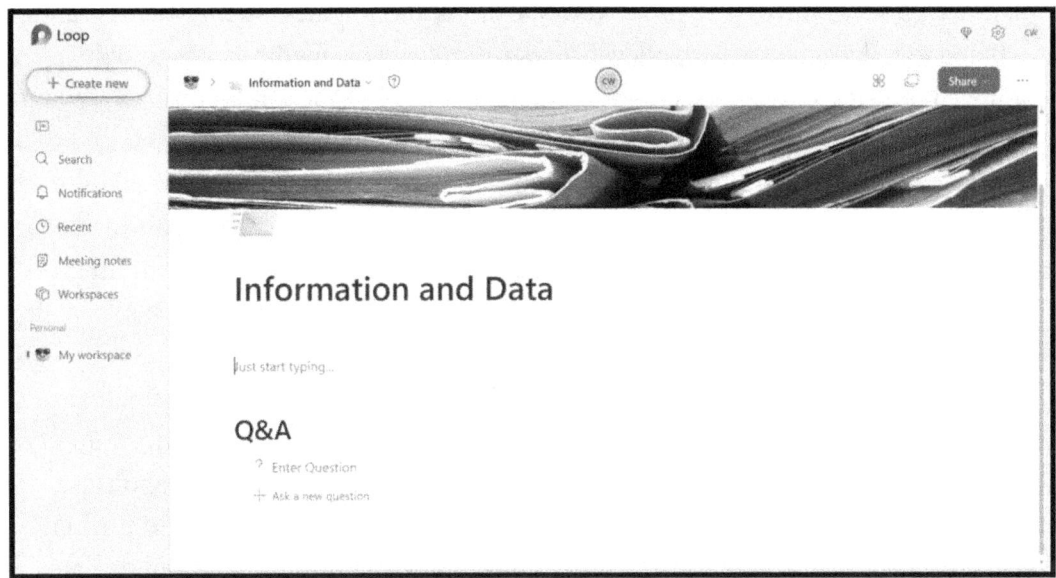

Figure 6-13. Display for Q&A Session

The core of the Q&A component is a series of entries, each consisting of a question paired with its corresponding answer. These entries are editable and may be commented on, tagged, or assigned to specific individuals. The structured format is designed to help teams organize information effectively. For example, a project manager might use the Q&A component to gather input from stakeholders with questions like "What are the key risks for this phase?" or "What dependencies should we be aware of?" Team members can respond directly within the component, making responses visible to all participants in real time.

A notable feature of the Q&A component is its **real-time collaboration** capability. Any changes made to Q&A entries are immediately reflected wherever the component is embedded, including Teams chats, Outlook emails, and Word documents. This approach is intended to ensure that information remains current and eliminates the need for version control or manual updates. The component also supports asynchronous collaboration, enabling users to contribute at different times while maintaining a centralized discussion record.

The Q&A component can be used in **onboarding scenarios**, where new team members require access to frequently asked questions and organizational knowledge. By embedding a Q&A component in a Loop page or workspace, organizations can create a dynamic FAQ that evolves over time. New questions and updated answers can be added as needed to reflect changes in policy, process, or tools. This method aims to reduce repetitive inquiries and helps team members find answers independently.

In **project planning and execution**, the Q&A component is utilized for clarifying requirements, resolving ambiguities, and documenting decisions. During sessions such as sprint planning, developers might ask questions about expected behaviors for features or potential edge cases. Product owners or designers can respond directly within the component, providing transparency and creating a record of dialogue accessible to all relevant parties.

The Q&A component also accommodates **feedback collection and brainstorming**. Teams can submit open-ended questions, such as suggestions for future improvements or ways to enhance customer satisfaction. Multiple users can contribute responses, and the component includes options for reactions and comments to support further discussion. This format is designed to encourage participation and bring out diverse perspectives.

From a **design and usability** perspective, the Q&A component offers intuitive and customizable features. Users can format text, add labels, tag people using the @ symbol, and insert other Loop elements such as dates or links. Each question–answer pair is displayed in a clear layout, and entries can be reordered or grouped by theme. The drag-and-drop functionality enables users to organize content as discussions progress. Integration with Loop Pages and Workspaces makes it possible to embed Q&A sessions within wider collaboration contexts.

The component integrates with **Microsoft Copilot**, the AI-powered assistant in Microsoft 365. Copilot can analyze Q&A entries, summarize key points, and suggest follow-up actions. For instance, after a brainstorming session, Copilot may generate a summary of main areas for improvement and recommend steps such as creating checklists or updating documentation. This output is intended to assist teams in moving from discussion to action efficiently.

The Q&A component aims to support a **culture of transparency and shared learning**. By documenting questions and answers in a centralized manner, teams build repositories of information for current and future reference. This approach is designed to foster open communication, minimize reliance on informal channels, and reinforce accountability. Decisions documented via Q&A entries can be referenced later to explain rationale or revisit context.

Security and compliance features are included, as the component inherits Microsoft 365's protections. Access controls determine who can view or edit the component, and data is encrypted during transfer and storage. Permissions can be managed at the workspace or page level, balancing security needs with collaboration.

With respect to **use cases**, the Q&A component has broad applicability. It is used for team retrospectives, customer support documentation, training session Q&As, and product development clarification, among others. Its structured format and real-time capabilities allow for use in both formal and informal settings, supporting synchronous and asynchronous work.

To summarize, the Microsoft Loop Q&A Session component provides a means for structured dialogue and collaborative knowledge management. Its editing capabilities, customizable layout, integration with Microsoft 365 apps, and support for AI-based insights are features within the Loop platform. The Q&A component is employed for onboarding, project planning, feedback collection, brainstorming, and other collaborative activities, aiming to enhance clarity, continuous learning, and effective teamwork. It transforms question-and-answer exchanges into ongoing, collective experiences that adapt to team requirements and workflows.

Calender

The Calendar component in Microsoft Loop is a scheduling tool that supports teams in managing activities, meetings, and deadlines within shared workspaces. As part of the Loop system, which focuses on modular and real-time collaboration across Microsoft 365 applications, the Calendar component integrates time management into daily workflows. Users are able to embed calendar views and date elements into Loop pages, enabling planning and coordination without needing to switch between other apps like Outlook or Teams. Using "+" option, a Calendar can be accessed and published inside a loop page, as shown in Figures 6-14 and 6-15, respectively.

CHAPTER 6 EXPLORING ADVANCED FEATURES AND CUSTOMIZATIONS

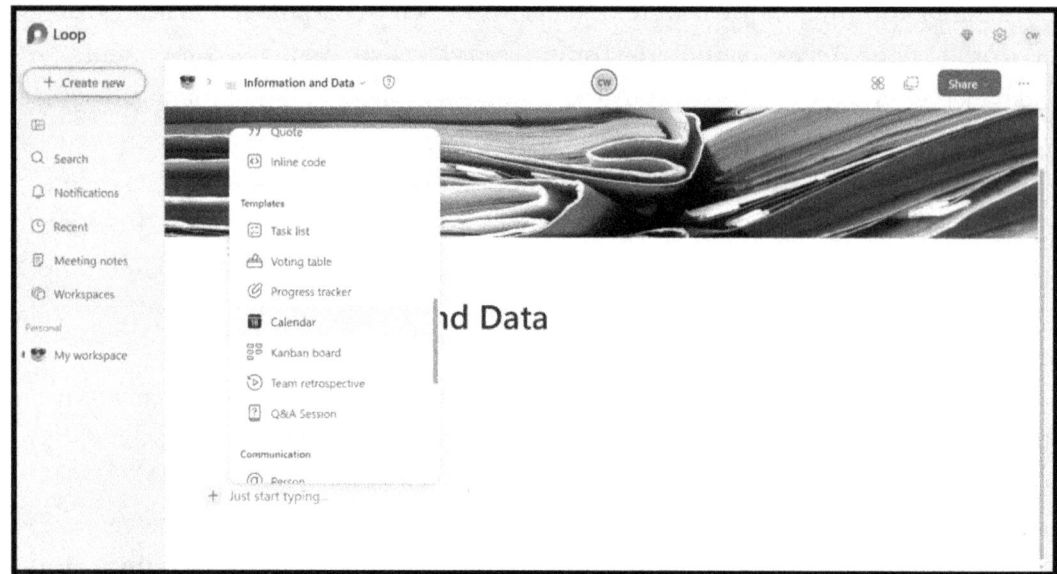

Figure 6-14. Access Calendar component

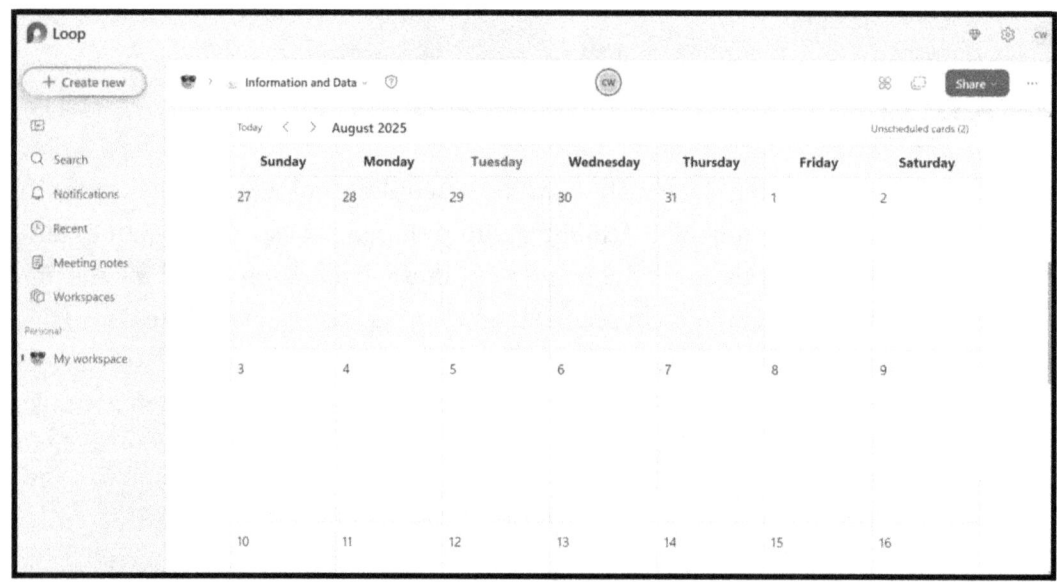

Figure 6-15. Display of Calander component

Although Microsoft Loop does not yet provide a stand-alone calendar comparable to Outlook Calendar, it offers calendar-like features using components such as the Date Picker, Task List with due dates, and Meeting Notes integration. These can be used together within Loop pages to support interactive scheduling. For instance, users may insert a Date component in a table to assign deadlines or use a Task List to monitor project milestones. These components update in real time and are accessible from different Microsoft 365 applications, ensuring consistency on timelines and responsibilities.

A frequent application of the Calendar component is meeting management. Teams may add Loop components to recurring meetings scheduled through Microsoft Teams or Outlook. For example, a weekly meeting might employ a Loop agenda, notes, and action items associated with particular dates. If a meeting's schedule changes, related Loop components can be updated or removed accordingly.

To manage recurring meetings, some users set up a dedicated Loop workspace for storing meeting documentation. Each meeting occurrence can have an individual Loop page featuring a calendar-linked agenda and notes. This centralization allows participants to reference previous meetings and observe ongoing progress. The "Add to Workspace" feature is available to organize notes by date or topic.

The Date component operates as a calendar element that users can place into tables, task lists, or paragraphs. It enables date selection from a calendar picker and association with tasks, events, or notes. This is applicable for planning purposes where deadlines and milestones are tracked. Teams planning campaigns, for example, might link specific tasks to dates and update them collaboratively, with instant synchronization across all instances.

Loop also offers calendar-style views via integrations with other components. Users may convert Kanban Boards or Task Lists to calendar views, showing tasks organized by due date. While this is not the same as a traditional calendar grid, it provides a timeline-based visualization for planning and prioritization.

Real-time synchronization is supported for calendar-related components. Changes to dates made in Loop pages, Teams chats, or Outlook emails are reflected consistently wherever embedded, supporting collaboration and reducing miscommunication. This feature accommodates both synchronous and asynchronous teamwork.

The Calendar component integrates with Microsoft Copilot, the AI assistant in Microsoft 365. Copilot can analyze schedules, identify potential conflicts, and suggest adjustments based on existing Loop data. It can also generate summaries of approaching deadlines or meeting agendas.

From a usability perspective, the Calendar component aims to offer an intuitive experience. Dates can be inserted with slash commands (/date), tasks moved between dates, and views filtered by time frame. Tagging and comments are available for annotation, while integration with labels and person tags adds additional context.

Regarding collaboration, embedding dates and schedules in shared workspaces aims to improve alignment on timelines and responsibilities. This approach makes information visible within the team and supports workflows requiring frequent updates.

Security and compliance features are consistent with Microsoft 365 protections. Access controls determine who is authorized to view or edit calendar data, with encryption applied in transit and at rest. Permissions can be managed at various levels to protect sensitive information.

In summary, Microsoft Loop currently does not include a stand-alone calendar, but its Calendar component—through date elements, task scheduling, and meeting integration—provides tools for collaborative time management. Real-time editing, integration across Microsoft 365, and AI insights are available. The component is suitable for uses such as meeting agendas, project timelines, or campaign planning, helping teams coordinate and stay organized within their workflow.

General Features to Support and Improve Content

In Microsoft Loop, there are features to support and improve content. These features helps to collaborate and share using content with multiple people team. As shown in Figures 6-16 and 6-16-1, examples of these features are New Subpage, Table, Checklist, Bulleted list, Numbered list, Date, Callout, Code, Mermaid, Math equation, Table of content, divider, and inline equation. In Figure 6-16-1, there are text styles such as Paragraph, Heading 1, Heading 2, Heading 3, Collapsible Heading 1, Collapsible Heading 2, Collapsible Heading 3, Quote, and Inline Code.

CHAPTER 6   EXPLORING ADVANCED FEATURES AND CUSTOMIZATIONS

Figure 6-16. *Examples of General feature in Microsoft Loop*

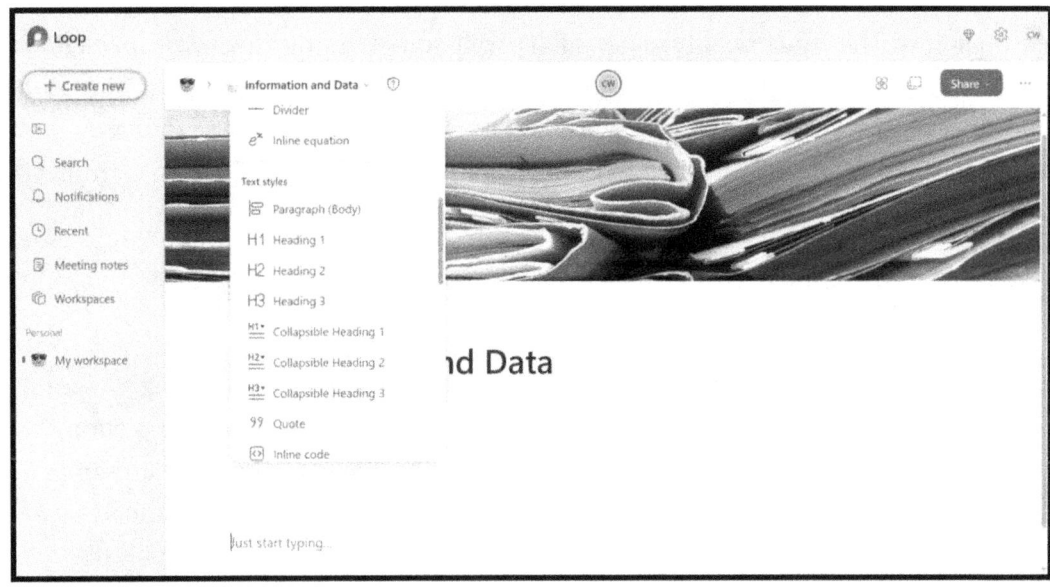

Figure 6-16-1. *Examples of General feature in Microsoft Loop*

193

New Subpage

A *New Subpage* in Microsoft Loop enables users to establish a nested page within a primary Loop workspace, facilitating hierarchical organization of content. This functionality is particularly useful for managing complex projects or ideas by segmenting topics into manageable sections, such as meeting notes, task lists, or research components. Subpages are compatible with all Loop components and support full collaboration, allowing team members to edit and comment in real time. To create a subpage, simply click the "+" icon or enter /subpage. This feature significantly enhances document clarity and structure, particularly in extensive collaborative environments.

Table

The *Table* component within Loop is a versatile grid designed to organize data in rows and columns. It accommodates multiple content types, including text, dates, checkboxes, and links. Tables are live and collaborative, enabling all contributors to view updates in real time. Users can sort, filter, and format columns according to their requirements. This functionality makes tables well-suited for tracking tasks, managing inventories, or planning events. Additionally, tables can be embedded across Microsoft 365 applications to provide seamless accessibility. To create a table, type /table; customization options include headers and formatting adjustments to align with specific workflows.

Checklist

A Checklist in Loop serves as an efficient and versatile solution for managing tasks and to-do items. Each entry features a checkbox that users may select upon completion. Checklists support collaboration, enabling multiple users to contribute updates in real time. Tasks can be assigned using @mentions, and comments may be added to provide additional context. This component is particularly well-suited for daily task management, project planning, or tracking action items from meetings. It facilitates team alignment and accountability. To create a checklist, type /checklist. Items can be reordered, nested, and embedded within other Loop pages or Microsoft 365 applications.

Bulleted List

The *Bulleted List* component enables users to organize information, ideas, or tasks in a non-sequential format. Each element is denoted by a bullet point, facilitating easy scanning and comprehension. Bulleted lists are particularly useful for activities such as brainstorming, agenda outlining, or discussion summarization. They offer support for rich text formatting, including links, mentions, and emojis. As with other Loop components, they are collaborative tools that update in real time. To create a bullet list, type /bulleted list. Items can be indented to establish sublists, allowing for hierarchical organization of content. This functionality promotes clarity and supports efficient idea documentation.

Numbered List

A Numbered List serves to organize information in a sequential or prioritized manner. Each entry is automatically numbered, making this format well-suited for step-by-step instructions, ranked concepts, or ordered assignments. Within Loop, numbered lists facilitate rich formatting and collaborative editing, enabling users to provide comments and make updates in real time. Items can be nested to create sublists and reordered as necessary. This component is particularly valuable for outlining workflows, procedures, and any content that requires systematic progression. To initiate a numbered list, enter /numbered list. Such lists support the maintenance of structure and clarity in team-based documents.

Date

The Date component enables users to insert and monitor specific dates within Loop pages. This feature is particularly beneficial for setting deadlines, scheduling meetings, or recording milestones. Users can select dates via a calendar picker, and each date is interactive, clicking on it opens additional scheduling options. Furthermore, mentions allow dates to be assigned to individuals or tasks. The Date component integrates seamlessly with other elements such as tables and checklists, supporting effective team coordination and schedule adherence. To add a date, type /date. This enhances time management and ensures all team members are informed of essential timelines within the shared workspace.

Callout

A *Callout* is a visually distinctive element designed to draw attention to critical information, reminders, or key concepts. This component features an icon, background color, and structured text, ensuring it stands apart from standard content. Callouts are well-suited for highlighting deadlines, identifying risks, or delivering motivational messages. They offer support for rich text and collaborative editing, enabling users to modify and comment in real time. To create a callout, simply enter /callout and tailor its appearance to your requirements. This functionality enhances the prominence of essential information and helps prevent important details from being overlooked within broader content.

Code

The *Code* component in Loop is intended for developers and technical teams to share and collaborate on code snippets. It offers syntax highlighting for multiple programming languages, enhancing readability and comprehension. Code blocks can be formatted using /code, and are editable in real time by multiple users. This functionality is well suited for documenting scripts, providing examples, or collaborative troubleshooting. Although not a full integrated development environment (IDE), it serves as an efficient solution for incorporating technical content into collaborative documents. The feature also facilitates communication between technical and non-technical team members.

Mermaid

The *Mermaid* component enables users to create diagrams and flowcharts utilizing Mermaid syntax, a text-based tool for diagramming. This feature is well-suited for visualizing processes, workflows, and organizational structures. By typing /mermaid and entering the required syntax, users can generate diagrams directly within Loop, allowing for real-time editing and seamless collaboration. Mermaid supports a variety of diagram types, including flowcharts, sequence diagrams, and Gantt charts. It is particularly beneficial for technical teams, project managers, and designers who require effective visual communication of complex concepts within the Loop environment.

Math Equation

The *Math Equation* component enables users to insert mathematical expressions using LaTeX syntax. This functionality is particularly suited for academic, engineering, or financial teams requiring the inclusion of complex formulas in documentation. By typing /math, users can begin composing equations, which are rendered in a clear and readable format. The component accommodates advanced notation such as fractions, integrals, and matrices. Collaborative features allow multiple individuals to edit or comment on equations in real time, thereby enhancing clarity and precision within shared quantitative documents.

Table of Contents

The T*able of Contents* component automatically compiles a list of headings from a Loop page, facilitating efficient navigation and structural organization. It updates dynamically in response to additions or modifications of headings, making it highly effective for lengthy or intricate documents. Users can implement this feature via /table of contents, enabling easy access to specific sections. This capability significantly improves readability and overall document organization, especially in collaborative settings where numerous contributors are involved. It offers a robust solution for enhancing document usability and structure.

Divider

A *Divider* is a horizontal line designed to separate sections within a Loop page. This element enhances the visual organization of content, contributing to improved readability and efficient navigation throughout the document. Users can insert a divider by typing /divider; this feature is particularly beneficial in lengthy pages containing various components, such as tables, lists, and callouts. While dividers do not influence the functional aspects of a document, they significantly improve its layout and clarity by subtly guiding readers through distinct sections or topics. As a result, the overall user experience in collaborative documents is elevated.

Inline Equation

The *Inline Equation* feature enables users to incorporate mathematical expressions directly within a line of text using LaTeX syntax. This capability is valuable for referencing formulas or calculations while maintaining the continuity of written content. By typing /inline equation and entering the desired expression, users can display math notation—ranging from basic to advanced—in a clear and organized manner. This tool is especially suited for technical documentation, academic writing, and financial analysis. Inline equations preserve readability, add precision, and support collaborative editing, in alignment with other Loop components.

Paragraph

The *Paragraph* style represents the standard text formatting within Microsoft Loop, designed for composing regular body content. It supports sophisticated rich text options, including bold, italics, underline, hyperlinks, and emojis. Paragraphs are optimal for general writing, serving explanations and descriptions, and can embed inline elements such as dates, mentions, and equations. This style maintains readability and consistency throughout the document. Users may begin typing directly or select "Paragraph" from the style menu. It is best applied to comprehensive content that does not require hierarchical emphasis, making it a foundational element of most Loop pages.

Heading 1

Heading 1 serves as the highest-level heading in Loop, designated for principal sections or titles within a page. It features increased size and weight relative to other headings, facilitating rapid identification of the main topic. This format is instrumental in structuring content into distinct segments, including project names, meeting titles, or document themes. Additionally, Heading 1 integrates with the Table of Contents component for streamlined navigation. Application includes selecting text and choosing "Heading 1," or entering # followed by a space. It improves document structure and clarity in collaborative settings.

Heading 2

Heading 2 denotes secondary headings, organizing subsections below Heading 1. While slightly smaller, it remains bold and noticeable, assisting users in segmenting content efficiently. Ideal for topics such as agenda items, task categories, or discussion points, this style also synchronizes with the Table of Contents for effective navigation. Users apply it via the "Heading 2" option or by typing ## followed by a space. It enhances readability and supports efficient information retrieval within Loop pages.

Heading 3

Heading 3 defines tertiary headings, allowing additional sub-level differentiation beneath Heading 2. With reduced size and prominence, it remains sufficiently distinct to provide organizational separation. This style is well-suited for detailed items like sub-tasks, examples, or notes, ensuring document hierarchy and continued Table of Contents compatibility. It can be applied by selecting "Heading 3" or entering ### followed by a space. It is particularly valuable in complex documents requiring multiple levels of clear visual separation.

Collapsible Heading 1

Collapsible Heading 1 mirrors the function of Heading 1 while offering the capability to expand or collapse underlying content. This feature facilitates management of extensive documents by enabling selective visibility of key sections. It effectively reduces visual clutter and enhances user focus. Users toggle content display with a click, making it ideal for organizing meeting notes, project phases, or documentation. Selection of "Collapsible Heading 1" from the style menu applies this formatting, providing dynamic control over content presentation and maintaining document structure.

Collapsible Heading 2

Collapsible Heading 2 presents a collapsible variant of Heading 2 for concealing or revealing subsections. It is highly beneficial for organizing granular content such as task breakdowns, discussion threads, or nested concepts. Users can expand or contract sections to prioritize relevant details. This style supports structured navigation and integrates seamlessly with the Table of Contents. Applying it is accomplished through the "Collapsible Heading 2" selection in the style menu, thereby improving usability in environments with rapidly growing collaborative content.

Collapsible Heading 3

Collapsible Heading 3 offers the collapsible functionality at the tertiary heading level, suited for hiding or displaying detailed subpoints, case examples, or annotations beneath broader divisions. It ensures document tidiness while allowing thorough coverage of subject matter. Support for real-time collaboration and integration with navigation tools is maintained. Users apply this style by selecting "Collapsible Heading 3" from the style menu. It is especially appropriate for technical documentation, brainstorming sessions, or layered planning where both accessibility and organization are priorities.

Quote

The *Quote* style highlights quoted text or emphasizes critical statements by displaying them with indentation and visual distinction from paragraphs. This format is apt for citing sources, sharing feedback, or drawing attention to insights. Quotes support rich formatting and collaborative features consistent with other Loop components. They are applied by selecting "Quote" from the style menu or typing > followed by a space. It reinforces clarity and emphasis, enabling readers to swiftly identify key or referenced material within a document.

Inline Code

Inline Code formats concise code snippets or technical terms within textual lines, utilizing a monospaced font and distinctive background for easy identification. It is intended for referencing commands, variables, or syntax in documentation or discourse but is unsuitable for complete code blocks—use the Code component for those cases. Users can apply Inline Code by selecting the text and choosing "Inline Code" or enclosing it in backticks (`). This approach improves clarity in technical writing and distinctly separates code from standard text.

CHAPTER 6 EXPLORING ADVANCED FEATURES AND CUSTOMIZATIONS

Communication, Media, Microsoft, and Other Apps

Microsoft Loop has communication, media, Microsoft, and other apps feature to support the content gets cocreated in the Loop. Communication features contain, person, Emoji picker, and Label, as shown in Figure 6-17. In-addition, Media features Image and Record Video, as shown in Figure 6-17.

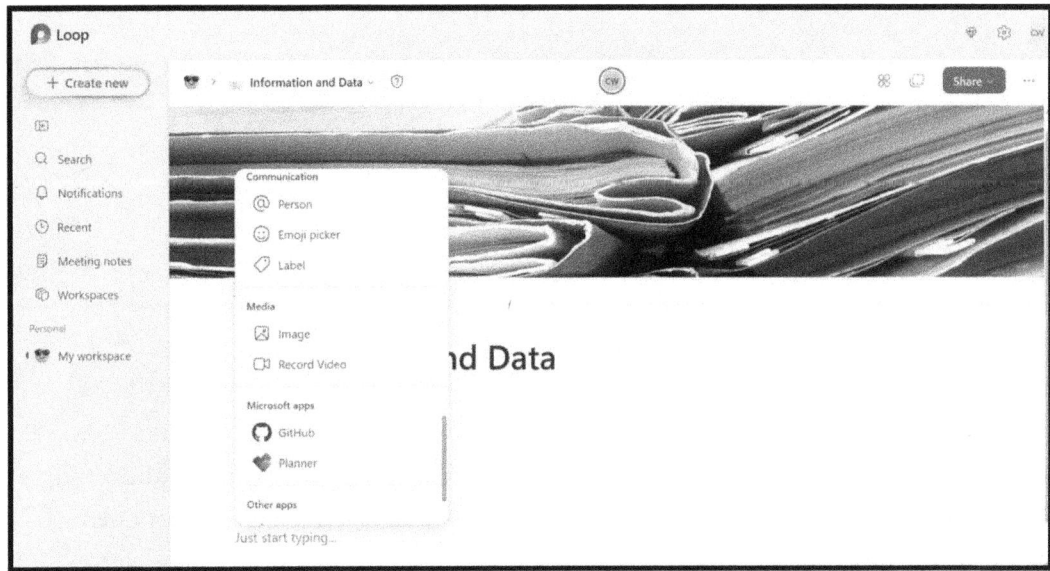

Figure 6-17. *Communication and Media features*

Finally, Microsoft app includes GitHub and planner apps. Loop allows you to import and manage your GitHub issues and Pull Requests. **Everyone will be able to view imported issues and Requests.** And Other apps include Jira and Trello, as shown in Figure 6-18.

CHAPTER 6 EXPLORING ADVANCED FEATURES AND CUSTOMIZATIONS

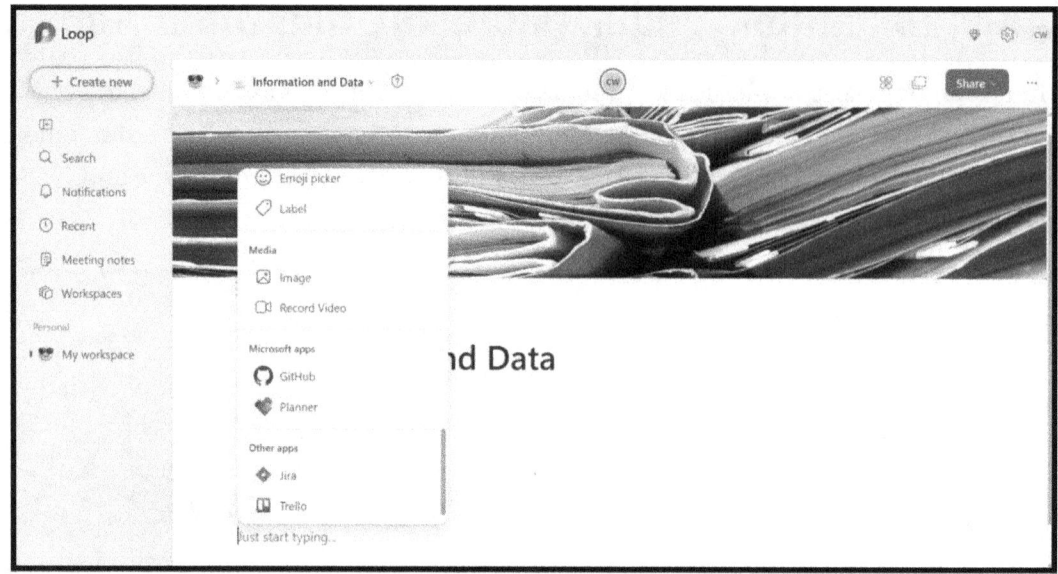

Figure 6-18. *List of Microsoft and other apps*

We conclude our chapter here. In this chapter, we have learnt about Microsoft Loop component and content supporting features, in which collaborating and sharing of content provides an awesome experience. We have covered Loop component such as Task List, Voting Table, Progressive Tracker, Kanban Board, Team Retrospective, Q&A Session, and Calendar. Further, we saw general features supporting content such as New Subpage, Table, Checklist, Bulleted list, Numbered list, Date, Callout, Code, Mermaid, Math equation, Table of content, divider, and inline equation. In addition, text styles such as Paragraph, Heading 1, Heading 2, Heading 3, Collapsible Heading 1, Collapsible Heading 2, Collapsible Heading 3, Quote, and Inline Code. Finally, we covered communication, media, Microsoft and other apps features which are part of Loop journey.

The final chapter of this book examines team collaboration, addressing various perspectives such as the value and impact of collaboration, essential elements of effective collaboration, challenges faced during team collaboration, strategies for successful collaborative efforts, collaboration in the digital era, the influence of technology on collaboration, and possible future developments in team collaboration. Additionally, a Microsoft use case will be discussed within these contexts.

CHAPTER 7

Use Cases for Team Collaboration Using Loop

In the previous chapter, we explored advanced features of Microsoft Loop and took a deep dive into features such as Kanban Boards, Ideas Tab, Page Linking, Templates, customization to fit real-time needs and others, and customization of Loop for your team needs. In this chapter, we will explore the meaning of Team Collaboration, under Team collaborating perspective in value and impact of collaboration, core components of effective collaboration, challenges in team collaboration, strategies for successful collaboration, collaboration in the digital age, the role of technology in collaboration and the future of team collaboration, and finally, we look at possible Microsoft loop use cases related to these perspectives.

Introduction

Team collaboration is a complex and multifaceted process central to the success of organizations, projects, and communities. It involves the coordinated efforts of individuals who work collectively toward shared objectives, utilizing their varied skills, experiences, and perspectives to achieve results unattainable by individuals working alone. In an environment characterized by increasing complexity, interdependence, and rapid change, collaboration has evolved into an essential requirement for fostering innovation, effective problem-solving, and sustainable development. This in-depth examination of team collaboration will address its definition, significance, core components, associated challenges, strategies for effective implementation, and its changing role in the digital era.

CHAPTER 7   USE CASES FOR TEAM COLLABORATION USING LOOP

Fundamentally, team collaboration is predicated on the principle of synergy, wherein the collective output surpasses the capabilities of individual contributors. When individuals unite with a clear, common purpose, they combine unique talents, insights, and viewpoints that, when effectively harnessed, promote innovation, enhance productivity, and strengthen results. Effective collaboration extends beyond mere colocation or task sharing; it necessitates active participation, mutual respect, transparent communication, and a readiness to both offer input and consider others' contributions. Cultivating a collaborative environment requires prioritizing group achievement over individual accolades and recognizing the value of diverse perspectives in supporting optimal decision-making. Introduction leads to different Team collaboration perspectives, which is shown in Figure 7-1, and following Figure 7-1, we will go through the details of each perspective.

CHAPTER 7   USE CASES FOR TEAM COLLABORATION USING LOOP

Figure 7-1. *Perspectives of effective collaboration*

Value and Impact of Collaboration

The value and impact of collaboration lies in innovation and creativity, efficiency and productivity, and problem-solving and adaptability, as shown in Figure 7-1-1.

CHAPTER 7 USE CASES FOR TEAM COLLABORATION USING LOOP

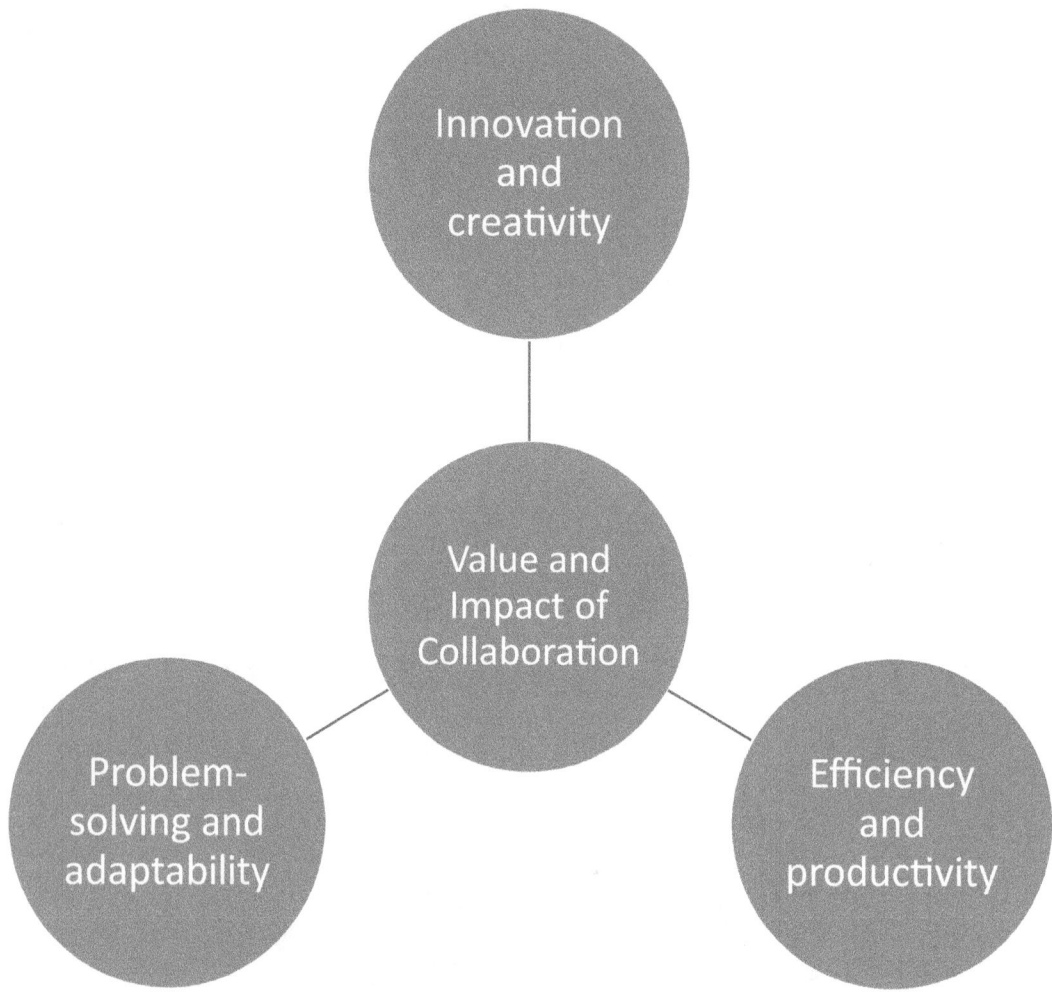

Figure 7-1-1. *Value and Impact of Collaboration*

The significance of team collaboration is paramount across various domains. In business, it propels innovation by cultivating an environment conducive to the open exchange and refinement of ideas. Within healthcare, collaboration facilitates comprehensive patient care through the coordinated contributions of physicians, nurses, specialists, and support staff. In the education sector, collaborative efforts promote improved learning outcomes by encouraging peer engagement, knowledge sharing, and the development of critical thinking abilities. In technology and engineering, effective teamwork supports the creation of sophisticated systems and products that necessitate cross-disciplinary expertise. Overall, collaboration strengthens adaptability, resilience, and the capacity to respond efficiently to both challenges and opportunities within any field.

CHAPTER 7   USE CASES FOR TEAM COLLABORATION USING LOOP

Core Components of Effective Collaboration

Core components of collaboration are Communication, Trust, Shared Goals, Defined Roles, Diversity and Inclusion, and Leadership, as shown in Figure 7-1-2.

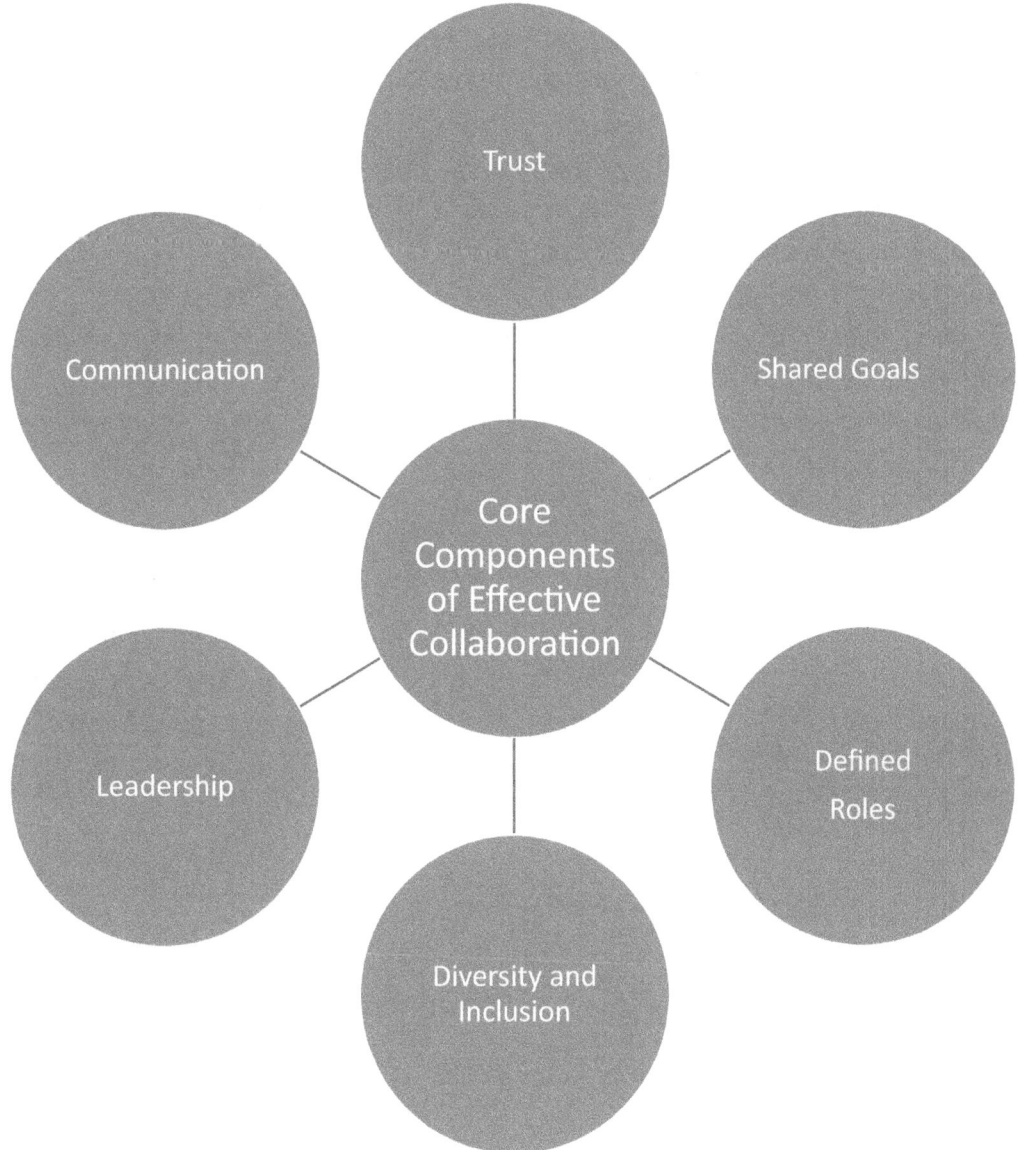

Figure 7-1-2. *Core Components of Effective Collaboration*

Effective team collaboration is supported by several fundamental components. Chief among these is communication; clear, open, and honest communication is critical for information sharing, goal alignment, conflict resolution, and trust-building. Establishing appropriate channels and norms—such as face-to-face meetings, digital platforms, or asynchronous tools—is necessary to suit the team's context. Furthermore, collaborative communication is enhanced by active listening, empathy, and constructive feedback.

Trust constitutes another essential pillar of team success. In its absence, team members may hesitate to share ideas, shy away from calculated risks, or engage in counterproductive competition. Trust develops through consistency, transparency, accountability, and mutual respect, empowering individuals to express themselves candidly, acknowledge mistakes, and depend on one another.

In addition, shared goals and a well-defined sense of purpose are imperative. Teams must have a clear understanding of their objectives and the underlying rationale. Such a shared vision provides direction, fosters motivation, informs decision-making, aligns individual efforts with collective aims, and cultivates both ownership and commitment within the group.

Challenges in Team Collaboration

Challenges in team collaboration are miscommunication and misunderstandings, conflicting priorities and goals, personality clashes and interpersonal dynamics, remote and hybrid work complications and cultural and time zone differences, as shown in Figure 7-1-3.

CHAPTER 7 USE CASES FOR TEAM COLLABORATION USING LOOP

Figure 7-1-3. *Challenges in Team Collaboration*

Clearly articulating roles and responsibilities is essential to prevent misunderstandings, duplication of tasks, or lapses in accountability. While collaboration necessitates collective effort, it is equally important to delineate individual responsibilities. Such clarity promotes coordination, operational efficiency, and optimizes the utilization of each team member's capabilities.

Diversity and inclusion are fundamental to enhancing collaborative outcomes. Teams comprising individuals from varied backgrounds, experiences, and viewpoints are better positioned to develop innovative solutions and mitigate the risks of groupthink. However, true diversity must be complemented by an inclusive environment—one that ensures every perspective is acknowledged, valued, and incorporated into the team's work.

Successful collaboration is also contingent upon effective leadership. Leaders who foster collaboration act as facilitators rather than directors, empowering team members rather than exerting control, and inspiring rather than commanding. These leaders promote a culture of transparency, encourage engagement, and exemplify the behaviors expected within the team. Additionally, they adeptly manage conflict, oversee team dynamics, and ensure sustained focus and cohesion among members.

Strategies for Successful Collaboration

Strategies for successful collaboration are Use of collaboration tools such as Microsoft Loop, establishing team norms and agreements, regular check-ins and feedback loops, training in soft skills: emotional intelligence, conflict resolution, and building and maintaining psychological safety, as shown in Figure 7-1-4.

CHAPTER 7 USE CASES FOR TEAM COLLABORATION USING LOOP

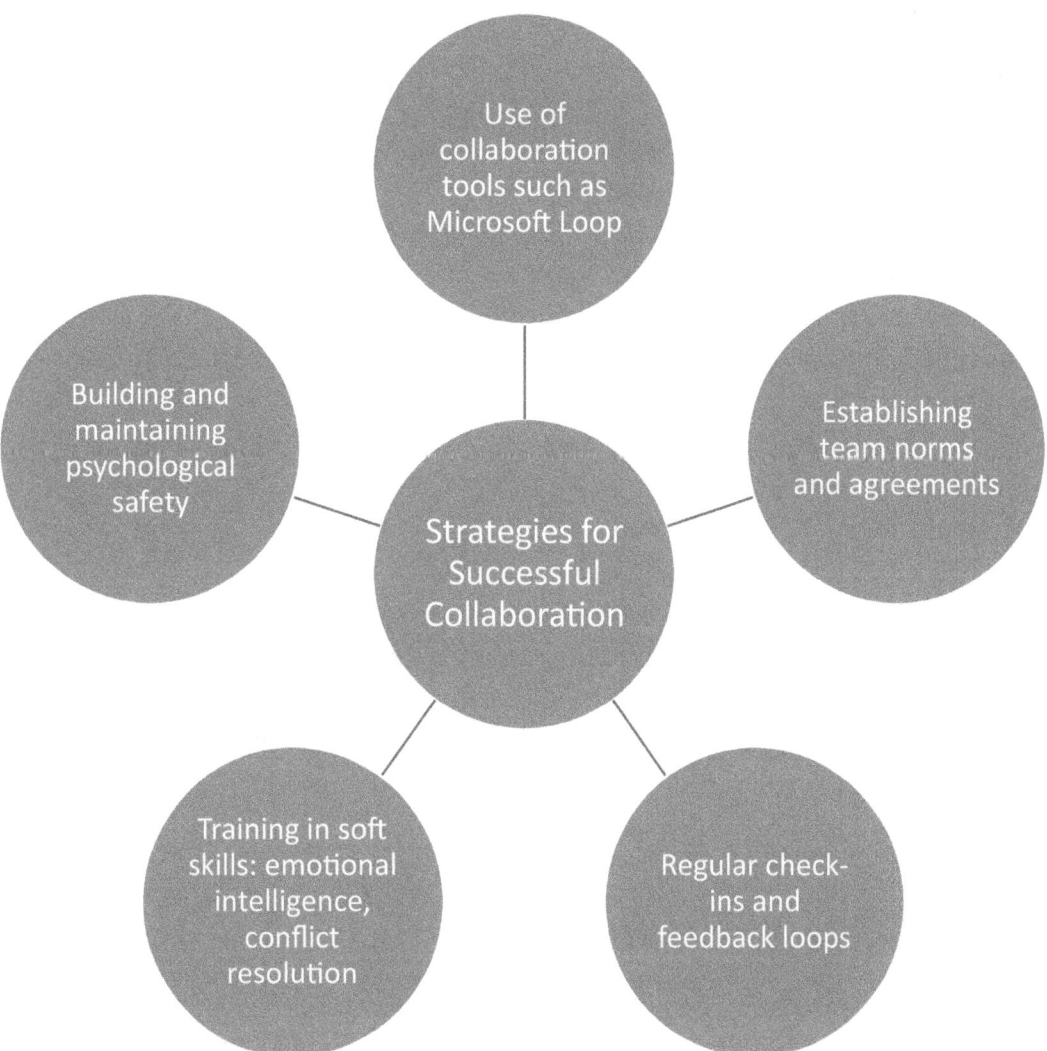

Figure 7-1-4. *Strategies for Successful Collaboration*

While team collaboration offers significant advantages, it is not without its challenges. Factors such as miscommunication, diverging priorities, personality conflicts, and power dynamics can impede effective teamwork. Remote or distributed teams may encounter additional obstacles, including time zone discrepancies, cultural differences, and technological constraints. Addressing these issues requires deliberate action, adaptive strategies, and an ongoing commitment to improvement.

The implementation of collaboration tools and technologies—such as Microsoft Loop—can facilitate communication, project management, and information sharing. These platforms help bridge geographical gaps, streamline processes, and promote transparency. Nevertheless, technology should be complemented by intentional practices and a human-centered approach.

Establishing team norms and agreements is another effective strategy. Defining guidelines for communication, decision-making, conflict resolution, and accountability helps set clear expectations and reduces misunderstandings. Regular check-ins, retrospectives, and feedback sessions contribute to continuous reflection, learning, and adjustment.

Ongoing training and development are essential for strengthening collaborative capabilities. Teams benefit from cultivating skills in communication, emotional intelligence, cultural awareness, and conflict management. Such investment enhances both individual and collective performance.

Psychological safety has become increasingly recognized as crucial for effective team collaboration. Introduced by Harvard professor Amy Edmondson, psychological safety refers to a shared belief that the team environment permits interpersonal risk-taking. In psychologically safe teams, members feel comfortable expressing ideas, posing questions, acknowledging errors, and challenging prevailing norms. This culture fosters learning, innovation, and resilience.

Collaboration in the Digital Age

Collaboration in digital age falls into rise of remote and hybrid teams, digital literacy and virtual communication, managing digital fatigue and maintaining engagement, and designing inclusive and equitable hybrid work environments, as shown in Figure 7-1-5.

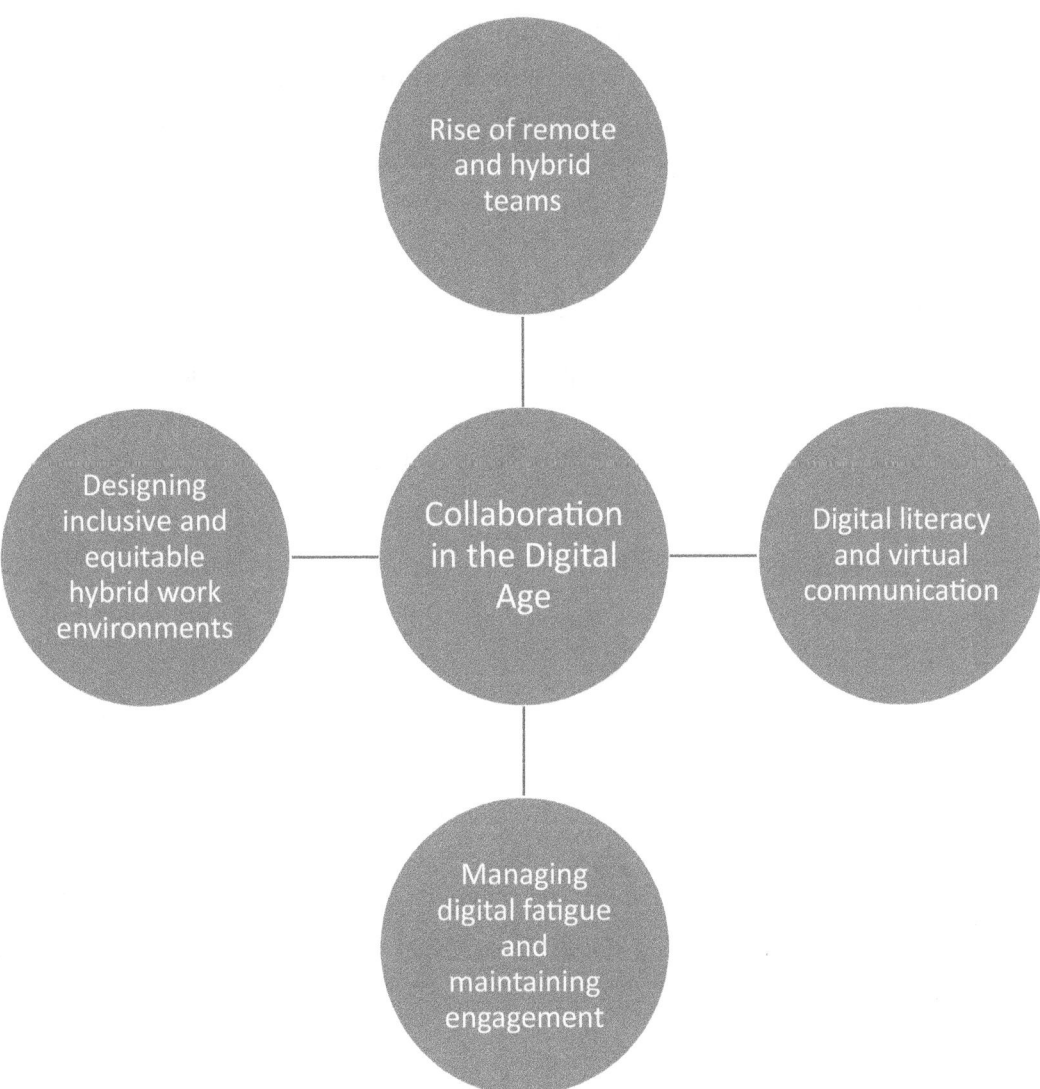

Figure 7-1-5. *Collaboration in the Digital Age*

The advent of the digital age has fundamentally altered the nature of collaboration. Developments such as remote work, virtual teams, and increased global connectivity have broadened collaborative opportunities while introducing additional complexities. Effective digital collaboration now necessitates proficiency in digital literacy, self-management, and virtual communication. Furthermore, it requires consideration of factors such as digital fatigue, maintaining work-life boundaries, and fostering purposeful connections.

CHAPTER 7 USE CASES FOR TEAM COLLABORATION USING LOOP

Hybrid work models, integrating both in-person and remote elements, present unique advantages and challenges. These models provide greater flexibility and access to a wider talent pool but also demand thoughtful coordination, equitable involvement, and inclusive practices. Consequently, organizations must reassess the design of workspaces, meetings, and team dynamics to effectively support hybrid collaboration.

The Role of Technology in Collaboration

Role of technology in collaboration happens through collaborative platforms and project management tools, AI and automation in supporting team workflows, and ethical considerations and human–AI collaboration, as shown in Figure 7-1-6.

CHAPTER 7   USE CASES FOR TEAM COLLABORATION USING LOOP

Figure 7-1-6. *The Role of Technology in Collaboration*

Artificial intelligence and automation are transforming collaborative work environments. AI-driven tools facilitate tasks such as scheduling, data analysis, content creation, and decision support, thereby allowing teams to focus on more complex, value-added collaboration. Nevertheless, these advancements also introduce important considerations regarding trust, ethical standards, and the evolving role of human participants in collaborative processes.

Future of Team Collaboration

The Future of Team Collaboration lies with Trends: agility; adaptability; purpose-driven teams; emphasis on well-being, inclusion, and continuous learning; integration of emerging technologies; and evolving leadership and organizational culture, as shown in Figure 7-1-7.

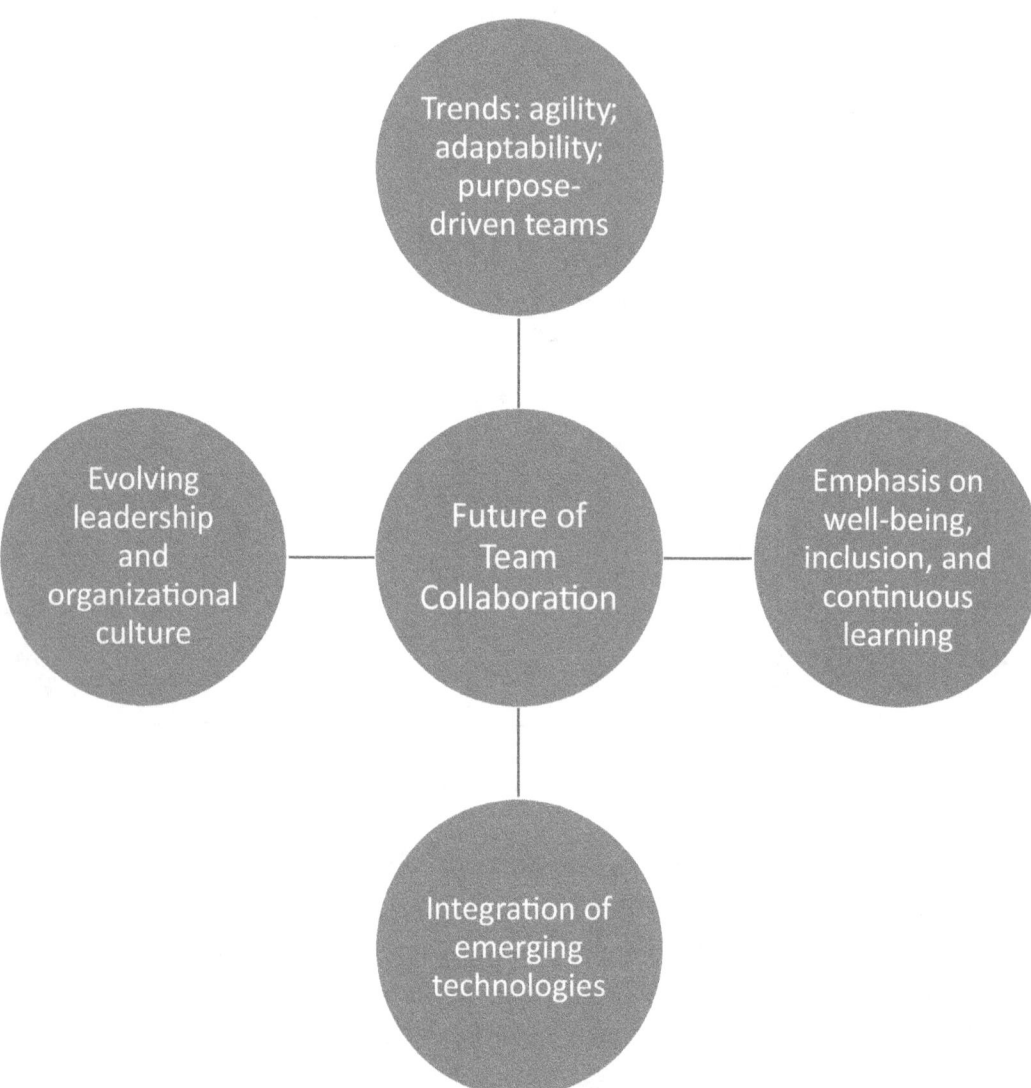

Figure 7-1-7. *Future of Team collaboration*

Looking ahead, team collaboration is expected to feature deeper technological integration, a heightened focus on employee well-being and inclusivity, and a transition toward more agile, adaptable, and purpose-driven teams. As the landscape of work changes, it is imperative that our strategies for effective collaboration evolve accordingly.

In summary, team collaboration serves as a critical mechanism for uniting individuals, leveraging their diverse strengths, and accomplishing shared objectives. It encompasses both structured methodologies and adaptive practices, necessitating thoughtful planning, ongoing development, and a keen understanding of interpersonal dynamics. Regardless of the setting—be it a corporate environment, educational institution, healthcare facility, or virtual platform—effective collaboration remains fundamental to realizing potential, advancing innovation, and collectively shaping improved outcomes.

Use Cases with Microsoft Loop

In this section, we will discuss possible use cases with Microsoft Loop in scenarios such as value and impact of collaboration, core components of effective collaboration, challenges in team collaboration, strategies for successful collaboration, collaboration in the digital age, the role of technology in collaboration, and the future of team collaboration.

Value and Impact of Collaboration

A possible use case on Microsoft Loop using value and impact of team collaboration lies in innovation and creativity, efficiency and productivity, and problem-solving and adaptability and is described as follows:

In the context of rapid product development at a global technology company, a cross-functional team was assigned to design an AI-powered customer support bot. This group comprised product managers, UX designers, software engineers, data scientists, and marketing strategists operating across multiple time zones. To address challenges related to asynchronous communication, fragmented documentation, and siloed workflows, the team implemented Microsoft Loop as their primary collaboration platform.

CHAPTER 7   USE CASES FOR TEAM COLLABORATION USING LOOP

From the beginning, Loop fundamentally enhanced the team's approach to innovation and creativity. Rather than relying on static documents or extensive email exchanges, the team utilized Loop components—dynamic, real-time content blocks such as task lists, tables, and notes—embedded throughout Microsoft Teams, Outlook, and Word. This enabled both synchronous and asynchronous brainstorming within shared Loop workspaces, fostering collective input. Designers uploaded initial wireframes directly into Loop pages, engineers contributed feasibility annotations, and marketers integrated customer insights—all consolidated within a single collaborative document.

This real-time co-creation environment fostered a culture of innovation, allowing ideas to develop through ongoing contributions and iterations. The team leveraged Loop's task-tracking components to delegate responsibilities and monitor progress effectively. With integration to Microsoft Planner and To Do, updates in one area were instantly reflected elsewhere, reducing duplication and ambiguity. This seamless synchronization notably improved efficiency and productivity by eliminating time spent searching for updated documents or clarifying task assignments.

Loop's adaptability was also evident when project requirements changed. For instance, in response to a client request for a new feature mid-project, the team swiftly established a new Loop page to evaluate the impact. Engineers detailed technical considerations, product managers revised timelines, and designers proposed user interface modifications—all accomplished within hours. Such agility demonstrated the team's adaptability in navigating dynamic project demands.

Further, Loop's commenting and emoji reactions facilitated open dialogue and expedited feedback, minimizing the necessity for extended meetings. Integrations with Microsoft OneNote and SharePoint ensured comprehensive knowledge management and supported continuous improvement initiatives. As the project advanced, Loop served as a central hub for stakeholder review preparations, integrating live status updates and demo links into presentations—a practice that earned positive feedback from leadership and reinforced transparency.

The culmination of these efforts resulted in the early delivery of a high-quality product, featuring fewer defects and achieving higher user satisfaction compared to previous launches. Post-launch retrospectives highlighted that Loop had transformed team collaboration by breaking down silos, expediting decision-making processes, and cultivating a more inclusive and innovative culture. Consequently, Loop's adoption expanded to other departments, including HR and finance, establishing a benchmark for modern, agile collaboration.

In summary, Microsoft Loop evolved into an essential enabler of collaborative excellence, seamlessly integrating diverse expertise, ideas, and workflows into a unified, high-achieving team. This case underscores how the strategic application of collaborative technologies can drive innovation, enhance operational efficiency, and enable robust problem-solving in today's fast-paced business environments.

Core Components of Effective Collaboration

A possible case on Microsoft Loop using Core Components of Effective Collaboration lying in Communication, Trust, Shared Goals, Defined Roles, Diversity and Inclusion and Leadership is described as follows:

At a global consulting organization, a strategic transformation team was summoned to develop a new digital onboarding solution for clients spanning various industries. This cross-functional group comprised consultants, UX designers, IT specialists, and client success managers from offices in Bangalore, London, and Toronto. To address the complexities of time zone variations, cultural differences, and fragmented workflows, the team implemented **Microsoft Loop** as their primary collaboration platform.

From project initiation, Loop fundamentally improved communication. Instead of relying on static documents or dispersed chat threads, the team utilized Loop's dynamic components—such as editable text blocks, task lists, and progress trackers—which could be embedded across Microsoft Teams and Outlook. This approach enabled all members to contribute ideas, updates, and feedback within a unified, real-time workspace, regardless of their location or working hours. Features like commenting and emoji reactions encouraged transparent dialogue and prompt responses, allowing for efficient asynchronous collaboration and reducing dependence on excessive meetings.

This open exchange fostered **trust**, as contributions were visible in real time, change tracking was seamless, and recognition of individual input was straightforward. Loop's version history and collaborative editing capabilities further promoted accountability and transparency, assisting in both affirming effort and resolving misunderstandings.

The team set **shared goals** by jointly drafting a mission statement and success metrics within Loop; these remained accessible throughout the project to ensure alignment on client outcomes over departmental objectives. Loop's organizational flexibility enabled the structuring of the project into distinct phases, each with dedicated pages outlining objectives, timelines, and deliverables.

Defined roles were clearly demarcated using Loop's task assignment functionalities, which integrated with Microsoft Planner and To Do. Every member had a tailored overview of their responsibilities, while a central dashboard provided comprehensive insight into overall progress, eliminating redundant efforts and streamlining dependency management.

Diversity and inclusion were actively championed. Loop's collaborative canvas supported multiple content formats—text, visuals, links, videos—encouraging participation from individuals across different backgrounds and communication preferences. Ideation sessions leveraged Loop's inclusive environment, facilitating meaningful input from all team members, including those who preferred asynchronous contribution. Retrospectives were conducted within Loop, where anonymous feedback could be openly addressed, underpinning a culture of ongoing improvement.

Effective **leadership** was instrumental in sustaining this collaborative ethos. The project lead demonstrated transparency through weekly updates, celebrating collective achievements and addressing obstacles. Rather than issuing directives, leadership fostered shared decision-making via Loop, encouraging debate and consensus-building.

When faced with an abrupt shift in client requirements, the team swiftly adapted by creating a new Loop page to realign priorities. Updated timelines, reassigned tasks, and innovative solutions were developed collaboratively within hours, all facilitated by Loop's real-time, shared workspace. This level of agility was underpinned by strong foundations in communication, trust, shared objectives, clear responsibilities, inclusivity, and collaborative leadership cultivated throughout the project.

Ultimately, the team delivered a customized, scalable onboarding experience that exceeded client expectations and established a benchmark for future initiatives. Microsoft Loop served not merely as a technological tool, but as the **collaborative backbone** uniting a diverse and distributed team—transforming complexity into clarity and vision into reality.

Challenges in Team Collaboration

A possible case on Microsoft Loop containing challenges in team collaboration are miscommunication and misunderstandings, conflicting priorities and goals, personality clashes and interpersonal dynamics, remote and hybrid work complications and cultural and time zone differences is described as follows:

CHAPTER 7   USE CASES FOR TEAM COLLABORATION USING LOOP

During a global marketing campaign for a new product launch, a cross-functional team comprising brand strategists, content creators, data analysts, and regional marketing leads encountered considerable collaboration challenges. Distributed across North America, Europe, and Asia in a hybrid model with both in-office and fully remote members, the team initially struggled with frequent miscommunications and misunderstandings—missed emails, conflicting document versions, and meeting notes dispersed across various platforms. To address these issues, the team implemented **Microsoft Loop** as a centralized collaboration space. Loop's real-time, editable components—including shared checklists, status trackers, and comment threads—facilitated alignment and transparency by consolidating communication and reducing ambiguity. This transition significantly enhanced clarity and minimized friction caused by fragmented information.

Additionally, divergent priorities and objectives arose between regional leads, who advocated localized messaging, and the global team, which emphasized brand consistency. Loop provided a solution by enabling the creation of a collaborative goals page, where campaign objectives, KPIs, and regional adaptations were documented collectively. This transparent approach promoted alignment and compromise, offering clear visibility into how individual contributions supported the broader strategy.

Interpersonal dynamics and personality differences, particularly between assertive and more reserved team members, also presented obstacles. Loop's asynchronous collaboration features empowered all participants to contribute ideas and feedback without the constraints of live meetings. Features such as emoji reactions, comments, and suggestion capabilities fostered a more inclusive environment in which diverse perspectives were valued, thereby reducing tension and building mutual respect.

Remote and hybrid work arrangements introduced further complexities, especially regarding scheduling and coordination. Integration with Microsoft Teams and Outlook enabled the embedding of live Loop components within meeting invites and chat threads, granting all team members access to current updates irrespective of location or working hours. This innovation reduced the need for frequent status meetings and allowed flexible participation.

Cultural and time zone variations initially contributed to delays and misaligned expectations. However, Loop's persistent, flexible workspace supported asynchronous collaboration, allowing regional team members to seamlessly continue each other's work. Documenting communication preferences, holidays, and working hours within Loop pages cultivated empathy and improved coordination. Over time, the team established an efficient workflow with Loop as the central hub for brainstorming, planning, and execution. The platform was used to coauthor briefs, track deliverables, and conduct retrospectives.

By the campaign's end, the team achieved an on-schedule global launch, reporting higher engagement levels and fewer internal conflicts compared to previous projects. Ultimately, Microsoft Loop not only resolved logistical challenges but also enhanced the team's capacity for cross-boundary, inclusive collaboration, transforming a potentially disjointed project into an exemplar of effective modern teamwork.

Strategies for Successful Collaboration

A possible use case on Microsoft Loop containing Strategies for successful collaboration are Use of collaboration tools such as Microsoft Loop, establishing team norms and agreements, regular check-ins and feedback loops, training in soft skills: emotional intelligence, conflict resolution, and building and maintaining psychological safety is described as follows:

Within a regional operations team dedicated to enhancing internal workflows across several departments, collaboration was initially disjointed and inconsistent. To resolve this, the team implemented **Microsoft Loop** as their central collaboration platform, which significantly improved the way they worked together. Loop's versatile features—including shared task lists, progress trackers, and editable notes—enabled real-time co-creation and content updates within Microsoft Teams, Outlook, and Word. This integration effectively resolved version control challenges and centralized communication, facilitating enhanced alignment.

At the outset of deployment, the team utilized Loop to **define team norms and agreements**, establishing a dedicated page to articulate expectations regarding responsiveness, meeting conduct, and decision-making protocols. Because these guidelines were both visible and editable by all members, the process fostered a sense of ownership and mutual accountability.

To sustain momentum and ensure ongoing alignment, the team organized **regular check-ins and feedback loops** through Loop's integrated task boards and comment threads. Weekly updates were posted on a shared Loop page, offering opportunities for team members to respond, pose questions, and suggesting enhancements asynchronously. This approach minimized the need for prolonged meetings while promoting continual, constructive feedback.

CHAPTER 7   USE CASES FOR TEAM COLLABORATION USING LOOP

Understanding the importance of interpersonal dynamics, the team also prioritized **soft skills training**, including emotional intelligence and conflict resolution. Loop supported these initiatives by hosting interactive learning modules and reflection exercises within its workspace, allowing team members to collaboratively engage with content and share insights. These activities contributed to improved empathy, active listening, and effective conflict management.

Significantly, Loop was instrumental in **establishing and sustaining psychological safety**. The platform's inclusive design enabled all voices to be heard through features such as anonymous feedback forms, suggestion boxes, and asynchronous brainstorming sessions. Team members felt secure contributing ideas, free from concern about judgment, while leaders modeled vulnerability by sharing personal reflections and acknowledging challenges via Loop. This culture of openness fostered trust, encouraged risk-taking, and paved the way for more innovative solutions.

Over time, the team evolved to become more agile, cohesive, and resilient. They leveraged Loop not only for project management but also as an ongoing hub for collaboration, learning, and professional growth. By integrating technological tools with intentional practices, the team progressed from operating silos to becoming a high-performing unit known for delivering consistent results and adapting effectively to change. Microsoft Loop emerged as more than just a tool—it became the cornerstone of a collaborative culture rooted in clarity, empathy, and shared purpose.

Collaboration in the Digital Age

A possible use case on Microsoft Loop containing collaboration in digital age falls into rise of remote and hybrid teams, digital literacy and virtual communication, managing digital fatigue and maintaining engagement, designing inclusive and equitable hybrid work environments is described as follows:

In a global software development company undergoing a digital transformation initiative, a cross-functional team was assembled to redesign the internal knowledge-sharing platform. The team comprised developers, UX researchers, content strategists, and IT administrators, many of whom worked remotely or under hybrid arrangements across different continents. Early in the process, the team encountered standard challenges associated with distributed work, such as coordinating across time zones, sustaining engagement in virtual meetings, and promoting balanced participation. To address these issues, the team implemented **Microsoft Loop** as their primary collaboration platform. Loop's real-time, adaptable components enabled collaborative document creation, task tracking, and brainstorming within a shared digital workspace accessible at any time and from any location. For remote and hybrid teams, this reduced the reliance on synchronous meetings and facilitated asynchronous contributions without loss of context. Integration with Microsoft Teams and Outlook allowed updates to be synchronized across systems, streamlining workflows and ensuring continuity.

As proficiency with Loop increased, the team explored its functionalities for supporting digital literacy and virtual communication. Its interface and modular structure permitted all team members, irrespective of technical expertise, to interact with content, provide feedback, and suggest modifications. A shared Loop page offering quick guides and best practices was developed to support onboarding and promote consistency in digital skills.

To address digital fatigue, the team restructured their collaboration routines using Loop. Asynchronous updates replaced lengthy video calls, with each member uploading weekly summaries and noting any challenges. This facilitated responses according to individual availability, decreasing required screen time and allowing for greater focus. Loop's visual elements, including progress bars, emojis, and embedded media, were used to present updates in an engaging manner. Additionally, Loop supported brief, interactive check-ins using emoji reactions or concise text inputs, supporting team connection.

Loop also contributed to developing an inclusive and equitable hybrid work environment by centralizing collaboration. It ensured that all members, regardless of work location, had equivalent access to information, participation in decision-making, and visibility. The team maintained a "Ways of Working" Loop page documenting meeting protocols, time zone overlaps, and cultural considerations to encourage inclusivity. Meeting times rotated to accommodate various regions, and Loop was employed to record notes and action items in real time, ensuring comprehensive documentation. Leadership utilized Loop for sharing feedback, collecting input, and acknowledging contributions. Over time, Loop served as the primary platform for team collaboration, facilitating effective work, sustained communication, and inclusive participation for all members.

The Role of Technology in Collaboration

A possible Microsoft Loop use case containing role of technology in collaboration happens through collaborative platforms and project management tools, AI and automation in supporting team workflows and ethical considerations, and human–AI collaboration.

In a rapidly expanding digital marketing agency, a cross-functional team was tasked with launching a multichannel campaign for a prominent client. The team consisted of content creators, data analysts, campaign managers, and client liaisons, all operating in a hybrid environment. To facilitate collaboration and manage project complexity, they implemented **Microsoft Loop** as their central platform. Loop's modular components enabled the team to co-develop campaign briefs, allocate tasks, and monitor deliverables within a shared workspace accessible through Microsoft Teams, Outlook, and Word. The integration of collaborative platforms and project management tools reduced the need to switch between applications and ensured access to consistent information. Loop's synchronization with Microsoft Planner and To Do provided real-time updates on tasks, while embedded checklists and status boards supported alignment and accountability.

As the project progressed, the team incorporated **AI and automation** features available within the Microsoft ecosystem to enhance workflows. AI-driven suggestions in Loop summarized meeting notes, generated content outlines, and proposed task assignments based on workload and expertise, which decreased manual tasks and allowed the team to focus on other responsibilities. For instance, when drafting social media copy, Loop's integration with Microsoft Copilot supplied AI-generated drafts for team refinement.

The team also addressed **ethical considerations in human-AI collaboration** by setting guidelines—documented on a shared Loop page—specifying that AI-generated content should be reviewed, attributed, and validated by team members before client submission. This process aimed at supporting transparency, accountability, and quality control. Discussions about data privacy and potential bias led to an agreement on limiting AI use for sensitive or culturally specific material. Loop's editing history and comment functionality assisted in tracking modifications and decisions.

CHAPTER 7   USE CASES FOR TEAM COLLABORATION USING LOOP

Over time, Microsoft Loop became a key component of the team's collaborative processes, supporting a balance between automation and human oversight. It facilitated faster workflow and structured ethical practices, demonstrating how technology can support both efficiency and integrity in team collaboration when managed appropriately.

Future of Team Collaboration

A possible Microsoft Loop use case containing agility; adaptability; purpose-driven teams; emphasis on well-being, inclusion, and continuous learning; integration of emerging technologies; and evolving leadership and organizational culture is described as follows:

In a sustainability consultancy, a newly established innovation team was assigned to develop a climate impact assessment tool for clients from various industries. The team members had diverse backgrounds, spanning continents, disciplines, and work styles, and worked in a hybrid model. To support this project, the team used **Microsoft Loop** as their primary collaboration platform. Loop's modular workspaces enabled the team to start new pages for ideation, prototyping, and collecting stakeholder feedback. As priorities changed due to client input and regulatory developments, workflows were adjusted in real time. Integration with Microsoft 365 tools and AI features such as Copilot helped automate repetitive tasks, summarize discussions, and generate initial content drafts, allowing more time for strategic planning. This approach allowed the team to focus on developing a climate impact tool.

Loop also contributed to well-being and inclusion within the team. Members documented work preferences, time zones, and availability, which helped minimize meeting fatigue and promote understanding. Asynchronous collaboration enabled contributions according to individual schedules, and design features like emoji reactions, comment threads, and multimedia options allowed for varied communication styles. The team used Loop to maintain "pulse check" pages, where individuals could note their status and highlight potential burnout, supporting a culture attentive to psychological safety.

For ongoing learning, Loop served as a knowledge base where the team collected articles, recorded lessons learned, and offered brief trainings on subjects such as climate science, data ethics, and stakeholder engagement. AI-supported tagging and summaries facilitated navigation and retrieval of insights. Leadership responsibilities

CHAPTER 7   USE CASES FOR TEAM COLLABORATION USING LOOP

shifted according to the project phase and area of expertise, and Loop pages were used to document decisions, assign tasks, and reflect on leadership approaches, promoting transparency and shared responsibility.

The team also connected Loop with Power BI dashboards, AI-based scenario modeling tools, and external APIs to create an information-rich environment for decision-making. By the pilot testing stage, the team had produced the assessment tool and demonstrated an adaptable, collaborative working model. Microsoft Loop functioned as the team's core platform, offering a combination of technical structure and collaborative features.

We conclude this section with the above possible use cases on Microsoft Loop in various scenarios such as value and impact of collaboration, core components of effective collaboration, challenges in team collaboration, strategies for successful collaboration, collaboration in the digital age, the role of technology in collaboration and the future of team collaboration.

With these we have come to the end of this chapter and end of this book. In the beginning of this chapter, we took a deep dive into Team collaboration, explored different perspectives of Team collaboration such as value and impact of collaboration, core components of effective collaboration, challenges in team collaboration, strategies for successful collaboration, collaboration in the digital age, the role of technology in collaboration and the future of team collaboration and finally, we have discovered a possible Microsoft use case in these different perspectives.

As we close this book, **Microsoft Loop** is designed as a platform to enhance team collaboration. It provides a workspace where ideas, tasks, and conversations can be managed and updated in real time. The platform aims to help teams move beyond static documents and disconnected communication by enabling more agile and inclusive workflows. With integration into Microsoft 365, Loop supports activities such as brainstorming, project planning, decision-making, and continuous learning. It seeks to address challenges specific to remote and hybrid work environments, support digital literacy, and encourage shared ownership.

As organizations respond to evolving workplace needs, Loop offers tools that align with changes in collaboration and technology. It is intended for users managing initiatives, working on cross-functional teams, or looking for methods to stay connected and productive. Adopting Loop involves learning new features and reconsidering approaches to teamwork in a digital context. We anticipate gaining valuable experience with the integration of Microsoft Loop into your daily jobs and across your organization.

Index

A
Agile workforce, 29
AI and automation, 225
Azure Active Directory account, 11

B
Bulleted List, 195
Business environments, 169

C
Calendar component
    access, 189, 190
    AI assistant in Microsoft 365, 191
    daily workflows, 189
    date component, 191
    display, 189, 190
    embedding dates and schedules, 192
    features, 190
    meeting management, 191
    in Microsoft Loop, 189
    "+" option, 189
    real-time synchronization, 191
    security and compliance features, 192
    style views, 191
    tagging and comments, 192
    teams planning campaigns, 191
    usability perspective, 192
Callout, 196
Checklist, 194
Class Algebra, 83
Code, 196
Collapsible Heading 1, 199
Collapsible Heading 2, 199, 200
Collapsible Heading 3, 200
Communication loop components, 73
Communication process and real-time collaboration
    Microsoft Loop
        accessibility and mobility, 128
        AI and Copilot integration, 128
        communication features, 123
        content collaboration, 123
        future, 129
        integration with Microsoft 365, 122
        limitations, 126
        portable components, 120
        purpose and philosophy, 121
        security and compliance, 127
        strengths, 126
        style, 121
        use cases, 125
        user interface and experience, 122
        workflow integration, 127
    Microsoft OneNote
        accessibility and mobility, 128
        AI and Copilot integration, 128
        content collaboration, 124
        digital notebook application, 120
        future, 129
        integration with Microsoft 365, 123
        limitations, 127
        purpose and philosophy, 121

INDEX

Communication process and real-time collaboration (*cont.*)
    security and compliance, 127
    strengths, 126
    style, 121
    use cases, 125
    user interface and experience, 122
    workflow integration, 128
  Microsoft Outlook
    accessibility and mobility, 128
    AI and Copilot integration, 128
    communication features, 123
    content collaboration, 124
    email and calendar platform, 120
    future, 129
    integration with Microsoft 365, 122
    limitations, 127
    purpose and philosophy, 121
    security and compliance, 127
    strengths, 126
    style, 121
    use cases, 125
    user interface and experience, 122
    workflow integration, 128
  Microsoft Teams
    accessibility and mobility, 128
    AI and Copilot integration, 128
    communication features, 123
    content collaboration, 123
    future, 129
    integration with Microsoft 365, 122
    limitations, 126
    purpose and philosophy, 120
    security and compliance, 127
    strengths, 125
    style, 121
    teamwork and streamline, 120
    use cases, 124
    user interface and experience, 122
    workflow integration, 127
Compliance, 29
Content in Microsoft Loop
  Bulleted List, 195
  Callout, 196
  Checklist, 194
  Code, 196
  Collapsible Heading 1, 199
  Collapsible Heading 2, 199, 200
  Collapsible Heading 3, 200
  communication features, 201
  Date, 195
  Divider, 197
  general feature, 192, 193
  GitHub and planner apps, 201
  Heading 1, 198
  Heading 2, 199
  Heading 3, 199
  Inline Code, 200
  Inline Equation, 198
  Math Equation, 197
  media features, 201
  Mermaid, 196
  New Subpage, 194
  Numbered List, 195
  Paragraph style, 198
  Quote style, 200
  Table, 194
  Table of Contents, 197
Copilot, 21–23

D, E, F

Date, 195
Digital age, 212–214, 223–224
Divider, 197

G

General loop components, 71

H

Heading 1, 198
Heading 2, 199
Heading 3, 199
Human-AI collaboration, 225

I, J

Inline Code, 200
Inline Equation, 198

K

Kanban Board
    "+" option, 180
    access, 180
    AI-driven assistance for task
        management, 182
    attributes, 181
    cards, 181
    design teams, 181
    display, 180
    dynamic tracking, 179
    integration, 181
    in Microsoft Loop serves, 179
    parameters, 181
    professional use cases, 182
    Ribbon Menu, 181
    security and compliance, 182
    sorting and filtering, 181
    transparency and accountability, 182
    typing, 181
Keyboard shortcuts, 23, 24, 26

L

Landing page, 31, 32
Loop app
    eligibility, 12
    Microsoft Entra accounts, 11
    Task Lists, 15
Loop components, 5, 97, 131
    atomic units of productivity, 1
    Calendar component, 189–192
    coauthor, 90, 91
    co-creation, 67
    communication, 73
    copied into OneNote, 88
    Copy List, 18
    Copy loop component, 87
    Copy URL, 18
    create teams meeting agenda
        Add an agenda, 77
        add Meeting notes, 80
        agenda component gets
            added, 76, 77
        agenda section, 78
        @-mention, 79
        create follow-up tasks using task
            components, 80
    email, 6
    find, 88–90
    general, 71
    icon, 5
    Insert Menu, 6
    Kanban Board, 179–182
    .loop file, creator's OneDrive, 68
    Loop files across M365, 89
    Loop files across Teams, 90
    manage access, 92
        add recipient name and
            message, 93, 94

INDEX

Loop components (*cont.*)
    interface, 95
    owner of component, 94
    select "More Actions", 92
    select "Share" option, 93
  media, 73
  Microsoft Teams, 4
  OneNote, 9 (*see* OneNote Notebook)
  Outlook (*see* Outlook)
  paragraph-formatted component, 70
  "+" option to add components, 70, 71
  portable elements, content, 4
  portable, interactive content blocks, 67
  progress tracker, 176–179
  Q&A session, 186–189
  set up loop task list component
    "Add a Title" option, 86
    Add option, 84
    "Add Task" option, 86
    inserted new task list component, 83
    Insert Menu, 81
    Message Menu, 82
    "Not done", 83, 85
    Task List, 82
    "To Do" bucket, 83, 84
  share loop component across Microsoft 365 Apps, 86, 88
  Task List, 169–173 (*see also* Task List)
  Team retrospective, 182–186
  Teams Chat, 19, 69
  templates, 72
  text style, 72
  types, 8
  voting table, 173–176
    hybrid work, 75
    predefined columns, 74, 75
    published for collaboration, 76
    selection, 74
    whiteboard, 7, 8
    Word document, 9, 10
Loop pages, 27, 68, 131, 132
  creation, 10
  flexible canvases, 1
  task lists, 1
  versatile workspaces, Loop app, 10
Loop's adaptability, 218
Loop workspace pages
  Access Copilot, 110
  add instructions, 116, 117
  additional, contextually relevant prompts, 111, 113
  with brainstorming, 115
  chat feature of Copilot, 113, 114
  choose Copilot to rewrite the idea, 115, 116
  clipboard, 111
  compose your own prompts, 110, 111
  content creation, modification, and editing, 109, 118–119
  Copilot history, 113, 115
  Copilot result work-in-progress, 110, 111
  default prompt, 112, 113
  draft of new idea in progress, 116, 117
  new idea created by Copilot, 116, 118
  prebuilt prompts designed to facilitate prompt writing, 110
  raw idea, 115, 116
  result from Copilot, 113, 114
  suggestion, 113
  summary content, 111, 112
Loop workspaces, 1, 10, 11, 68, 131, 132
  access favourites, 48
  access permissions, 38
  account information, 32

INDEX

add workspace description and files, 37, 38
assign name, 33, 34
choose icon, 33, 35
collaboration, diverse materials, 32
Copy link, 50
create new workspace, 33
create pages and subpages
    collapse subpage, 43
    create new page, 40
    create new pages option, 45, 46
    expand subpage, 44
    new page creation, 39
    new pages, 41, 45
    new untitled page creation, 41
    option to create new subpage, 42
    option to rearrange pages, 44
    rearrange, 44
    settings, 45
    subpage creation, 43
creation, 38
delete workspace, 62
    access recycle bin, 63, 64
    empty all recycle bin, 65
    option, restore content, 64
    permanent delete, 65
favourites, 46–48
Invite and manage members, 48, 49
invite colleagues to join, 35, 36
name/email address, 49
navigation area, 32
page versions
    More Options menu, 58
    page's version history, 58
    restore previous version, 60
    version history, 59
print/export workspace page
    formats, 62
    Print and PDF option, 61
programs, 32
projects, 32
remove user, 50, 51
rename and style
    availability, cover types, 55
    icons, 53
    Information and Data, 53
    option, random cover, 56
    rename workspace/page, 52
    revised title, icon, and cover design, 56, 57
    select information-related cover, 56
    selection icon, information, 54
    stack of files, 56, 57
    title field, 52
    update cover option, 54, 55
untitled page, 39
workspace creation, 36, 37

M

Math Equation, 197
Media loop component, 73
Mermaid, 196
Microsoft 365, 81
    subscriptions, 11
    tools, 96
Microsoft 365 Apps
    Cloud Policy settings, 132
    E3 and E5 enterprise subscriptions, 132
    information and data management professionals, 132
    Loop components
        OneNote (*see* OneNote Notebook)
        Outlook (*see* Outlook)
    platforms, 132
Microsoft 365 Copilot License, 99

INDEX

Microsoft Entra accounts, 11
Microsoft Loop, 131, 219
    accessibility and mobility, 128
    AI and Copilot integration, 128
    Android, 31
    benefits
        Agile workforce, 29
        collaborative workforce, 28
        compliance, 29
        information sharing, 29
        knowledge management, 29
        Microsoft 365 integration, 27
        modular content structure, 27
        productivity, 28
        Project management, 28
        real-time collaboration, 26
        security, 29
    brainstorming, 13
    coauthoring, 13
    cocreation challenges
        adoption and change management, 96
        compliance, discovery, and legal risks, 97
        governance and administrative control, 97
        integration and ecosystem maturity, 97
        overlap with existing Microsoft 365 tools, 96
        performance and scalability issues, 98
        security and privacy concerns, 97
        storage and data management complexity, 97
        strategic alignment and ROI, 98
        user experience and learning curve, 98
    co-creation/collaboration platform, 67
    collaborative technology, 2
    communication features, 123
    compliance, 2, 127
    components, 2
    content collaboration, 123
    Copilot, 21–23
    data compilation, 13
    desktop version, 31
    directing a discussion, 12
    elements, 1
    features, 2, 11
    formats, 2
    future, 129
    Home page, 3
    integration (*see* Microsoft 365 Apps)
    integration with Microsoft 365, 122
    iOS mobile devices, 31
    keyboard shortcuts, 23, 24, 26
    limitations, 126
    loop components, 1 (*see* Loop components)
    loop pages, 10
    loop workspaces, 1, 10, 11
    Microsoft 365 applications, 95
    Microsoft 365 ecosystem, 96
    network environment, 12
    Personal workspaces, 96
    portable components, 120
    project management, 13
    purpose and philosophy, 121
    real-time collaboration, 98 (*see* Real-time collaboration)
    recent components and pages, 4
    security, 2, 127
    Shared workspaces, 96
    strengths, 126
    style, 121

Task List (*see* Task List)
Team collaboration (*see* Team collaboration)
types, professional scenarios, 2
use cases, 14, 125 (*see* Use cases)
user interface and experience, 122
workflow integration, 127
Microsoft Loop Access, 99
Microsoft Loop app, 31
Microsoft LoopKeyboard shortcuts, 24
Microsoft OneNote
    accessibility and mobility, 128
    AI and Copilot integration, 128
    content collaboration, 124
    digital notebook application, 120
    future, 129
    integration with Microsoft 365, 123
    limitations, 127
    purpose and philosophy, 121
    security and compliance, 127
    strengths, 126
    style, 121
    use cases, 125
    user interface and experience, 122
    workflow integration, 128
Microsoft Outlook
    accessibility and mobility, 128
    AI and Copilot integration, 128
    communication features, 123
    content collaboration, 124
    email and calendar platform, 120
    future, 129
    integration with Microsoft 365, 122
    limitations, 127
    purpose and philosophy, 121
    security and compliance, 127
    strengths, 126
    style, 121
    use cases, 125
    user interface and experience, 122
    workflow integration, 128
Microsoft Teams
    accessibility and mobility, 128
    AI and Copilot integration, 128
    communication features, 123
    content collaboration, 123
    future, 129
    integration with Microsoft 365, 122
    limitations, 126
    purpose and philosophy, 120
    security and compliance, 127
    strengths, 125
    style, 121
    teamwork and streamline, 120
    use cases, 124
    user interface and experience, 122
    workflow integration, 127
Modular content structure, 27

N

New Subpage, 194
Numbered List, 195

O

OneNote Notebook, 9, 88, 95–97
    Add Title to component, 157
    adjust size of component using double-headed arrow, 158
    board view of restrospective, 165, 166
    choose team retrospective, 155, 156
    chosen "Add Card" option for "Start doing" group, 158, 161
    insert group left or right, 161, 165

INDEX

OneNote Notebook (*cont.*)
   Loop component, 155
   move group left or right, 161, 164
   option to add additional group, 161, 162
   post selecting "Add Card" option, 158, 160
   post selecting team retrospective component, 155, 156
   rename existing group, 161, 163
   retrospective component with "Getting this ready" Title, 156, 157
   select "Add Card" option, 158, 159
   select Loop component from insert menu, 155
   table view of restrospective, 165, 167
   team retrospective, 155
Organizations, 29
Outlook, 68, 69, 95, 97
   access "sort" option, 150, 151
   access dropdown menu of "Certification Name" column, 143, 144
   added two new columns, 140
   adjust row height, 152
   board view of content, 149, 150
   calendar view of content, 149, 150
   change column of certification status column to label, 143, 145
   Click on Table component, 135, 137
   column type, 140, 142
      changed to text, 143, 144
      choose person, 140, 143
      default is text, 140, 142
      employee name changed to person, 140, 143
      selection, 140, 141
   copy table component, 153, 154
   data entry for all columns, 147
   different content views, 149
   drafted email message, 133
   email subject line is prepopulated, 135, 137
   emails, 133, 134
   explore conditions for data filter, 151, 152
   export data to excel and ".CSV", 152, 153
   hide existing columns, 152, 153
   insert ribbon, 134, 135
   label values visible after saving changes, 144, 146
   list of users, 153, 154
   Loop Components, 135
   message ribbon, 134
   messages, 81, 86, 98
   missing title message, 148
   plus sign, 138, 139
   renaming of the Columns, 138, 139
   SAP certification List@, 148, 149
   SAP Certified, 140
   select dropdown menu, 140, 141
   Select Table component, 135, 136
   setup in process with "Getting this ready" message, 135, 136
   shared location to copy across other Loop workspaces, 153, 154
   sort content based on a chosen field, 150, 151
   status, 144, 145
   Table component with prepopulated columns, 135, 138
   table data, 147
   update label values, 144, 146

P

Paragraph-formatted component, 70
Paragraph style, 198
Productivity, 28
Progress tracker
    access, 176, 177
    advanced and user-friendly solution, 176
    advantages, 178
    coordination and decision-making, 176
    culture of transparency and accountability, 179
    design, 178
    display, 176, 177
    elements, 178
    feature, 178
    human resources teams, 178
    Loop ecosystem, 176
    "+" option, 176
    security and compliance, 179
    systematic framework, 176
    usability perspective, 179
    use cases, 178
    utilizes, 178
Project management, 28
Psychological safety, 212, 223

Q

Q&A session component
    access, 186
    culture of transparency and shared learning, 188
    design and usability, 188
    display, 186, 187
    feedback collection and brainstorming, 188
    interactions within teams, 186
    Microsoft Copilot, 188
    onboarding scenarios, 187
    "+" option, 186
    project planning and execution, 188
    real-time collaboration, 187
    security and compliance features, 189
    series of entries, 187
    structure, 186
    structured format, 187
    use cases, 189
Quote style, 200

R

Real-time collaboration, 26
    and communication process (*see* Communication process and real-time collaboration)
    Copilot
        content generation, 100
        content generation is in progress, 101, 102
        Expand Copilot Overlay, 100, 101
        "Keep draft" or "Go back and start now" options, 102, 103
        Loop workspace pages, 109–118
        option to setup page, 101
        prompt for demonstration, 101, 102
        reference files, 103, 104
        resulting page, 102, 103
        rewriting content, 104–109
        set up your page with, 100, 101
    Microsoft 365 Copilot License, 99
    Microsoft Loop Access, 99
    Microsoft 365 subscription, 100

INDEX

Rewriting content with Copilot assistance
- appearance, 105, 106
- draft in progress, 108, 109
- file reference to rewrite paragraph, 107, 108
- paragraph or paragraph title, 105, 106
- prompt box, 105, 107
- prompt initiation, 104, 105
- prompt to expand on the existing paragraph topic, 107, 108
- query loop content using default and custom prompts, 104, 105
- resultant content, 108, 109
- selection of paragraph, 105, 107

S

Security, 29
Soft skills training, 223

T

Table, 194
Table of Contents, 197
Task List, 1
- access loop component
  - Outlook, 20
  - Teams Chat, 19
- advantages, 172
- appearance, 170, 171
- benefits, 171
- checkbox, 171
- checklist, 169
- completed tasks, 172
- components, 169, 170
- Copy URL of Loop component, 19, 20
- creation, 17
- cultures, 173
- design, 172
- features, 171
- Loop app, 15
- Loop Pages, 172
- Loop Workspace, 172
- marketing teams, 172
- Microsoft Teams meeting, 171
- M365 services, 21
- multiple users, 171
- names assign, 16
- "+" enables insertion, 16
- "+" option visible, 170
- portable and dynamic, 169
- product teams, 172
- security and compliance, 173
- "/" enables insertion, 15
- synchronization distinguishes Loop, 169
- use cases, 172
- Whiteboard, Copy URL of Loop component, 21

Team collaboration
- challenges, 208–210
- complex and multifaceted process, 203
- core components, 207–208
- in digital age, 212–214
- future, 216–217, 226–227
- mere colocation/task sharing, 204
- perspectives, 204, 205
- principle of synergy, 204
- role of technology, 214–215
- strategies for successful collaboration, 210–212
- value and impact, 205–206

Team retrospective
- access, 183
- agile methodologies, 182
- Cards, 184

categories, 184
collaborative tool, 182
cultures, 185
design and usability, 184
digital workspace, 182
display, 183
features, 184
integration with Microsoft Copilot, 185
Loop component within OneNote Notebook (*see* OneNote Notebook)
Loop Pages, 185
"+" option, 183
real-time collaboration, 184
real-time synchronization, 184
robust, flexible, and intelligent tool, 186
security and compliance, 185
use cases, 185
Teams, 68, 69, 89, 90, 95, 96
Templates Loop Component, 72
Text style loop components, 72
Trust constitutes, 208

U

Use cases
    challenges in team collaboration, 220–222
    collaboration
        in digital age, 223–224
        role of technology, 225–226
    core components of effective collaboration
        client requirements, 220
        defined roles, 220
        diversity and inclusion, 220

        features, 219
        leadership, 220
        shared goals, 219
        static documents/dispersed chat threads, 219
        strategic transformation team, 219
        trust, 219
    strategies for successful collaboration, 222–223
    value and impact of team collaboration, 217–219

V

Versions, 58
Voting table
    access controls, 176
    appearance, 173, 174
    broader Loop platform, 173
    decision-making solution, 173
    democratic and inclusive culture, 175
    design and usability, 175
    feature, 175
    Loop Pages, 176
    permission management, 176
    "+" option, 173, 174
    rationales and suggestions, 175
    security and compliance measures, 176
    spreadsheet/matrix, 175
    use cases, 175
    utility, 175

W, X, Y, Z

Whiteboard, 95
Word, 69, 95

GPSR Compliance

The European Union's (EU) General Product Safety Regulation (GPSR) is a set of rules that requires consumer products to be safe and our obligations to ensure this.

If you have any concerns about our products, you can contact us on

ProductSafety@springernature.com

In case Publisher is established outside the EU, the EU authorized representative is:

Springer Nature Customer Service Center GmbH
Europaplatz 3
69115 Heidelberg, Germany

www.ingramcontent.com/pod-product-compliance
Lightning Source LLC
LaVergne TN
LVHW081450060526
838201LV00050BA/1750